The Healing Power of Crystals

Front Cover Jewelled Pin

This enchanting Kiss pin, designed by Elizabeth Gage, features a mandarin Garnet to the centre, surrounded with yellow Beryls and silver South Sea cultured Pearls held in fluted cones. The piece is finished with Diamonds, hand carved gold detail and matching orange enamel. Another version of the Kiss Pin can be seen in the Victoria and Albert Museum/London.

Elizabeth Gage has won many accolades including the prestigious Queens Award for Export, British Jewellery Designer of the Year and the coveted De Beers Diamond Award for her Agincourt ring which was described as an engineering masterpiece. Elizabeth is a Freeman of the City of London and a Liveryman of the Worshipful Company of Goldsmiths. Her most recent honour being the Lifetime Achievement Award presented in 2008 by Retail Jeweller, a UK Jewellery publication.

About the Author

Magda Joy Palmer Cordingley was born in Melbourne, Australia. She studied Gemmology at London's City Polytechnic (now the City University) and Jewellery Design at the Gemmological Association of Australia. She holds a Diploma of Clinical Hypnotherapy and is trained in Remedial and Therapeutic Massage, Shiatsu, Iridology and Aromatherapy. She is a member of Book Creators Circle—Tropical Writers Group, Tropical Writers Cairns/North Queensland, and Cairns Art Society and Inkmasters Cairns Inc. Magda has won both writing and art prizes.

She was employed as a consultant on the mythological associations and healing properties of crystals for "Nature Sculpture", a shop-within-a-shop at Harrods. After returning to Australia Magda concentrated her energies on her passions which are art, poetry, writing for ensemble theatre and public speaking. She lives in Far North Queensland with her husband Tom Cordingley who is an inventor of software products and has degrees in Mathematics, Computer Science and Electrical Engineering and their pet family.

Magda is determined to promote beauty, knowledge, decency and honour. Her code of conduct is to live without malice, devoid of greed and gluttony so she does not eat, wear or use animal derived products. She is against animal experimentation and animal to human organ transfers.

Her wish is to effectuate an enlightened planetary civilization deserving of the creation of which we are an integral part.

THE HEALING POWER OF
Crystals
*Birthstones and Their
Celestial Partners*

MAGDA PALMER

iUniverse, Inc.
Bloomington

The Healing Power of Crystals
Birthstones and Their Celestial Partners

Copyright © 2013 by Magda Palmer

iUniverse books may be ordered through booksellers or by contacting:

iUniverse
1663 Liberty Drive
Bloomington, IN 47403
www.iuniverse.com
1-800-Authors (1-800-288-4677)

First published in 1988
10 9 8 7 6 5
Copyright © Magda Palmer 1988
Published in 1988 by Rider, an imprint of Ebury Press, Random House, 20 Vauxhall Bridge Road, London SW1V 2SA
Random House Australia (Pty) Limited 20 Alfred Street, Milsons Point, Sydney, New South Wales 2061, Australia
Random House New Zealand Limited 18 Poland Road, Glenfield, Auckland 10, New Zealand
Random House (Pty) Limited
Endulini, 5 A Jubilee Road, Parktown 2193, South Africa
The Random House Group Limited Reg. No. 954009 www.randomhouse.co.uk
Reprinted 1988, 1989, New edition 1992, Reprinted 1994, Reprinted 1997
Originally printed and bound in Great Britain by
Cox & Wyman Ltd, Reading, Berkshire
A CIP catalogue record for this book is available from the British Library
ISBN 0-7126-7151-X
Printed in the United States of America
St Martin's Press. New York, NY 10010
Library of Congress Cataloguing-in-publication Data
Palmer, Magda.
Precious Stones.
1, Gems Miscellanae. 2. Occultism. 1. Title.
BF1442.P74P35 1988 133.3'22 87-28503
ISBN 0-312-01495-3

Original print Germany—Heyne Bucher ISBN: 3-453-13279-3

Original print Brazil—Edicoes 70, LDA-Street Rasa Village 1734400

New legal deposit Gaia 36421/90

ISBN: 978-1-4759-7220-7 (sc)
ISBN: 978-1-4759-7222-1 (hc)
ISBN: 978-1-4759-7221-4 (e)

Library of Congress Control Number: 2013901012

Printed in the United States of America
iUniverse rev. date: 02/01/2013

Dedication

*This book is dedicated to
Rivers Scott, my first editor, my mentor.*

CONTENTS

PART THREE

PART FOUR

PART FIVE

TABLES

Introduction to 2012 Edition

Since the day when the first edition of this book blazed its trail into the annals of alternative medicine, orthodox medicine itself has changed dramatically. Never before in history can humanity have returned in such large numbers to ancient traditions and the start of a drugless renaissance.

No longer does it surprise one to see a cluster of crystals beside a stethoscope, thermometer, tongue press and skeletal structure on the local GP's table. It would, by contrast, be amazing to notice the absence of carved crystal tools in the treatment room of any modern practitioner of massage.

As though in echo of ancient Rome, brightly coloured bits of rock lie alongside the beige folders and their accompanying red ribbons on cluttered lawyers' desks, while onyx ashtrays adorn the reception areas of smart fashion houses.

Clumps of amethyst cluster near computers and crown *microwaves, agate bookends support the works of reference in* the offices of financial giants and most corner shops sell local stones.

Works on the subject now abound in public libraries, while parents of newborn babes are as likely to receive gifts of bedside rocks, talismans and precious gems with which to celebrate the happy event as bonnets, bootees and cuddly koalas or teddies.

In fact, crystals span society, linking those engaged in places as diverse as factories, law courts, restaurant kitchens and kindergartens.

Perhaps most important of all is the way in which the study of crystals has infiltrated the realms of government subsidised adult education where, alongside other tertiary programmes, the gentle methods of natural healing are taught regularly.

My book was the first to bring a truly scientifically informed technique to the matching of stones to planets and to tabulate from modern testing the power of crystals to heal. During the years since it first appeared astronomers have further refined their knowledge of our solar system's heavenly behaviour, though they have learned little more about its chemical constitution.

One discovery was of water on our Moon, but as that water is not abundant and is, in any case, in solid form often encased in crystals, no change was necessary in my original evaluation when matching crystals to the Cancerian part of the zodiac.

Nor did the find in Antarctica of a 1.9kg meteorite, chock-a-block with what appear to be chemical and fossil remains of microscopic organisms that lived on Mars 3.6 thousand million years ago alter parallel birthstones for Aries. Then astronomers decided to change their rules as to what size and behaviour a planet should have so little Pluto was demoted to a dwarf planet but that didn't cause any changes either.

This new edition allows me to pay tribute to all those who have given me wholehearted support by setting up healing circles and clinics specialising in treatment based on my research. Their enthusiasm is an endorsement of my deep belief in the healing power of crystals, in the part they can play in all medicinal therapies, and in the enrichment of the lives of countless people, young and old.

Finally since the publication of my book many articles and websites have used its title, "The Healing Power of Crystals". I wish to make quite clear that these writings, teachings and sites have nothing to do with the nine year study and research I originally carried out for this work nor have they asked my permission to use the title although it is generally taken as manners to do so.

Original Introduction

When I was twelve, my adoptive father took me to visit Jenolan Caves in the Blue Mountains situated in New South Wales. One of these awesome limestone caverns, named "The Cathedral", is acoustically perfect meaning a person standing at one end has only to utter a word or sing a few notes and every soft syllable can be heard clearly throughout the whole, vast area. I remember my father, a convent trained singer, giving a rendering of Gounod's "Ave Maria" and "Little Grey Home in The West" to prove this point for the benefit of the rest of the party.

But this was not the only this aspect of Jenolan Caves which won my admiration. Everywhere I looked there were great, breathtaking columns of stalagmites and stalactites and tiny, glittering settings which to a child's eyes resembled pictures from fairy tales and golden and pink shawls draping Greek columns seen in photos in history books, all still imperceptibly growing, though I did not understand this at the time. So was my first introduction to the world of minerals which has entranced me ever since.

This book is about rough and polished minerals and gemstones, the latter being minerals in their most refined form. It will tell you how to use them; how to discover which are the right ones for you, according to your month of birth, western astrological birth sign and your physical and spiritual needs; how to enlist them as healing agents for yourself and others.

My work as a consultant for Harrods store in London and for individual healers and astrologers in Britain and elsewhere in the world has shown me how significantly the whole study of precious stones has broadened out in recent years. Gone are the days when the traditional lore concerning them was dismissed as mere superstition, when the only thing donors and recipients saw in them was superficial beauty, wonderful though that can be, and all that interested them was the price.

Now there are even surgeons who like to have a nest of crystals placed nearby when they are carrying out operations though few of them will yet admit the fact. But if you enquire about fine surgical instruments you will find listed among the most prized are Diamond, and corundum blades. Sapphires and Rubies are members of the corundum family.

Science has stepped in to revalidate many ancient beliefs, to reinterpret the links between the planets and ourselves, and to show minerals for what they are, essential mediators between outer space, our solar system, ourselves and planet Earth.

This then is the moment to look at gems with a fresh eye. The aim of this book is to help the reader to do so, adding thereby to the store of knowledge and pleasure, the spiritual enlightenment and physical wellbeing and health, that all of us would like to attain.

PART ONE

History of Birthstones
The Planets

History of Gems and Birthstones

The first rocks which eventually formed the inner planets of our solar system were more like fluff than hard stones according to modern science. Today the whole of our planet is made of rocks and minerals, the mountains, the valleys and the riverbeds — everything.

Minerals are mostly composed of elements and salts with crystalline structures and shapes which identify which family of chemicals they belong too. Rocks are a combination of two minerals or more. A great example of a single mineral is a Diamond because it is made solely of compressed carbon, while Lapis Lazuli and Granite are rocks, Lapis more usually has a combination of five separate minerals and Granite contains three. Crystals are minerals which form from molten chemicals which, when cooling have space to grow in their natural shape, determined by their chemical composition. When the cooling in smaller spaces they form in chunks and are called massive. Most minerals take thousands, and sometimes millions of years to solidify, while others such as rock salt have been seen to grow while you watch!

It wasn't until six thousand years ago, in ancient Mesopotamia, that first the Sumerians and then the inhabitants of Ur of the Chaldea's started looking at minerals and precious stones, as well as at the stars, with a view to improving their crops, protecting themselves from enemies, human or natural, foreseeing the future and generally attempting to probe the secrets of the universe about which they knew more than our materialistic age gives them credit for. At that time the roles of priest, doctor, seer, astronomer and astrologer were merged into one. These sages knew much about the Dog Star Sirius (Sirius A, as it is now called), and its companion planet, Sirius B, despite the fact that these two bodies are right outside our solar system. Certain primitive tribes, far removed from Mesopotamia, knew about them too, and believed that messengers from the Sirius System had descended to Earth to teach their ancestors good government and a method of counting. The Sumerians knew about the great density of Sirius B, about its fifty year orbit round Sirius A, and because Sirius A is the brightest star in the night sky, linked both it and its accompanying star with the indigo-blue mineral, Lapis Lazuli, which they also allocated to their gods.

But this was not the end of the Sumerians' esoteric knowledge. They cut, polished and set such hard and precious substances as Rock Crystal, Amethyst and Banded Agate; they used beautiful stones to adorn their buildings and statues, and to accompany the royal and wealthy to the grave. They had also begun to grasp, though in a different way from ourselves, the general connections between planet Earth and the rest of the solar system, and the function of minerals as a link between the two.

Their method of making these connections was by colour: rose and scarlet stones to match the rusty-red tint of Mars which mounted the horizon in April when the Sumerian year began; green jewels for Venus, which appeared as the crops started and the people settled down to enjoy the green plenty of summer; blue for Mercury, lord of blue skies and balmy days; violet tints for autumnal Saturn; and pale blue to reflect the melting snows on far off mountains which occurred during Jupiter's reign.

To the Sun were allocated all yellow stones, and to our Moon Pearls and sea shells fetched or traded from the Persian Gulf.

Over simplified though these associations undoubtedly were, and misleading in many respects, they were intelligent interpretations of the facts then known (chemistry was unknown); and the lore of the inhabitants of ancient Mesopotamia, inherited by the Egyptians and later echoed in the Old and New Testaments, laid foundations of knowledge on which we can still build. The question to be asked in the scientific climate of today is how can links between precious stones and the planets be shown to be genuine?

To answer this question we should reflect first of all on the fact that the ninety or so elements that constitute all matter on Earth, including minerals and the human body, are represented out there in the planets, as are Earth's minerals themselves. Thus not only is it true that no man is an island, but no planet is an island either, and our bodies reverberate to celestial vibrations through the medium of precious stones. If you stand near the wall of a room and clap your hands, the disturbance will ruffle a feather placed on a table near the wall opposite. Just so will planetary forces ruffle or soothe human beings. Putting the matter another way, it could be said that a precious stone will fulfil the role of an electrical substation, receiving the heat and vibrations from its owner's planetary ruler and transmitting them with increased power.

Scientific evidence suggests that all things are one, in the sense that all the chemicals and elements on Earth and on other planets are particles of our galaxy, the incredible Milky Way, which could well contain over one hundred million other solar systems besides our own, all born with the universe at the moment of the "Big Bang", the hypothetical creative instant. Thus, throughout our lives, we have the "melody" of our ruling planets in our bodies, and never is this planetary influence as strong as at the moment when we are born and are forcing our way into the world. Both mother and child need their appropriate stones near them at that time, to strengthen the planetary influences even further. And these influences remain.

Another argument can be drawn from the activity of nature, even of inorganic nature. Minerals can probably boast the most spectacular and protracted prenatal history of any substance there is. When a miner or prospector discovers a gem laying in the Earth it has not been there in that state forever. On the contrary, it has been subjected several times, and over a period of millions of years, to a devastating alternation of expansion and shrinkage, heat and cold, brought about by the giant upheavals of the earth.

There are four substances that are loosely termed mineral but belong in fact to the animal or vegetable kingdom. Two of them are Amber and Jet. They are found in the earth's crust and can be cut and polished like stone. The other two are Coral and Pearl. These come from water and water creatures. They are classed as "mineraloids". True minerals are different. Inorganic in composition, they contain exactly those elements to be found in every piece of matter in our solar system, from planets and moons, asteroids, comets and meteorites down to mere dust. Therefore, though formed on our planet, they are directly linked with their corresponding elements in celestial bodies other than Earth.

This mysterious process of creation is still going on. While we stand surveying a beautiful stretch of countryside, enjoying the shade of a forest, or getting our breath back at the top of a steep hill, minerals are constantly assembling under our feet, just as they are still being produced in the planetary masses. The correspondence between this activity on Earth and in the planets is another reason why we should try to live in harmony with them both.

The main part of this chapter will be devoted to listing and describing the stones appropriate for those born under each sign of the western zodiac, but first some explanations are necessary. As will be seen, this section is divided not into signs but into half signs first half Scorpio, second half Pisces, and so on. It is often forgotten that when the science of astrology was first devised, each sign of the zodiac filled an exact month Capricorn filled January, Aquarius February, and so on. Down

5

the centuries, in the course of each celestial mass's journey round the Sun, the heavenly bodies have crept into different positions, so that now each sun sign begins earlier than the first day of its original month and ends part way through the next. The division dates for each astrological sign are correct for 2013. They will vary thereafter from year to year according to the astronomical almanac of that year.

It is the intention of the writer that each person should know their correct Birthstone, the Birthstone which correlates with the heavenly bodies which greatly influenced this planet at the person's date of birth.

The word "birthstone" implies a gemstone, mineral, or mineraloid which has been matched either chemically, structurally or by colour/s to a planet or satellite.

Most people believe a mineral sold as a birthstone has therapeutic or talismanic benefits connected to the heavenly body which greatly influenced our planet on the day they were born. These same individuals will be shocked to know that there is no truth in their belief because there is absolute proof that the "traditional" birthstones were chosen by shrewd minds in the gem industry to boost sales, and have absolutely no connection with heavenly bodies.

Sloppy research and wishful thinking has some saying there is a connection between birthstones and the breastplate of Aaron who was a high priest of the Old Testament. Ask the person sprouting this information to prove their claims and they can't because many great scholars, including Josephus (1st century AD Jewish historian) and St. Jerome (fifth century AD translator and Christian monk), have failed to prove any correlation. This is because the breastplate was a religious garment set with twelve gemstones representing the twelve tribes of Israel and no connection with celestial bodies.

Yet many "authorities" blatantly name birthstones correlating with months and sun signs saying they have been used throughout history and in biblical times!

The original idea of Birthstones was, without doubt, the brainchild of 18th century Jewish Gem traders who, upon settling in Poland, cleverly boosted sales by spreading word that each person should wear a gemstone corresponding to the month of his or her birth.

In 1912 the so called "traditional" birthstones list was created by the American Jewellers Association to standardise the list of birthstones across countries to financially benefit the jewellery industry.

Well according to the University of Adelaide the word traditional means consisting of or derived from tradition, also conventional (in accord with or being a tradition or practice accepted from the past), also handed-down (having been passed along from generation to generation), long-standing (having existed or continued for a long time) and time-honored (acceptable for a long time and pertaining to time-honored orthodox doctrines.

The perpetrators did not confer with astrologers, astronomers, gemmologists or geologists, they cunningly chose gemstones which were easy to obtain and always available to pop into (more often) pre-made settings and those which the public favoured for colour. The list is as follows;

January birthstone. . . . . . Garnet
February birthstone . . . . . Amethyst
March birthstones . . . . . . Aquamarine
April birthstone . . . . Diamond
May birthstone . . . . Emerald
June birthstones . . . . Pearl & Moonstone
July birthstone . . . . Ruby
August birthstones. . . . . . Peridot
September birthstone . . . Sapphire
October birthstones . . . . . Opal
November birthstones . . . Topaz
December birthstones . . . Turquoise & Zircon

Then the "traditional list" changed again because in 1938, the American Gem Society (AGS) adopted the list. When they did, they added a new birthstone-Citrine.

Then in 1952 this "traditional" list of birthstones changed again. In 2002 the American Gem Trade Association (AGTA) announced that they added Tanzanite as a birthstone for December, even though that month already had two birthstones-Turquoise and Zircon.

The Jewellers of America made this press release "JA sees the addition of Tanzanite for December as a way to build business. Any step that helps retailers sell more jewellery is a good one." The chief executive office of The American Gem Trade Douglas K. Hucker said "Once Tanzanite became a staple gem meaning constant supply was assured, and once supplies showed no sign of letting up, it seemed as worthy of membership on the birthstone list...". "All of the major industry associations agreed that the public would respond positively to a dynamic new birthstone choice for December."

In February 2006, the Tanzanite cartel TanzaniteOne Ltd, announced a marketing strategy to make Tanzanite a birthstone.

But TanzaniteOne (name of the group who own the only mine that yields Tanzanite) weren't content for Tanzanite to be just another birthstone. They found another way of extracting money from the public and wanted Tanzanite to be given to every child at birth, regardless of which month, referring to contestable Masai tribal birth practices. The planned advertising slogan was "be born to Tanzanite." Oh dear more changes to grab money from the gullible public. To date the following commercial list of so called "traditional" birthstones matched to months of the year according to the jewellery trade is as follows;

January birthstone. . . . . . Garnet
February birthstone . . . . . Amethyst
March birthstones . . . . . . Aquamarine & Bloodstone
April birthstone . . . . Diamond
May birthstone . . . . Emerald
June birthstones . . . . . . Pearl, Moonstone & Alexandrite
July birthstone . . . . Ruby
August birthstones. . . . . . Peridot & Sardonyx
September birthstone . . . Blue Sapphire
October birthstones . . . . . Opal & Pink Tourmaline
November birthstones . . . Topaz & Citrine
December birthstones . . . Turquoise, Zircon & Tanzanite

Sadly, this list (and a myriad of other lists on the net) of month stones is often referred to by western astrologers as set "astrological stones". This in turn infers that each astrological sign is contained in one whole month which we know they are not and that an astrological stone carries the characteristics of the planetary ruler of that sign.

Now we must ask why do authors of books and western astrologers list stones which are supposed to correspond to celestial bodies, when few if any have studied astronomy or the chemical compositions, density, weight, electrical qualities and water content of minerals, which they should if they are going to advise on such an important subject. The answer must be that they are getting on a bandwagon. Many books on all subjects are written by professional authors who simply rewrite books which have been written by others. These professional writers do not care if facts are correct, they write to sell their books. Often consulting individuals give copycat information instead of simply saying "This is not my subject so I cannot advice".

One has to consider purposeful misinformation as dishonest and it should be pointed out that all crystals, minerals and rocks are made of undiluted chemicals and often contain positive and negative energies which have an effect on the human body, mind and soul. To back this up one only has to look at the high success of homeopathic remedies, which are typically made of inert substances such as sugars and lactose upon which a drop of healing liquid derived from a known healing source is placed to understand a pure mineral is obviously much stronger and so must have a stronger effect on the body and mind.

Therefore we should see that a gemstone, mineral or rock out of synchronization with our birth planets/satellite may not give us the result we expected. One wonders what astrologers would say if a gemmologist entered their field and set up business without study astrology?

Returning to the "traditional" list compiled for the benefit of sales for the jewellery trade, it must be made clear the intention was to boost sales, not to mislead people we hope.

True healers, mystics and shamans know that individual stones have unique properties which can be aids to healing, knowledge, mediation, protection, and to attract the law of supply, harmony and romance.

Surely birthstones should express the strength of their corresponding heavenly bodies. The myriad lists of birthstones have got out of hand and those who advise can't give any valid explanations as to their choice, although some say they were given the information through meditation or were channeled.

With so much doubt as to what corresponds with whatever it is blatantly obvious we must start from scratch to give credence to this beloved and most important subject. To begin and to help you the reader understand why certain minerals have been chosen for the different zodiac signs, we should study our major heavenly bodies which contain a vast astronomical treasure house of gasses, colours, weights, and strengths. In the light of this, and to ensure the most accurate predictions possible, conscientious astrologers take care to consult the astronomers annual Almanac, or solar system calendar. As the heavenly bodies move forward on their journey round our sun, the ruler of each zodiac sign varies in the degree of influence it exerts on Earth at any given moment, hence the need for the designation of "mutable" which accompanies the ruling body.

To take Aries as an example: although its main ruler is Mars, its first half has overtones of the Sun while the second has a subsidiary influence in Jupiter; likewise the Mercury ruled house of Gemini has overtones of Venus in the first half with a Uranian influence in the second.

Next, it will be noted that each division of the zodiac is allotted not one classification of stones but three it's "precious crystal", its "talisman" and its "bedside rock". In rough and ready terms, these generally represent three orders of value, precious crystals being, as their name implies, the most suitable for setting as jewellery or being carried in the pocket, preferably wrapped in silk. Next comes the talisman, a lucky charm, as the dictionaries tell us, worn to ward off negative happenings and so bring strength and good fortune to their owner. Often less costly but not least delightful is the humble bedside rock, often uncut (in rough) but not less closely matched with its zodiacal sign than the other two categories indeed, if anything, more so. The two or more choices of stone offered in almost every entry allow wearers to indulge their tastes also to accommodate their purchases to their pockets and not be floored if some stones are hard to obtain. No one should be deprived of the chance to wear lovely gems or build up a collection of them. Using the appropriate stones in any of the ways here indicated will contribute to your general wellbeing by putting you more closely in tune with the energies of your astrological sign and its ruling planet.

Although this book is about the beneficent powers of stones, rather than their aesthetic qualities (though these are often referred to), and is not intended as a compendium for dealers, a few definitions may be found helpful. Common or garden minerals are generally called stones (that is, anything loose and detachable from the surface of the earth), but when two or more minerals of set but distinct composition join together; the resulting formations are called rocks. Stones suitable for cutting or wearing are called gemstones more usually after they are cut, and are few in comparison with all the minerals to be found on Earth. Yet nature is prodigal in her production of these too, and while most varieties have been known for thousands of years, new types of existing species appear from time to time, and occasionally a completely new gem is discovered, amid much rejoicing and excitement. Several are listed and described in the following pages.

The value of gemstones mostly depends on their beauty, rarity and durability, the more they show usually the higher the retail price. For these qualities we must thank nature's magic, for she manages to make the most glittering and glorious stones out of the commonest basic materials. A Diamond is no more than compressed and aged common carbon. The most famous mineral of all, Rock Crystal, is simply a clear variety of quartz, made up of two of the world's most abundant substances, silicon and oxygen. Rubies and Sapphires are a mixture of aluminium and oxygen, with traces of different metals, inclusions or irradiation causing their colour variations.

Indeed colour in gemstones is itself a further paradox, for with one or two exceptions (notably Tourmaline and Opal) those glorious tints which add so much to pleasure and price are the result not of some natural grand design but of accidental impurities, a small change in structure or irradiation. (Amethyst, for instance, is basically Rock Crystal, its purple tint caused by an impurity in the form of iron.) To be distinguished from colour is lustre, which depends on reflection and the nature of a stone's surface. Turquoise has a waxy lustre, Diamonds, Topaz and Zircons have a hard lustre, and Moonstones appear silky, and so on.

The beneficial action of stones is automatic. Because each variety's individual atomic structure is always the same, they will help you equally whether they are cut or uncut, mounted or unmounted, worn, carried about, or lying on a table or desk. Your choice should be the variety which attracts you most. Minerals will benefit your wellbeing even when the planets with which they are matched are furthest away from our planet, though the closer the better, of course.

Nor is it true that the only stones you can usefully wear are the ones astrologically matched with your planet. Nobody is under the rule of one planet alone. We are a mixture of many elements, and everything that goes on in our solar system affects everything that happens on Earth, in one way or another. So relax. Let your stones work for you, however "passive" you or they may seem. If you want to be busy, the best thing you can do is to '"orchestrate" your collection of stones, composing them into beautiful groupings, patterns of interesting colours and shapes. That way, they will work on each other and on you at the same time. Your stones are there to tune you, and that is all.

Finally, reference will be made in the following pages to the Mohs scale of hardness. By this form of measurement the Diamond scores highest, with a mark of ten out of ten; talc is lowest, at one out of ten. The Mohs is a purely practical test devised by a Viennese mineralogist called Friedrich Mohs, more than a century and a half ago, for the benefit of dealers and others for their own specialist purposes, and still applied, despite diversity between numbers. What concerns us here is the esoteric use to which the numbers on the Mohs scale and other numbers can be put. To explain these, we will end these introductory remarks with a note on Numerology.

A Note on Numerology

In simple terms, the law of numerology "the study of the occult significance of numbers"'(Webster's Dictionary) states that all numbers are single and lie between the digits one and nine inclusive. Thus the number 10, comprising two digits, is broken down to a single number by adding together its first and second digits, one and zero, to arrive at the calculation 1 + 0 = 1. On the same principle, 23 becomes five (2 + 3 = 5), but nineteen becomes 1 by the addition of an extra step: first, add one and nine (1+9 = 10), then add one and zero (1+0 = 1). Final score: 1. So far, so easy. But now we need to know the number allotted by western astrological tradition to each of the heavenly bodies in our solar system. They are as follows:

- The Sun. 1;
- Our planet's Moon . . . 2;
- Jupiter. 3;
- Uranus 4;
- Mercury. 5;
- Venus 6;
- Neptune 7;
- Saturn. 8;
- Mars . . . . 9.
- Pluto . . . . on account of its very recent discovery (1930), has no traditional number, but Western Astrologers, by a near unanimity, seem to be settling for the double digit 22. So that number, plus its multiples of 2, 3 and 4 that is, 44, 66 and 88 are treated as special cases and all are attached exclusively to this dwarf planet-come-lately.

In the following pages, listing jewels and their heavenly partners, certain numerological associations deriving from these numberings will be mentioned from time to time, in connection with the Mohs scale of hardness. It will be pointed out, for example, that Diamonds, with a hardness of 10 on the Mohs scale, are linked with the Sun (1+0=1) as well as with Neptune, on which these jewels are thought to proliferate. Pink Sapphire (hardness 9) corresponds with Mars (astrological number 9); Peridot (hardness 5) goes with Mercury (astrological number 5); and so on.

In the section on anniversaries towards the end of this book the numerical calculation is crucial. An eleventh birthday falls under the influence of the Moon (1+1=2, the Moon's number), a twenty seventh under Mars (2+7=9), a sixty sixth under Jupiter (6+6=12=3). So ancient astrological lore and a branch of esoteric mathematics (now suited to the needs of the computer age, incidentally) combine in keeping man in harmony with the universe, the greatest boon he can enjoy.

The Astrological birth sign dates given in this book are correct for 1988, the year before the original publication of book was first released. They will continue to vary according to astronomical calendars thereafter from year to year, but more usually, only by a day or two.

The Solar System

"The planets in their radiant courses", as the poet felt inspired to write of them, are less romantically described in Hutchinson's invaluable "New 20th Century Encyclopaedia" as "non-luminous globes revolving around the Sun at various distances and in various periods".

Five (in addition to our own Planet Earth) have been known since the earliest times. Three are newcomers. Uranus was discovered two centuries ago, Neptune in 1846, and dwarf planet Pluto as recently as 1930. Since then science has taken an even more spectacular hand, beginning with the Mariner II space probe of 1962 which transformed our knowledge of Venus. Soon the mysteries of Mars may be partially unveiled at least. And that is not to mention the landing of the first man on our Moon.

Before getting down to the detailed listing of stones and signs, the reader is invited to take a journey into space, beginning, as is proper, with our own Sun and Moon, and working outwards to almost unimaginable distances. Mercury spins at 57.91 million kilometres (36 million miles) from the Sun, a mere stone's throw by astronomical standards and plainly visible. Pluto, poised on the very edge of our Solar System, is no more than a speck in the scientist's telescope and over a hundred times more remote.

But near or far, all planets are equal, astrologically speaking, in terms of their influence even though they are geologically different. All inner planets are "rocky planets", those beyond the Main Asteroid Belt are "gas planets", "ice planets" and most likely a "water planet".

The Sun

The Sun is our daytime star, just one among a hundred billion in the galaxy of the Milky Way, and is mostly composed of the gases hydrogen and helium, hydrogen having been converted to helium by natural nuclear reactions within the Sun's body. Scientists class the Sun as rather an ordinary medium size star because it has shown relative stability during the past three billion years, even though it constantly wobbles, shakes, bubbles and rolls, and presents us with a vast variety of confusing surface features such as "sunspots" (magnetic storms), "flares" (violent outbursts) and weird atmospheric structures. Deep in its heart this blazing, spherical inferno has a natural dynamo which reverses itself every eleven years, ensuring, through its output of energy, the continuance of explosive fires which heat and light all surrounding planets, moons and matter far beyond the orbits of Neptune and Pluto in the Kuiper Belt at the outer edge of our solar system.

At more than 300,000 times the size of Earth and nearly 100 times that of every planet, satellite and solid object in our section of the Milky Way put together, the Sun has a diameter of 1,392,684 kilometers (865,374.5 miles). So mighty is its attraction that all the bodies in its domain dance round it like courtiers in attendance on their king. The planet we inhabit is third in distance from the Sun, preceded by Venus and Mercury and followed by Mars, Jupiter, Saturn, Uranus, Neptune and little Pluto, although sometimes the latter two change places. Pluto, as far as we know, is our guardian planet on the very edge of the Solar System, a big job for a little dwarf. The temperature at the Sun's core has been estimated at about seventeen million degrees Celsius and the surface heat evaluated at 5,500 degrees. Therefore the Sun has no affinity with water.

The Sun is sometimes called our "solar bulb" because it makes all things visible and is our natural form of light, its white rays holding a combination of every colour of the rainbow, from red and orange through yellow and green to blue, indigo and violet. Each tint has its own frequency wave and gives a visible display only when interference breaks the merging of the spectrum.

Surrounding the outer atmosphere of the Sun is a corona, visible during total eclipses as a pearly white crown displaying a variety of features including streamers, plumes and loops. Charged particles, mainly protons and electrons, known as solar winds escape from the Sun's upper atmosphere streaming in all directions at about 400 km (about 1 million mph) showering our solar system with ionised gasses, and many known elements including carbon, nitrogen, oxygen, neon, magnesium, silicon and iron.

Solar winds create a vast bubble that surrounds our solar system called the heliosphere which strength can cause geomagnetic storms capable of knocking out power grids on Earth and causing the tails on comets to always point away from the Sun whether travelling to or away from it.

Besides other phenomena solar winds gift us the once seen never forgotten awesome curtains of fluorescent light known as the aurorae borealis (the Northern Lights and the aurora australis (the Southern Lights) seen in the night sky usually at altitudes between 90 and 130 km above sea level. The best places to view this celestial light show is near the magnetic poles— Northern Lights in Greenland, the Scandinavian coast, Siberia, Alaska and Aberdeen/Scotland, Southern Lights in Antarctica and the surrounding ocean, Tasmania, there have been reports the aurora has been seen from as far north as northern NSW/Australia and in the southern most states of the United Sates in the past after massive solar flares which are in the 30 degree latitudes. The Northern and Southern Lights occur simultaneously and are almost mirror images of each other.

The solar winds reach our planet a mere forty hours after leaving the Sun, they ride the lines of magnetic force generated by the Earth's core then flow through the magnetosphere dumping electrons in the upper atmosphere where dancing patterns and flowing curtains are born through magnetic and electrical forces re-acting to each another in constantly shifting combinations along atmospheric currents reaching 20,000,000 amperes at 50,000 volts. The aurora's neon colours depend on which atom is struck and at what altitude. Green and red—oxygen, green up to 241.35 km (150 mph) in altitude, red above 241.35 km in altitude. Blue, violet and purple —nitrogen, violet up to 96 km (60 mph) in altitude, violet and purple above 60 miles in altitude. There have been reports of sound associated with the aurora, but so far none has been recorded.

The outer border of our System lies beyond Pluto's realm and that is where the strength of Solar Winds are no longer great.

NASA has employed Solar Winds as a relatively inexpensive form of interstellar travel.

The one zodiac sign under the sovereignty of the Sun is Leo. Though recognized by both Indian and western astrologers, it is the western school that conferred on it its Leonine designation, calling it "The Lion" and allotting "Fire" as its primary substance.

The Moon—Our Satellite

The lunar world is aptly dubbed "The Sea of Tranquillity", for on its erosion free surface nothing is ever disturbed. From the cosmic rubble of ages to the footprints of the Apollo astronaut, all is still there, and will be for billions of years.

There is evidence that much eruptive activity occurred in Moon's remote past, but that was before this sleeping beauty became the gentle, persuasive counterpart to bustling Earth, but she is not as dead as a dodo because recently planetary scientists have cited shallow valleys in her slowly expanding surface caused by "Moonquakes". Without our lunar dancing partner working with the Sun we should have no gravitational energy to draw and deplete the waters of our world; nor would our dark evenings be lit by a silvery reflection of the Sun's light.

Romantic fiction turned to fact when actual pictures of the ghostly white landscape with its stark mountain ranges, deep winding canyons, flat plains of lava and vast, circular craters left by ancient bombarding meteorites, came back to us via satellite control. Our Moon, over which the fabled cow once jumped, was no longer merely an inaccessible light in the sky.

To scientists Earth's Moon is a sort of "Space Museum" from which dust can be gathered and analysed to assist in discovering secrets of our planet and the solar system's history. Its airless surface has trapped billions of tons of solar atoms, still as fresh as at the moment when, three billion Earth years ago, they were carried over by the Solar Winds. Green crystalline rock fragments, formed an estimated four million years ago, and shiny, transparent black crystals hiding in a moon rock three and a half million years old, look fresher now in the space scientist's photograph than would a much younger stone spat from a volcano on Earth. On our planet these minerals would long since have been eroded by one thing the Moon lacks our liquid water, or H2O.

Less romantically then, the Moon, with the same side always facing us, is a battered, lifeless globe formed either separately from Earth or from a spray of material ejected into space from our planet, but its origin has yet to be decided. Still, we do at least know that it is not made of cheese and that the Man in the Moon about whom we told our children so many stories is a figment of our imagination alas!

The Moon has many minerals similar to our own. They contain silicon, calcium, iron, titanium and magnesium, but not lead sodium or potassium. It also reveals particles of orange soil which are really minute glass beads formed through a former burst of intense heat. It has plentiful rocks, mostly composed of a sort of feldspar. Its diameter measures 3,476 kilometers, or 2,160 miles, a mere quarter of that of Earth.

One would wonder why the moons of other planets have names and our moon is simply called "Moon". The noun Moon derives from moone (1380) which came from mone (1135) which derives from Old English mona (before 725). This was the name of Earth's satellite. The Ancient Greeks called it "Selene", the Romans "Luna", the Celts sometimes called her "Artio", while America's Red Indians named each full moon as a separate identity such as "Full Wolf Moon" for the howl of wolves in Winter, "Full Snow Moon" for the heavy snow falls in February, and "Full Pink Moon" after the herb Moss Pink which flowers in April. Each nation had its own word, but they all simply meant "Moon". People were simply not aware that there were other moons accompanying other worlds until 1610 when Italian astronomer Galileo Galilei discovered four moons orbiting Jupiter in 1610 then these were given individual names to separate their identities. From then on the word moon became the given name of our satellite.

Both Indian and western astrologers agree that Cancerians are Moon ruled. Water is their element, because our Moon, working with our Sun controls the tides and all the waters under the Earth, including the preponderance of water in our own bodies. The Cancerian emblem is the Crab.

Mercury

Sun baked and covered by a colourless coating of bleached, pummelled rock dust and volcanic glass, planet Mercury's perilous position as the Sun's closest neighbour shows in its pock marked face, rough, cratered body and vast volcanic plains on the side facing the Sun and a mysterious, and very cold dark side facing planet Venus. Corresponding with the pitch black Mercurian sky, satanic shadows mark the rise of intensely lit white hills while shimmering plains spread below cliff paths curling and zigzagging a thousand metres above. This pale, confused landscape is shaped by volcanic action and major shrinkage which occurred long ago in Mercury's distant past while dark glassy lava regions display pitted rock where the planet's lighter material has been hardened by the Sun's splitting rays.

This is the eastern, Sun scorched side of the planet, with a super-heated day temperature of 400 degrees Celsius. In direct contrast, and as if touched by an angel, is the western side, this time exposed to Venus, in which evening covers the brutal countryside with a saintly shroud of dark grey and the temperature drops dramatically to minus 183 degrees Centigrade. The setting Sun's tenacious fingers throw skyward streamers of blue, gold and green which fly into distant space till they eventually fuse in aerial flight. Our Earth and Moon are seen as twin blue stars and the light of bright planet Venus shines with cut crystal clarity, casting hypnotic shadows over the lulled land. Solar Winds replenish Mercury's surface with helium.

Yet this apparently waterless, rocky world might be hiding ice in its deep craters which, because they are on the dark, shaded side of Venus can have temperatures hundreds of degrees below zero. Mercury has an ultra-slow axis spin which lengthens each day and night to the equivalent of nearly fifty nine complete rotations of Earth, yet its 87.969 Earth day year is the shortest in the solar system. Sprinting alone through space on an eccentric orbit, this lonely planet has no companion moon. The smallest world in our heaven (at 4,878 km or 3,049 miles in diameter), Mercury is fittingly named after the swift messenger of the gods, son of almighty Zeus and of Maia, the goddess of night. In Roman mythology Mercury is the god of commerce, travel and thievery.

NASA's "Messenger" orbiter is the second spacecraft to visit Mercury. It made three flybys before working its way into orbit in March 2011. Messenger was the first spacecraft to orbit Mercury.

By Indian astrological lore, Gemini comes under the domain of Mercury's light side and Virgo under its dark. Astrologers of the western school also place these two signs in Mercury's charge. Virgo's emblem is a woman carrying a sheaf of wheat with the element earth. Gemini's emblem is the twins, Artemis and Apollo, children of Zeus, who inhabit air.

Venus

As the only planet named after a female in our male orientated Solar System, Venus shows her individuality by making her days last longer than her years. She obtains this result by rotating at a snail's pace, making each individual day equivalent to about 243 Earth days. Yet the comparatively giddy speed at which she circles our Sun would cut Earth's year to 224.7 days. Her slow rotation has another unusual effect. Venus is the only world to have an even temperature day and night.

This steamy, torrid namesake of the Roman goddess of love has a surface heat of about 425 degrees Celsius, hot enough to melt lead. The drab, grey terrain has a strong orange cast and is constantly threatened by sulphuric rain from a highly charged electrical sky whence lightning and thunder precede gales of typhoon like violence which bully and catapult cart sized boulders over a punch drunk surface. Yet suddenly this volatile mistress of heaven can undergo a change of attitude and, although the globe remains flaming hot, light winds caress the broken rocks and stones of lava, salt and sulphur. Then change of heart again and quick as a blink, hurricane-force winds whip the planet.

Estimated to measure 12,104 kilometres (or 7,565 miles) across and with an atmospheric density about 100 times that of Earth, planet Venus gathers and traps heat and light, re-radiating precious little to her tiny neighbour Mercury.

Mexican mythologists used to say of their major god: "After his death Quetzalcoatl's heart rose to become silver Venus". From Earth, this perfectly shaped second world from the Sun appears heavily veiled by a curtain of cloud and water, her smooth, whitish orb pocked with craters, valleys and volcanoes, the whole resembling an austere, waterless seabed. Venus has no moons.

The European orbiter—Venus Express-since reaching Venus in April 2006 logged signs that Venus has been volcanically active in the last three million years suggesting the planet may still be geologically active.

Indian and western astrologers consider Taurus and Libra are ruled by Venus. Western sages allot the Bull of Minos as the Taurean emblem with an Earth element, while Libra has the Scales of Justice and air.

Planet Earth—Our Celestial Home

Believe it or not, our world is the only identity in our solar system which seems not to have been officially named. With the exception of some of Uranus' moons all other planets and satellites in our solar system are named after Greek or Roman gods or goddess.

The English word "Earth" derives from an 8th century Anglo Saxon word— Erda meaning "the ground" or "opposite to the sea" and there are, of course, many different interpretations of the word in other languages such as "Terra" — Portuguese, Dutch — "Aarde", "Terre" — French, Finnish — "Maa", "Bumi" — Malay, "Zeme" in Czech and so on. Imagine the confusion if there were a council of planets and those beings who were alien asked our planet's name. An embarrassing situation to say the least. A planet with no name is like calling a child "human" and we certainly think little of those humans who called their feline companion "cat" or their canine companions "dog one and dog two".

Thinking people have noted this horrendous state of affairs and have tried to correct it by giving our planet a feminine gender and calling her Gaia (or Gaea) after the mother of all Olympian gods, known through an epic poem written by Hesiod (8th-7th century BC).

He tells that before the solar system there was chaos from which arose the primeval divinity, the great mother of all, whose name was Gaia. She gave birth to the starry sky and a son named Uranus whom she lay with and consequently gave birth to our planet. Many scholars still use this name and all people give our planet a feminine gender. So perhaps we are on the way to giving a name to the nurturing mother of all life as we know it. For the respect our world deserves the remainder of this write-up will refer to our world as Gaia.

Gaia was born approximately 4.54 billion years ago; she is third planet from our Sun, the densest and the fifth largest world in our solar system. She is mainly composed of iron, oxygen, silicon and magnesium. Her nickel-iron core is molten and creates a magnetic field (magnetosphere) making Gaia a giant magnet with poles at the top and bottom of the planet. The magnetosphere extends beyond her surface for thousands of kilometres which, together with the ozone layer, protects us from radiation carried by the super-sonic solar wind, channelling it around the earth and then out to space. The glorious aurora borealis (Northern and Southern Lights) are particles from the Sun carried by the solar wind and trapped in Gaia's magnetic field which ionize the atmosphere as they enter causing glorious curtains of coloured lights which people travel the world to view.

Within the magnetosphere and near Gaia's body is an ocean of air (atmosphere) consisting of much nitrogen, a fair amount of oxygen and a small percentage of other ingredients. The oxygen and nitrogen molecules are comparable in size to the blue wave length entering our atmosphere from the sun and it is this that makes the sky, oceans, lakes and large rivers appear blue. Long-term climate change and short-term weather conditions are caused by the way vapour is distributed through the atmosphere.

Gaia's four seasons are the result of her axis of rotation which is tilted more than 23 degrees, but near the equator Gaia changes her notion of seasons and simply chooses a period of "Wet" and "Dry", phenomena of the "tropical savannah".

Gaia's oceans are at least 2.5 miles (4 kilometres) deep and water covers nearly 70% of Earth's surface; the remaining 30% is solid ground. When one speaks of water, it includes all the seas, lakes and underground water. Gaia's abundance of water is what sets her apart from other planets.

In space Gaia presents as a twin blue planet, meaning her moon (the Moon) is part of her. She has another two satellites named 3753 Cruithne and 2002 AA29. The former is 5 km across and is often referred to as Earth's second moon but is actually following its own distinct track around the Sun and doesn't orbit our world as our Moon and the other tiny (60 metres across) satellite 2002 AA29. 2002 AA29 follows a horseshoe orbit around the Earth that brings it close to Gaia every 95 years. There is some talk of a future space exploration mission to 202 AA29.

Earth is a terrestrial planet meaning she has a rocky body rather than a gas planet like Saturn, Jupiter and Uranus. Gaia is composed of five layers and two cores;

1. *Inner core* composed almost entirely of solid iron;
2. *Outer core* composed of a molten nickel-iron alloy;
3. *D layer* — unknown composition,
4. *Lower mantle* composition includes silicon, magnesium, and oxygen and probably also contains some iron, calcium, and aluminium.
5. *Transition region* mainly comprises basaltic magmas with amounts of calcium, aluminium and garnet;
6. *Upper mantle* is believed to comprise is made of crystalline forms of Olivine and pyroxene;
7. *Crust* is mostly made up of 8 elements which are Oxygen, Silicon, Aluminium, Iron, Magnesium, Calcium, Potassium, and Sodium.

There are 4,124 valid species of minerals according to the International Mineralogy Association. Gemstones and collector minerals are formed in various environments under Gaia's crust, it has not been proven but it is believed that the Diamond, Peridot and possibly Garnet and Zircon may be formed in the mantle.

All mining for gems takes place in Gaia's crust and it is up to the public to be on the backs of politicians to make them aware of environmental issues related to the gem mining industry such as soil erosion, sedimentation and destruction of river banks. The gem industry generates direct and indirect work opportunities and the beauty of Gaia's purest offspring gives pleasure to many.

As the author of this book "The Healing Power of Crystals" I am often asked if there is a precious gem directly connected with our planet more than any other body in our solar system. I answer without hesitation that it has to be Precious Opal because it is a gem which colours and patterns depend completely on the original stacking of tiny silicon spheres, not on a crystal structure, impurities or radiation. Silica is an essential trace mineral required by our and all free standing bodies for strong bones, healthy hair, nails, skin elasticity, flexible joints and general, radiant health. It is abundant in sea life and Silicon is the second most common element in Gaia's crust.

The early Roman Empire's famous author, naturalist and natural philosopher Gaius Plinius Secundus (23 AD – August 25, 79 AD), better known as Pliny the Elder, wrote of the Opal "There is in them a softer fire than the Ruby, there is the brilliant purple of the Amethyst and the sea green of the Emerald — all shining together in incredible union. Some by their splendour rival the colours of the painters, others the flame of burning sulphur or of fire quickened by oil".

Finally how could one write about our world without mentioning the genius and fate of the Italian Galileo Galilei physicist / mathematician / astronomer / philosopher who was born on 15th February 1564.

As a seventeenth century professor of astronomy he was required to teach the accepted theory of his time that the Earth was stationary at the centre of the universe and the sun and all other heavenly bodies revolved around it.

But Galileo publically upheld the new theory that the Earth was not flat, but spherical and it rotated around the sun.

The Holy Office in Rome threatened to execute him if he didn't speak the "truth" that being ignorantly based on Biblical references Psalm

93:1, 96:10, and 1 Chronicles 16:30 text stating that "the world is firmly established, it cannot be moved", Psalm 104:5 "the Lord set the earth on its foundations; it can never be moved" and Ecclesiastes 1:5 "And the sun rises and sets and returns to its place" etc.

Galileo was tried by the Inquisition and was found "vehemently suspect of heresy" and was required to publically withdraw his support for the theory and to abjure, curse and detest those opinions.

He was sentenced to formal imprisonment at the pleasure of the Inquisition. On the following day this was commuted to house arrest, which he remained under until he died aged 77 years.

Mars

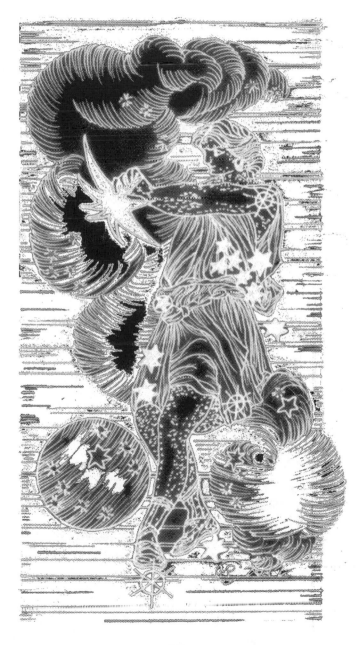

Named after the god of war, because this planet shows reddish in our evening sky which reminded the ancients of spilled blood, Mars is in fact a curiously peaceful planet which boasts a fragile atmosphere and soft, scattered clouds in a pinkish-orange sky. Blissful winds whose gentleness belies their speed (24 km or 15 mph) brush over the mid-green terrain with its cracked craters peppered with meteorite scars. They are hurrying to reach the other side of the planet where the undulating landscape comprises crushed strawberry and orange-toned sand dunes with bracken tinted shadows. In contrast to its arthritic looking green side, here the setting Sun will illuminate and light the rock masses and bronze the ribbons of dry riverbeds which coil their way through pinky brown deserts for hundreds of kilometres, fading at last into tributary arms which reach into snow-capped mountains.

Mars is always much colder than Earth, with temperatures capable of dropping to -207 degrees Fahrenheit or -133 degrees Celsius. The Martian evening is truly dark, for the planet's two moons, Phobos and Deimos, named after the sons of Greek god of war Ares, are fashioned from sombre, irregular lumps of matter thought to be captured asteroids. However, at 7.30 a.m. local time a theatrically lit early morning will find the peak of a colossal, extinct volcano called Olympus Mons (25 kilometres or 15 miles high) looking down on an orchestral space dance in which the performers are frolicking patches of blue and green vapour disappearing into a pink heaven from the valleys and crater basins. The valleys' fluted edges recall wind and rain erosion on Earth but there so far there appears to be no liquid water here. Scientists know that liquid water once flowed in rivers across the surface of Mars long ago was because the clay-like soil is coloured by rusted iron and the rocks are similar to the sulphur and water compounds and the lava found on Earth. Sadly, this fourth globe from the Sun and the planet most favoured by science fiction writers past and present is so far giving little indication of whether it did or did not support life as we know it. That said, where there is water there is usually life and NASA's Mars Odyssey spacecraft detected huge deposits of water in the form of ice underneath and across the planet's surface.

At this point in time—December 2012—the world is waiting in anticipation to be told what NASA's aptly named robotic rover "Curiosity" has discovered. Certainly Martian caves are a promising location for future human settlement and perhaps the warmer environment of the sub-surface will offer proof of life which once was or still is on or inside our immediate, planetary neighbour.

We do know this apricot coloured star which shines in our night sky was once Earth-like and both planets have many similarities. Although one

Martian year is the equivalent of twenty three months on Earth, both take approximately 24 hours to rotate on their axes, each enjoys four seasons and has ice caps which aren't quite centred on their North and South poles. Mars has a rotational 30 degree tilt similar to that of Earth, although its diameter is smaller at about 6,794 kilometres (4,246 miles), making this intriguing planet about 53% of our planet Earth's mass.

Pink is the colour of unconditional love and Mars on the outer side of the Sun shines for us with softer brilliance than Venus does on her Sun side.

Indian astrologers say Mars shows its pink side for Aries and its green side for Scorpio. Western astrologers place Mars as the Arian ruling planet, designate the golden fleeced ram (Mars spelt backwards without the S) as the sign's emblem and give "fire" as its substance. Some astrologers say Scorpio has a sub-influence of Mars.

Asteroid Belt

When the sun formed, about 4.5 billion years ago, it was surrounded by a disk of gas and dust. During the next few million years, our major planets formed from the contents of that disk, and the remaining dust and gas concentrated in the main Asteroid Belt, between the orbits of Mars and Jupiter, where numerous irregularly shaped bodies have repeatedly crashed into one another to form asteroids or/and minor, dwarf planets. Asteroids are rocky, airless worlds that orbit our sun, but are too small to be called planets. It seems that perhaps half the mass of the belt is contained in the four largest asteroids: Ceres, Vesta, Pallas, and Hygeia.

Ceres, about 950km (about 590 miles) In diameter, named after the Roman goddess of growing plants, the harvest, and motherly love by Giuseppe Piazzi (1746-1826) an Italian Catholic priest, mathematician, and astronomer, is the Asteroid Belts only identified dwarf planet at this moment. Scientists suspect she is divided into core and mantle, and may have ice caps and a thin atmosphere.

Vesta, named after the Roman virgin goddess of home and hearth, the second largest member of the Asteroid Belt, around 530km (about 329 miles) in diameter and density make it massive enough for its gravity to keep it roughly spherical, like a proper planet. Evidence suggests it has a nickel iron core like our Earth's, overlain by a rocky mantle.

Pallas round 530.565 km (about 329 miles) named after Pallas Athena (an alternate name for the goddess Athena) is slightly larger than Vesta but it is however, 20% less massive. Pallas is possibly the largest irregularly shaped body in our solar system.

Hygeia, named after the Greek goddess of health, has oblong diameters of 350x500 km (about 217x311 miles), and is the fourth largest asteroid by volume and mass.

The remaining bodies range down to the size of a dust particle. The Asteroid Belt material is so thinly distributed that multiple unmanned spacecraft have traversed it without incident. But collisions between large asteroids do occur, the result being a fine dust that forms a major portion of the zodiacal light, a faint, whitish glow sometimes seen in the night sky. When asteroids pass close to Earth they are called a "Near-

Earth Objects" (NEOs).Many modern, western astrologers consider Virgo is strongly influenced by our main Asteroid Belt. If one believes in signs then this thinking should be considered because Virgo's symbol is a female carrying a sheaf of grain and each of the four dwarf planets have been named after female deities of harvest, home, food and health by scientists who, in the main, scoff at astrology. Interesting?

Year 2012, NASA's Dawn mission is on a journey to the Asteroid Belt to orbit asteroid Vesta and dwarf planet Ceres, hoping to understand the conditions of the solar system's earliest days by studying these two very different worlds.

Shooting Stars

These magical night-sky features are small chunks of rock and debris from space which fall through Earth's atmosphere showing a bright tail as they are heated to incandescence by the friction of our atmosphere and those pieces that to land on Earth are called meteorites.

Science has tagged almost 260 minerals found on our planet in meteorites and another 40 minerals exclusive to extra-terrestrial habitat. "Stony Meteorites" known as "Chondrites" are the most common. Chondrites are characterized by small spheres of formerly melted minerals that have come together with other mineral matter to make solid rock. They are believed to be among the oldest minerals in the solar system. "Iron Meteorites" and "Stony Irons" are the other common groups. Magnetite, an ore of iron, is found in the crusts of most meteorites. Meteorites can contain chromite an ore of chrome, clay, Olivine (Peridot), many of the feldspar group, carbon (as graphite and Diamond) and corundum—the mineral family Sapphire and Ruby belong to but the colour is more usually grey, not red or blue. Scientists are still trying to unravel the truth about glass meteorites. They may be from meteorites impacting our atmosphere, or perhaps they are the result of silicone-rich earth that melted and fused from a fallen meteorite's heat. Then it is thought perhaps some items sold as "Glass meteorites" may not have extra-terrestrial origins but could be natural glass from our planet's volcanic activity. School's still out on that one.

The Antarctic search for meteorites (ANSMET) program which began in 1976 has recovered more than 10,000 from Antarctica. They are currently considered the only reliable, continuous source of new, non-microscopic extra-terrestrial material.

Astrologically speaking Shooting Stars can affect all signs, but no sign is completely under their influence. They are included in this book because they contain minerals from on our planet and (other) mystery minerals from extra-terrestrial sources.

43

Jupiter

Positioned in the dynamic middle path of the Solar System, belching huge aerial waves, Jupiter well deserves its occasional nickname of "Enraged Bull of the Universe". Its gyrating mass abounds in swirling tints of yellow, black and brown, relieved by smaller patches of mid-blue and pink. A vehement storm in the guise of a great red spot has menaced its anguished face for the past three hundred years. Named after the Roman equivalent of the great god Zeus, lord of the thunderbolts and giver of victory, this titanic ball with the density of very weak gravy shows unremitting fury at its dismissal to outer space.

In Jupiter's immediate sky, rapid, whining wind changes tear wretched clouds to pathetic excuses, while from the depths of its gaseous atmosphere feathery plumes of some vivid, unknown substance throw intense and immeasurable ultraviolet light, promising death to any Earthman insolent enough to venture there.

Above the melee and like a flock of frightened angels, four large alabaster coloured moons float in semi-stillness. These frozen combinations of ammonia, carbon dioxide and nitrogen glitter and gleam as spidery webs of crackling orange and blue electrical currents flick icy spangles from their frosty mantles. They are called the Galilean Satellites after Italian astronomer Galileo who discovered them in 1610. Named Io, Europa, Ganymede, and Callisto, each Moon has a distinctive character of its own.

As they orbit Jupiter Io is in a tug-of-war with Ganymede and Europa, and Europa's orbital period around Jupiter is twice Io's period, and Ganymede's period is twice that of Europa yet the moons always face Jupiter as if they are afraid to turn their backs on their torrid master. Io is Jupiter's principal satellite and queen. She glows bright red and yellow due to the presence of iron and sulphur elements formed from the first active volcanoes found outside of our planet. Myriad shimmering golden haloes crown her surface and can be seen through the telescope reflected intermittently in white snow patches patterning its otherwise charred, jet-black terrain.

Europa's water ice surface shows signs it may be covering an ocean of water or slushy ice, possibly hiding twice as much water as that of planet Earth. Astrobiologists think Europa may have a habitable zone because life forms have been found thriving near similar subterranean volcanoes on Earth.

Ganymede is the largest moon in the solar system and is the only moon known to have its own internally generated magnetic field.

Callisto's face is extremely heavily cratered and ancient but the very few small craters on Callisto indicate a small degree of current surface activity.

Also witnessing their master's wrath are 50 named, unattached moons and another sixteen provisional moons waiting for an opportunity to get closer to their master.

Jupiter was the king of the gods in Roman mythology, making the name a good choice for the largest planet in the Solar System. At the enormous measurement of 142,800 kilometres (89,500 miles) it has a diameter more than eleven times that of Earth and is an astonishing 3,018 times greater in mass. Its rotational spin takes just under ten hours, against Earth's 24, though it takes nearly twelve years to make its journey round the Sun. Seen from our planet it glows with a steady, yellow based, blue-green light a deceptive appearance of calm. It is hideously cold.

NASA's Pioneers 10 and 11, Voyager 1 and Voyager 2 showed great colour views and global perspectives from flybys of the Jupiter system and later the Galileo spacecraft passed as low as 260 km (162 miles) over Jupiter's moons resulting in images with incredible detail.

Western astrologers consider Sagittarians are influenced by this powerful globe, while Indian astrologers place both Pisceans and Sagittarians in the Jovian domain. Western sages give the Archer cum Centaur as the Sagittarian emblem and "Fire" as its essence.

Saturn

A great, flattened, golden brown balloon surrounded by speeding circular bands of luminous light resembling rainbows such is the appearance of Saturn, "the Charmer of the Universe" named after the second oldest deity in the Roman Empire, god of agriculture and fertility.

No other world can compare with this illustrious masterpiece about (diameter 120,536 kilometres or 74,900 miles). Fifty three named moons accompany this beauty while nine, unnamed, provisional moons lie in wait, hoping to become part of the spectacular gas giant's unique beauty.

Saturn's rings—also referred to as bands or hoops—are spectacular. Measuring no more than one km (3,200 ft.) or less in depth, they span up to 282,000 km (175,000 miles) from the planet which is about three quarters of the distance between our own planet Earth and its Moon. These spinning hoops festooning Saturn are composed of thousands of ringlets of countless miniature moons and others as large as mountains fashioned from cosmic dust which reflect the Sun's light through their coating of frozen gases. Formed into at least seven major hoops they speed in their own orbits round planet Saturn which takes about 10,759.26 Earth days, or 29.46 Earth years, to circle the Sun. Scientists believe there may be life on one of Saturn's moon named Enceladus because NASA's Cassini spacecraft discovered ice geysers gushing from the moon's southern pole and the thought here is that wherever we find water on our planet we find life. Back to Saturn itself; because of this slow, deliberate trudge, or perhaps because it was named after an aged god, Saturn has suffered from mistaken classifications and been wrongly identified with heavy corresponding Earth minerals. In fact this gossamer globe has the lightest body weight of all planets in our area of the Milky Way and very pretty shadows of bright indigo and deep violet mark its whitish and yellow-brown surface with fuzzy edged patches. A most unusual feature of Saturn's sky is an extra-long, ribbon-like cloud which floats below at least twenty extravagantly fashioned water ice moons of much larger proportions than those fairy domains which comprise its reflective rings.

Being so far from the Sun, Saturn is dimly lit, although it is easy to see a small, revolving red spot which stalks its face and is thought to be a hideous storm. Its weather conditions seem stable, doubtless because this sixth world in our planetary system emits uninterruptedly and at a constant rate three times the amount of heat it receives from the Sun. After this incredible world the Solar Wind weakens somewhat, sprinkling its ebbing strength on the nine gyrating haloes whose billions of rainbows effectively crown Saturn with more jewels than any king could acquire.

To enter Saturn's orbit, NASA's Cassini flew through a gap between two rings, during which time it logged incredible information and footage.

Indian Astrologers give Aquarians and Capricorns a Saturnian ruling, but their Western counterparts allow only the latter to come under Saturn alone, placing Aquarians under the sign of Uranus. So Aquarians reading this book must look under Uranus for their minerals. For Capricorns, the Western school designates the Sea Goat as their emblem and Earth as their substance.

Uranus

The glacial temperature on Uranus the coldest planet in our Solar System is hardly friendly at minus180 degrees Centigrade but the icy sunlight, roughly 1,000 times brighter than that of the full moon on Earth, invites strange reveries. All shades of turquoise from green to bright, mid blue to blue green, through Sherwood to olive, suffuse the planet's genteel hollows, making them appear deeper, while airborne icicles, similarly coloured, suggest fairy tale forests.

This green giant, its girth measuring 51,800 kilometres (32,375 miles) contains the low temperature, lighter-than-air gas Methane in its mainly hydrogen and Helium atmosphere which gives Uranus its stunning blue colour. Methane is a major constituent of natural gas and petroleum and on Earth often found near water. Many scientists have consequently been tempted to deduce the presence of water on Uranus, and also that the planet produces oxygen, Carbon, nitrogen, silicon and Iron. These in turn produce between them hydrogen, helium, methane and ammonia.

No internal heat emanates from this extraordinary globe, which, like a tubby man who can't rise after a fall, rolls sideways during the 84 Earth years, that it takes to circle the Sun. Believe it or not, the warmest place on this planet is probably either it's North or its South Pole, rather than it's Equator.

The moons of Uranus are mostly a lightweight group but the two largest moons; Titania (diameter of about half the diameter of the Earth's moon) and her partner Oberon are crowned by shimmering, ice frosted haloes. Named after the fairy king and queen in Shakespeare's A Midsummer Night's Dream, they faithfully act out their parts, the jealous and conceited Oberon not wanting the exquisite Titania to outshine him, and the proud queen not giving way, so that they both hurl effervescent bubbles of light far beyond themselves, propelling toxic vivacity towards the Sun.

Three smaller satellites are in attendance on Titania and Oberon. There is Umbriel, who betrays his presence by no more than a shy sparkle, Miranda in her dark cloak, and Ariel, who tries to win the admiration of the royal couple by throwing out shiny bubbles. Above them the known thirteen, watchful black rings of Uranus, seventh world from the Sun, arc narrow and steady, a reminder that this planet was named after the father of the antique gods, who with his wife Ge (Earth) brought forth the Titans, the Cyclops, the Furies and other terrifying creatures of mythology. Uranus was discovered by William Herschel, court astronomer to King George III, who wrote that he was renaming the planet George, since "it first shone officially in his auspicious reign.

God save the King". The result was laughter, followed by a protracted stalemate. Was this new planet to be called by the name of its discoverer or his king, or the most ancient of the gods? It took sixty years to decide and then name it Uranus to honour the earliest supreme god, ancient Greek deity of the heavens.

Because this planetary system is nearly 4,828,032,000 kilomtres (3 billion miles) away little was known about the moons of Uranus or indeed how many he had in attendance until 1986 when Voyager 2 visited the system and did a headcount and found Juliet, Puck, Cordelia, Ophelia, Bianca, Desdemona, Portia, Rosalind, Cressida and Belinda. Since then astronomers have raised the total to twenty seven moons, all named after either a Shakespearian character or from the poetic mind of Alexander Pope.

Indian Astrologers do not recognize this jolly green giant as a ruling body, but Western seers place Aquarius under its domain. They allocate air as the Aquarian substance and the Water Bearer as its symbol.

Neptune

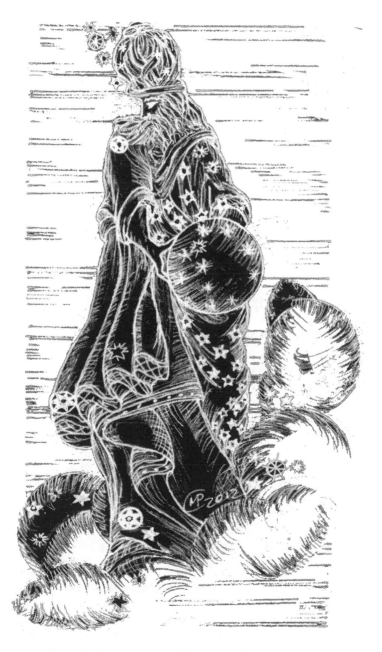

To the eye of the beholder Neptune is a stunning planet presenting as a glittering, bright blue balloon, poised in space and encircled by six white hoops.

This world truly wanted to be recognized as it was first recorded in 1612 as a fixed star by Italian astronomer Galileo Galilei, predicted mathematically as a planet by English and French astronomers John Couch Adams and Urbain Le Verrier in 1845, and then discovered by Johann Galle at the Berlin Observatory in 1846.

Neptune is the eighth world from the sun and the last of the great, gas giants in our solar system with a diameter of about 50,540 kilometres (31,400 miles) making it seventeen times the size of Earth. It is a fast mover, with a spin producing a sixteen hour day and an eighteen hour night. The rapidity of this spin causes pressure to build up, first, on the planet's slightly flattened top and base and, secondly, on its two sides. But it takes a tedious 164.80 Earth years to orbit the Sun. Scientists have decided Neptune is composed of the same chemicals that make up Earth's solid rocky crust—hydrogen, helium, silicates and water. Beneath the bright blue clouds Neptune presents a dark and chilly surface covered with thick layers of hydrogen sulphide cloud whipped to frenzy by supersonic winds traveling at more than 1,000 kilometres per hour (700 miles).

Named after the old Roman god of the sea the bright blue clouds surrounding this planet consist mainly of frozen methane and at least one other substance not yet decided. When methane atoms are broken down they become carbon which in turn, when compressed under great pressure, becomes the pure substance of Diamonds. And so the presence of Diamonds on Neptune may reasonably be deduced. But, unlike Earth, Diamonds may not be found in this world's interior because it has a non-solid surface of heavily compressed gasses above an ocean of water and liquid chemicals churning around an Earth sized, solid rock core.

Therefore one could be forgiven for imagining Neptune to appear as a raging sea of cloud capped by oodles of perfectly shaped Diamonds which shimmer in the light of the distant sun. This fairy tale description may sound far-fetched, but in fact Neptune's Diamonds would be composed of the same chemicals and elements as those on Earth and it is very likely the planet is rich in them.

Neptune's six known rings are unusual because NASA'S Voyager 2 in 1989 found they are not uniform but have three thick regions called arcs which have been named Liberty, Equality and Fraternity. The existence of arcs is explained by the gravitational effects of a moon named Galatea.

Neptune's largest moon—Triton—with a diameter of 2,700 kilometres (1,680 miles) is immense in comparison with our Moon. Named after the child of Neptune and Amphitrite, pleasing Greek goddess of the sea, Triton is represented in legend as a fish with a human head. This is the only large satellite in our solar system which circles its planet in the opposite direction to the rotation of the planet it accompanies.

Till recently many science fiction buffs thought that if an unspeakable catastrophe struck planet Earth, perhaps one of the best places to migrate to would be Triton for it was thought this satellite has an earth like atmosphere possibly capable of supporting human life. But NASA's Voyager 2 revealed Triton's surface is one of the coldest places in our solar system at about -400 degrees Fahrenheit (-240 degrees Celsius) so cold that ice volcanos spewing a mix of liquid nitrogen, methane and dust instantly freeze and then snow back to the surface.

Apart from that Triton rotates in an alarmingly precarious fashion, lurching backwards and off centre, with the consequence that this suicidal mass is likely to disintegrate (though perhaps not for ten, or even a hundred, million years) as it draws too near to its planet.

Science has much to discover about Neptune and its thirteen known moons, all named after ancient Greek sea gods and nymphs.

Planet Neptune is disregarded as a ruling body by Indian Astrologers, but Pisceans are ruled by it according to the Western tradition. Pisceans' badge of office is two fish joined head to tail and their primary element is water.

Pluto

On the rim of the Solar System, 5,900 million kilometres (or 3,666 million miles) from the Sun, dwarf planet Pluto rotates erratically accompanied by its five moons—Charon, Nix, Hydra and the temporally named P4 and P5. One of the most secretive entities in our area of the Milky Way, it is thought Pluto is one of the largest known bodies the Kuiper belt, a shadowy disk-like zone beyond the orbit of Neptune populated by a trillion or more comets.

But what is Pluto? Perhaps a new class of world which may be a giant comet that doesn't shoot out of its highly eccentric orbit, or perhaps it is a dwarf planet, a double planet or material once kicked off Jupiter or Neptune when they were forming, but whatever Pluto is, it certainly holds precious information because it was formed early in the history of our solar system. Astronomers have calculated that Pluto has a whisper-thin atmosphere of nitrogen, methane and carbon dioxide and its chemical composition is probably 70% rock and 30% water ice.

By calculations based on comparisons with our Moon, Pluto's estimated diameter is less than one-fifth that of Earth or only about two-thirds as wide as Earth's moon.

At only three hundred times the strength of full moon on Earth, the far away, midday Sun twinkles like a dazzling pin prick in the Plutonian sky, a twilight zone on a glazed, flat, frozen surface— roughly minus 375 degrees F (minus 225 degrees C). Coloured reddish stabbed with slate and hazy-purple shadows, Pluto was rightly named after the Roman god of the Infernal Regions, brother of Jupiter and Neptune by Venetia Burney of Oxford, an 11 year old girl, English girl. The first two letters of this world's name also honours Percival Lowell, an American astronomer who first caught hints of Pluto's existence in 1905 from odd deviations he observed in the orbits of Neptune and Uranus. Pluto's discovery came in 1930 from Clyde William Tombaugh at the Lowell Observatory, based on predictions from Lowell and other astronomers.

Pluto's largest moon with a pure, water ice mass roughly half that of its planet is named Charon after the Greek god, Ferryman of the Dead. This satellite is most unusual not only because it moves neither to North, South, East nor West in relation to its planet and hangs stationary above it in luminous complacency, but it is a giant in comparison with our own Moon, of which it is six times the size.

Together this pair of frosty entities, which at the birth of the Solar System were molten fireballs, slowly circumnavigates the Sun, taking the equivalent of 247.7 Earth years (or over 90,000 days) to complete each course. On their six day rotational period Pluto and its moon have a hair raising habit of crossing the orbital path of Neptune, their nearest planetary neighbour, in a sort of celestial bout of Russian Roulette, spurred on, say scientists, by the hypnotic attraction that Neptune has for Pluto's moon. Pluto and planet Earth, again according to astronomers, are the only two worlds with a double planetary system, but there the likeness between them ends, since Earth and our Moon are nearly five times further apart than Pluto and his Ferryman.

Soon Pluto will no longer be unchartered territory because NASA's current mission "New Horizons" launched in 2006 from Earth and using Jupiter's gravity field like a slingshot is due to make its closest approach to Pluto July 14th 2015. The ashes of Clyde Tombaugh (February 4, 1906-January 17, 1997) are on board and he will go where no man has ever gone before, not only to his beloved Pluto, but far beyond because after New Horizons has collected and relayed information for NASA it will travel to outer space to witness who knows what.

Though Western Astrologers take account of Pluto, Indian practitioners dismiss It as a vulgar interloper (it was discovered as recently as 1930 and then, in the first instance, by mathematical calculation rather than direct observation). In the Western scheme this dwarf planet, one of the furthest solar system identities from the Sun is designated as the ruler of Scorpio with Mars as a sub-influence. Its subjects have the Desert Scorpion or, anciently the Eagle as their emblem and water as their substance.

PART TWO

Sign by Sign and Stone by Stone

Notes:

1. *The approximate beginning and ending dates of each astrological sign (according to Tropical Zodiac dates printed in the following charts) differ from year to year by a day or two according to astronomical calendars which all meticulous astrologers study and abide.*

2. *On advice given by Astrologers Betina Lee and Jeff Meddle—both attached to the London Astrological Lodge, John Clarke of the Sydney Astrological Centre and Manika Gosh Astrologer and Tutor of the Indian School of Astrology, scientifically matched Birthstones for each Zodiac sign must also be in harmony with its mutable planet or satellite. Therefore sun signs on the following charts are divided into two parts because a different, mutable planet or satellite interplays with the major planet or satellite about half way through its cycle adding its own energy at the time of an individual's birth. Again dates vary by a few days annually according to the Astronomical Almanac.*

Zodiac Sunsign	Celestial Ruler	Mutable Body	Precious Crystal	Talisman	Bedside Rock
Aries 21/03 05/04	Mars	Sun	Pink Diamond, Pink Sapphire	Sunstone, Jasper	Cinnabar
Aries 06/04 20/04	Mars	Jupiter	Alexandrite Rhodonite	Bowenite, Carnelian	Youngite, Ruby Zoisite
Taurus 21/04 04/05	Venus	Mercury	Emerald, Green Sapphire	Azurite, Malachite	Marcasite, Pyrite
Taurus 05/05 21/05	Venus	Saturn	Spinel, Andalusite	Lavender Jadeite, Ammonite	Irish Fairy Stone
Gemini 22/05 05/06	Mercury	Venus	Orange Sapphire, Taafite	Green Garnet, Moss Agate	Staurolite, Verdite
Gemini 06/06 21/06	Mercury	Uranus	Cat's Eye Chrysoberyl	Jade, Green Garnet	Rubellite, Geode
Cancer 22/06 06/07	Moon	Pluto	Blue Moonstone, Scapolite	Pearl, Rose Quartz	Aragonite, Calcite
Cancer 07/07 23/07	Moon	Neptune	Water Opal	Coral	Desert Rose, Water Nodule Selenite
Leo 24/07 07/08	Sun	Jupiter	Yellow Diamond	Zircon, Phenacite	Vanadinite, Muscovite
Leo 08/08 23/08	Sun		White Diamond	Heliodore, Sphene	Suphur, Volcanic-Bombs
Virgo 24/08 07/09	Mercury	Saturn	Black Opal, Pietersite	Labradorite Orange Garnet	Hematite, Magnetite
Virgo 08/09 23/09	Mercury	Venus	Iolite, Red Garnet	Tiger's Eye, Vesuvian Lava	Meteorite, Obsidian

Zodiac Sunsign	Celestial Ruler	Mutable Body	Precious Crystal	Talisman	Bedside Rock
Libra 24/09 08/10	Venus	Uranus	Spinel, White (clear) Topaz	Dioptase, Tsavorite	Kyanite, Wavellite
Libra 09/10 23/10	Venus	Mercury	Blue Sapphire, Sillimanite	Green Jadeite	Adamite, Ilmenite
Scorpio 24/10 07/11	Pluto/ Mars	Neptune	Ruby, Benitoite	Blue John	Stibnite, Crocoite
Scorpio 08/11 22/11	Pluto/ Mars	Moon	Rhodocrosite Colour-change Sapphire	Amethyst	Okenite, Prehnite
Sagittarius 23/11 06/12	Jupiter	Mars	Melonstone Tourmaline, Phospho-phylite	Amber Eilat Stone	Chryso-colla
Sagittarius 07/12 21/12	Jupiter	Sun	Tourmaline	Turquoise Hauyne	Bornite Thunder-Egg
Capricorn 22/12 07/01	Saturn	Venus	Topaz, Chondrolite	Jet, Lazulite	Stichtite Amethyst
Capricorn 08/01 20/01	Saturn	Mercury	Tanzanite, Opal	Lapis Lazuli	Rock Crystal, Venus-Hair
Aquarius 21/01 04/02	Uranus	Mercury	Peridot, Braziliantite	Aven-turine, Onyx	Wulfenite
Aquarius 05/01 19/02	Uranus	Venus	Star Diopside, Tugtupite	Jade, Casiterite	Charoite, Torbenite
Pisces 20/02 05/03	Neptune	Moon	Diamond, Aquamarine	Smith-sonite, Satinspar	Opal-Fossil
Pisces 06/03 20/03	Neptune	Pluto	Kunzite, Hiddenite	Chryso-prase, Lace agate	Fluorite, Apophy-lite

First Half Aries Precious Crystal

PINK DIAMOND
A "fancy" is the term used in the diamond trade for fine quality gems exhibiting beautiful and unusual tints. One of the rarest in this class is the Pink Diamond, of which the finest specimens occur in Australia. It is the precious crystal which corresponds with the first half of Aries ruled by the planet Mars with the Sun as a mutable body.

To deal with the mutable mass first, it should be said that a Diamond is formed of one element only and is unique in that this one element (carbon) is self-bonding when exposed to elevated temperatures and extreme pressure, after which it becomes a crystal of carbon, better known as a Diamond. The Diamond, like the Sun, has no affinity with water. It can withstand very high temperatures and, in correspondence to the Sun's light, has the highest degree of brilliance possible in a transparent material.

Nobody knows for certain but currents thoughts are that pink Diamonds are coloured by some clever structural deformation. As first set Aries have the Sun as their mutable body and Mars as their true celestial sovereign they must have a Pink Diamond.

Moreover, in view of the fact that Mars has no liquid surface water and that popular astrology considers the Aries individual to be ruled by the "red" side of Mars, the Pink Diamond corresponds with this gentle planet of the rusty-pink terrain and the softly coloured pink sky down to the last detail.

PINK SAPPHIRE
This is the second precious crystal for first half Arians. Strong enough to deal with the Sun as a mutable planet at a hardness of 9 (the number allotted to Mars by numerologists) and thought to be coloured by a sniff of iron and chromium, this stone has a metallic element dominant in its composition and is one of the most intensely luminous crystals in existence.

Second Half Aries Precious Crystal

ALEXANDRITE
This scarce variety of the chrysoberyl family has a curious absorption of light in the critical yellow-green of the spectrum which gives it marked

hues of dark, mossy-green in day light and soft, columbine or raspberry-red under electricity. Sometimes Alexandrite occurs in paler shades, but still exhibits the pink to green colour-change. Coloured by the metallic element chromium, it actually comprises the rare metal beryllium, and also aluminium, the former giving it a correspondence with planet Jupiter, which scientists believe has rare metals swirling around in its mass. The Beryl is the only commercial source of beryllium, and this, being one of the lightest metallic elements, is a bodyweight match for both Jupiter and Mars.

Because of its colour-change, the Alexandrite is often thought of as an Emerald by day and an Amethyst by night and for this peculiarity is treasured by connoisseurs. It was also much valued by a scoundrelly old womanizer of days gone by, who used it to trick innocent girls. He told them that if the Emerald they saw by day turned into an Amethyst by night it would prove his undying love for them.

Discovered on the birthday of Tsar Alexander II, and sporting the Russian national colours, the Alexandrite is the first gem of Russia. It came to light first on the banks of the Takovaya River in the Urals, but since this lovely gemstone has been found in Brazil, Madagascar, Zimbabwe and Sri Lanka.

RHODONITE
Yet another precious gem for Arians born in this half. Whether transparent or translucent, this little known and rare crystal reflects the tranquil Martian rusty-pink terrain and it's pink to soft rose-red sky. In sympathy with Jupiter, Rhodonite has a greenish tone when containing impurities, but its basic composition is variable in that its manganese elements can be replaced by calcium or iron. This gemstone has a medium hardness of 5.5-6.5 out of 10, but is still very wearable and quite at home with frosty Mars and with Jupiter's distance from the Sun.

Semi-precious, translucent to opaque Rhodonite with its splendid spectrum of baby-pink, crushed strawberry and raspberry tints, the opaque variety often seamed by a black alteration product, was favoured by Carl Fabergé, whose aristocratic clientele commissioned petite vases of Rhodonite berries, boxes and farmyard animals. In view of this one would assume that the best quality came from Russia, but in fact much top quality Rhodonite occurs in the vicinity of the hot, dusty Australian town called Broken Hill.

First Half Aries Talisman

SUNSTONE

A reddish iridescence, brought about by minute inclusion of Hematite, Lepidocrite and like materials on a yellow or brownish-yellow background, is a characteristic of this gem. Lepidocrite is a mineral made of translucent red to orange-red crystals found in veins of iron, and hematite is a valuable iron ore. Both correspond with the Martian globe.

The Sunstone imitates the Sun by its red and gold spangled brilliance which glitters and gleams sensationally in jewellery. It is usually cut with a rounded surface or half round. When flecked with red, the Sunstone is called Jasper, another Arian birthstone.

HELIOTROPE

An alternative talisman for these Arians, the name of this dark-green gemstone with red flecks is derived from the Greek word meaning "sun turning". It is otherwise known as a Bloodstone. This legendary gemstone, which, it was once believed, would change the yellow of the Sun to crimson if immersed in water, has always brought its wearer good fortune. It lives with the chalcedony family which usually forms at low temperatures, making it an Earth mineral parallel to Mars in colour, composition and formation. The Red Indians, Arabs and Babylonians wore amulets of carved Bloodstone.

When Bloodstone lacks its red flecks it is called Plasma (another gemstone for the Arians in this set). The dark-green is coloured by a material known as "green earth" which is not what its name implies but rather a mineral derived from chemicals in molten lava which are rich in both iron and manganese.

Second Half Aries Talisman

BOWENITE

The ancient Persians called it "Sang-I-Yashim", the New Zealand Maoris "Tangiwaiit", and we know it as Bowenite, the talisman for Arians in the second half.

Previously the stones allotted as talismans to Arians have been of bright and harsh colours, perhaps through ignorance of the fact that their celestial sovereign's mass is muted, rather than brutal-red, and that the ancient side of Mars is green.

Bowenite with its soft, mystic green translucence belongs to the serpentine family of minerals, yet it is more than twice as hard as the other members of its clan at a count of 55. It contains the Martian metal (iron) amongst other metallic elements which correspond to that planet.

Wonderful specimens occur in America, Afghanistan, China, Kashmir and New Zealand, the last mentioned country producing green Bowenite with a touch of blue which noticeably deepens that normally pale stone. For the pocket of the average person, splendid Bowenite beads, assorted jewellery and carvings are available.

The carvings are generally fashioned in China and often sold as "New Chinese Jade". Apart from this the occasional Bowenite talisman from the Punjab may be found in genuine antique shops.

Carl Fabergé commemorated the birth of Tsarevitch Nicholas, heir to the Russian throne, by designing a presentation clock of Bowenite embellished with opalescent-pink and translucent-white enameling, Rose (cut) Diamonds, silver gilt figures and platinum doves.

CARNELIAN
Sometimes called "Sard" or "Cornelian" Carnelian is another talisman for second set Arians. Carnelian is a transparent tawny-red or translucent yellow-rust member of the chalcedony group. Around the middle of the sixth century the Greeks and Phoenicians started using cutting wheels and drills to embellish gemstones. Carnelian was the favourite material because of its fine, granular formula, its availability and its variegated shadings, which were carefully utilized. The artist used the drill as a brush and the stone as both paint and canvas. Paler zones were meticulously worked for intricate hairstyles and the upper folds of garments, the darker tints for the face and body. A popular subject was the Egyptian scarab, worn as a ring and used as a seal. The carved side of the beetle was set lengthways on a swivel, thus enabling it to be flipped over to reveal the underside engraved with personal insignia.

Carl Fabergé also worked Carnelian. His "Pumpkin Box", decorated with yellow-gold, white enamel and Rose (cut) Diamonds is magnificent.

First Half Aries Bedside Rock

CINNABAR
For the double-sided, Martian world ruling Aries, this is a Bedside Rock with triple combinations featuring scarlet Cinnabar with Quartz and Dolomite.

The Neolithic artist powdered Cinnabar to colour his gory pictures of animals and the chase and its modern name derives from the Persian word for dragon's blood. In about 100 BC the Romans ordered 4,500 tons of Cinnabar from Spain, where among other places, it is still being worked today. Now it is being put to many beneficial uses. It contains up to 86 per cent mercury and is the most important mineral bearing that metal.

The gentle Martian world with its light atmosphere is in harmony with this bedside rock's vermillion crystals and their fine, transparent edges, all the more so as Cinnabar is often found in veins near cooling volcanic disturbances, corresponding with the extinct volcanoes on Mars. In laboratory tests red Cinnabar gives off greenish fumes, their colour matching the ancient face of Mars.

Like Cinnabar, Dolomite is a soft material, transparent to translucent in appearance, and is usually tinted pearly-white or pearl-yellow — hence its other name, Pearl Spar. Its crystals are reasonably common and hard to distinguish from those of calcite. It was named after the man who first recognized the distinction, Deodat Dolomieu, in 1791. As a source of carbon dioxide it is a correct match for the Sun (mutable body).

Quartz, which completes the trio of bedside rocks for first half Arians, actually corresponds with planet Saturn, but Earth's most abundant mineral is acceptable visually to complete the dramatic display of scarlet in its triple textures, providing a sparkling finish in contrast with the matt of Cinnabar and the pearl-lustred surface of Dolomite.

Second Half Aries Bedside Rock

YOUNGITE
Imagine a craggy mass of solid mushroom-pink shimmering with Stardust, and you have Youngite, the second set Arian bedside rock. It is actually red Jasper with a re-crystallized surface, a tough opaque material that featured strongly in the jewellery of New Kingdom Egypt (1500-900 BC). The vogue in that era was for earplugs and earrings, broad collars, double-string girdle belts, armbands, bracelets and pendants, in a colour coordinated mixture of seeds, glass, metal beads and various stones, the link between them being reddish Jasper which was often cut in the form of a barrel shaped bauble. It corresponds to the soil of Mars which is now known to be pinky rust in all shades.

Nature changed the appearance of this long-loved member of the Chalcedony family by giving it a coating of transparent and minute rock crystals and set the "new model" Jasper in a place where man would discover it. He found it in America and named it Youngite. It sits well to Jupiter, the mutable planet for Aries in the second half, and to the outer planets too with their cooler position in space.

RUBY ZOISITE

As a glorious second bedside rock, fortunate Arians have the ornamental Ruby Zoisite. Looking like a bright-green cherry cake with dark chocolate bits, this gem cuts to superb dishes, ashtrays, eggs and even solitaire spheres. The cherries are actually big, blobby, opaque crystals of Ruby which are held fast in a black mineral running through the Zoisite, with its bright yellow to grass-green tints. The black mineral holding the Rubies is iron rich. Tanzania yields this wonderfully attractive stone.

First Half Taurus Precious Crystal

EMERALD

This gemstone has a fascinating, well charted history, going back to the earliest times. Emeralds were first found in Ethiopia and legend has it that Sargon I, Emperor of that country, always wore one. They were a prime source of wealth in ancient Egypt, and also Greece. Hieroglyphics have survived showing Greek miners at work in a mine near the Red Sea in the time of Alexander the Great their tools were rediscovered in the early nineteenth century and in Roman times, a famous Emerald was inscribed with Cleopatra's face.

In Latin America Peruvian temples were grass-green with Emeralds while in Mexico they were plundered in vast quantities by the conquistadors for use, among other things, in their own churches. Today the most notable Emeralds are found in Colombia, Egypt, the Salzburg Alps, Siberia, Zambia and Zimbabwe. The Emerald crystal always contains at least two metallic chemicals, aluminium and beryllium, but its glowing and seductive tints, which run through dark, rich to paler shades of green, are probably due to the presence of small amounts of chromium. Red Emeralds have occurred in nature, but few of gem quality have ever reached the market as they are a collector's prize. Large Emeralds are rare, which accounts for their high price, and so are clear specimens. Most are cloudy from imperfections and the inclusion of extraneous minerals, and the trade calls them "mossy". Under the microscope even absolutely clear Emeralds show a characteristic trait of uneven colour distribution, often in layers.

Although Emerald is of low bodyweight, and on this count ill matched for the ponderous Venus, its metallic elements make amends and Taureans can own or wear one of these stones with confidence.

ORIENTAL EMERALD
They can feel equally at home with the Oriental Emerald, which is actually a green Sapphire, and also contains aluminium. It is harder than the Emerald and slightly heavier, but lacks the other stone's intensity of colour. One good reason for its correspondence to Venus is that its toughness would make it impervious to acid rain.

Second Half Taurus Precious Crystal

SPINEL
This spectacular, naturally occurring gemstone is, in the main, unknown to the public because most jewellers set a synthetic (man-made) version of it in their pre-made jewellery, which has ruined the natural gemstone's reputation.

Natural Spinels are favourite gems of collectors and connoisseurs on account of their brilliance, hardness and wide range of spectacular colours. All colours suit this part of the zodiac because it has a Venus ruling (both Venus and Saturn emit much light which carries the colours of the spectrum).

Taureans will have to order this stone from a reputable jeweller because the average jeweller doesn't know about Spinels and often doesn't deal in special orders.

Through lack of gemmology knowledge and may even tell the would-be buyer that a Spinel is not a natural gemstone. Spinels are most famous for their rich red colours, the "Black Prince's Ruby" and the "Timor Ruby", both in the British Crown Jewel collection, and the "Cote de Bretagne" formerly from the French Crown jewels are among the famous.

Spinels are mined in Burma, Sri Lanka, Tanzania, and Tadzhikistan, part of the former Soviet Union. Until the 18th century Spinels and Rubies were both called Rubies because they are both red, both hard, and occur together in the same mines and locations.

Once discovered they were two different stones, for reason known only to those who made this decision, the softer and less flamboyant stone retained its name Ruby while the divine red stone was named Spinel and also the Balas Ruby.

ANDALUSITE

This is another gemstone for second set Taureans. Just as a caterpillar turns into a butterfly, so Andalusite has undergone a magical seeming change in the case of the transparent variety, from opaque, black rock to heavenly, colour variation crystal.

In the dark, amorphous Interior of the Earth, waves of heat once caused areas of solidified rock to evaporate and steam their way through splits in the crust. In the process, the liquid gases mixed and transferred parts of themselves to places where they either came to rest or received more pressure as they settled to cool. Some remained as they were but most continued to somersault, melt, mix, swim and restyle themselves until they reached an area near the surface of the Earth, where they took the form they have now. A great variety of stones was the result, but Andalusite's character is determined by aluminium, which accounts for its correspondence with Venus, giving it reflective powers to match those of the brightest star in the sky. Like Venus too, it can withstand great pressures of light and heat, and is a remarkable conductor of electricity. The Andalusite crystal presents itself in tints of yellow, green, grey, pink, flesh-red, red, purplish-red and brown, each variety displaying mineral magic in its ability to vary its shade when viewed from a different angle. A particularly lovely change is that from green to purplish-red; another is that from blue-purple to pale yellow. Both coloured and transparent crystals match Venus and Saturn, mutable planet for second half Taureans, in tone as well as hardness. Their hardness count is uneven, with a maximum rating of 7.5 and, like the Emerald, they are resistant to acid. Andalusite Crystals are often heated in Gemmological ovens which turn the mineral to a bright rich blue giving it more sales opportunities and a colour also very appropriate for correspondence with Venus and Saturn.

CHIASTOLITE

Some Taureans in this area of the zodiac may prefer Andalusite's sister gem, Chiastolite, which has the same composition but with added flecks of carbon that give the impression of a four-petalled flower, or cross. In northern Spain Chiastolite crystals are accordingly called '"Stones of the Cross" and have been sold to pilgrims since medieval times. Andalusite derives its name from the province of Andalusia/Spain. Today top quality gems come from Brazil.

SPHALERITE

And here is yet another precious crystal for this area of the zodiac. The richest colour of gem quality produced by this stone is a glorious brownish-gold with a play of intense yellow light, but Sphalerite can come in so many hues that not even experts always recognize it straight away. It usually contains iron along with a number of rarer elements, while non-precious Sphalerite is a major ore of zinc. Top gem quality crystals generally come from Spain.

First Half Taurus Talisman

AZURITE and MALACHITE

These are twin talismans for first half Taureans. They have similar compositions and the same hardness measure (3.5-4). Both, too, yield well over 50 per cent copper which, thanks to its content of sulphur and iron, establishes their correspondence with both Venus (ruling Taurean celestial body) and Mercury (first half mutable globe).

The intense, transparent to translucent azure-blue Azurite is the rarer stone of the two. It tends to occur either in rosettes formed of tiny powdered crystals, or in sparkling masses on minerals of other varieties. During the 15th and 16th centuries European artists used ground Azurite extensively, but it was then discovered that, when the paint dried, the brilliant blue Azurite colour changed to shades of stunning green which gave rise to some thinking their ancestors were unhappy with them!.

The more prolific Malachite is easily recognized by its swirling zones of light and dark colours, dramatic patterns resembling pale green cream in exotic emerald nectar. Sometimes called "Satin Ore", Malachite is the subject of many ancient, magic tales. Once upon a time, individuals in possession of this mineral were said to be able to understand the conversation of animals, and many a Russian Princess spent days of delight playing with Malachite trinket boxes filled with matching foibles, which were supposed to confer the power of invisibility upon their owner.

Don't buy ashtrays made of either of these minerals cigarette and cigar stubs mark them. But they are popular for other ornaments. Supplies of both stones come mainly from the Congo, which yielded over 2,000 tons in 1966, but large quantities are now found in Australia, America, Britain, France and Siberia.

Second Half Taurus Talisman

JADEITE

This stone can only be formed under high pressure – which makes it a worthy partner for planet Venus where the heavier than Earth atmosphere could crush anything. It is exceptionally resilient, with fibrous, interlocking crystals in its structure which give toughness greater than that of steel. Wonderful shades of Jadeite include black, brown, and lavender, pink, red, orange-brown and white, through many shades of green. Lavender Jadeite has been allocated to second half Taureans because planet Saturn of the purple and blue shadows is their mutable globe.

Jadeite is the symbol of purity, steadfastness and all things enduring. When struck it gives a musical note, which is doubtless the source of ancient belief that it was a "charm of harmonious omen". One terrifying lady who fancied this gem was Tz'e Hsi, the tyrannical last Empress Dowager of China, who died in 1908. In her long life she is thought to have collected over 3,000 carved Jadeite containers, all choc-à-bloc with trinkets of the same stone.

PYRITIZED AMMONITE
This is a lovely extra talisman for 2nd half Taureans, almost as ancient as life itself and a talisman sometimes so smooth that it can be carried in the pocket, placed in a locket or cut in half and set as cufflinks.

This fascinating mineral can be said to be history in silvered stone, for it is formed from a creature extinct for 60 million years the early forerunner of the octopus family.

Probably a vegetarian, it inflated its body with air, which enabled it to shoot through water like a modern submarine. Fine examples of Pyritized Ammonite come from Yorkshire in England, and from France. Its link with Venus is the iron ore and pyrite, which is used to produce sulphur dioxide for sulphuric acid.

First Half Taurus Bedside Rock

MARCASITE DOLLAR
For good reason the Marcasite Dollar has been allocated as the first bedside rock of first set Taureans, for it is formed in an environment of acid solutions, corresponding with Venus, the planet of sulphuric rain. It is a flat circular stone, formed of radiating and glittering crystals which vary gently in hue from silver-yellow to yellow-bronze.

Very little natural Marcasite jewellery is offered for sale as modern trade prefers steel; it's less expensive and easier to set. The surface of a Marcasite Dollar must, if sold as an adornment, be covered with some non-tarnishable substance or else the blaze of light which issues from its heart will become dim.

PYRITE
Cubes of silver tinted Pyrite, otherwise known as Fool's Gold, is a second bedside rock for these Taureans. Pyrite's composition is identical to that of Marcasite, but this stone is formed at a higher temperature and is darker in colour. Its high sulphur content has led to its being utilized in the manufacture of sulphuric acid: indeed in some acid solutions it is itself completely insoluble. Sometimes occurring with gold, Pyrite is a bright, silver-coloured, shiny mineral, formed in flat blocks with furrowed, straight lines on their faces. Its shape is so perfect that, when they see it for the first time, most people think this stone must have been sculptured by the hand of man. Its name comes from the Greek pyr, meaning "fire", because of the sparks Pyrite gives off when subjected to friction.

Both Pyrite and Marcasite have a measured hardness of 6, Venus's own number

Second Half Taurus Bedside Rock

IRISH FAIRY STONE
Second half Taureans have a Venus ruled, Saturn mutable influence in their horoscope and are therefore entitled to this admirable mixture of cubic, blue-grey Galena (the principal ore of lead), sparkling, clear Rock Crystal (the "seeing Eye" of fortune tellers), yellow and black metallic Sphalerite (the principal source of many rare metals and the most important ore of zinc), and brassy little blocks of Fool's Gold, or Pyrite which together form the Irish Fairy Stone. As Irish as its name, here is a truly unpredictable specimen in which not one of the crystals comprising it is what it originally set out to be.

The elements composing them started deep in Earth's crust as a conglomerate of dark rock mixtures. Then came pressures from deeper down still, in consequence of which these basic rocks were folded, broken, squeezed and melted, liquefied and re-hardened many, many times, on each occasion undergoing transformation into a completely new mineral. Finally they came to rest near enough to the Earth's surface, far enough away from the volcanic disturbances not to melt again and ready to be discovered by man.

Such is the history of the Irish Fairy Stone, with its glittering mass of crystals displaying proud and dark splendour after their rough ride through time.

First Half Gemini Precious Crystal

ORANGE SAPPHIRE (Padparadjah *or* Padmaraga*)*
In parallel to the bravest globe in our Solar System, the steeliest crystal next to a Diamond insists on furnace like conditions at birth. Belonging to the corundum family, which derived its name from Kuruwinda, the Sanskrit for Ruby, the Orange Sapphire has an age old reputation as the badge of truth, constancy and virtue. It exhibits a tone, transparency and tint which gained the corundum clan a status as flowers among gems, since glorious shades are habitual. Impurities are the cause the group's enormous colour range, the red is tinted by metallic chromium, and the blue is caused by a whisper of titanium and iron. Although some of the softer hues have possible titles, only three popular names are geologically accepted. "Ruby" for red, "Sapphire" for blue and all other shades except orange which is named Padparadjah or Padmaraga derived from the Indian, meaning "Lotus Blossom". The Padparadjah is dedicated to the Indian goddess of fertility as her first gemstone followed closely by all other Sapphires. Indeed Lalita is properly known as the Sapphire Devi of Fertility.

Mercury's nearest planetary neighbour, Venus, with its orange-lit soil, is the mutable body in this part of the zodiac and is constantly threatened with sulphuric rain, so again the Padparadjah qualifies by its immunity to acids. In sympathy with the most Sun-abused world in the Solar System, the Padparadjah is resilient and will not fuse under tremendous heat, its lustre is enduring, and the fire in its being splits light into almost as many colours as the Sun produces. It also has a hardness count only one below that of the Diamond nine out of ten.

In the corundum family three tints in one crystal are a frequent occurrence, and this phenomenon is beautifully displayed in a much celebrated statue of Confucius, carved from a three-colour stone. It shows a transparent, white head, pale-blue body, and yellow-orange limbs.

Finally, imitating its heavenly partner's pulverized rock-dust surface, corundum of poor quality has been used for centuries as an industrial abrasive. The ancient Chinese fitted bows with emery covered cords (emery is corundum dust) to shape other substances.

TAAFEITE
Although Taafeite is one of the rarest crystals known to man, it gives a splendid second choice to Geminis in the first half. Discovered along with other Spinels by Count Taafe in 1945, Taafeite is almost as hard as a Sapphire and about the same bodyweight. It is a brilliant gem but, like the colourless Sapphire, sometimes almost impossible to obtain.

Second Half Gemini Precious Crystal

CAT'S EYE

The Greeks called it Cymophane, meaning "Waving Light", but we know the precious crystal for part two Geminis as "Cat's Eye". This especially valued, translucent gemstone may have a golden-yellow, mid-yellow, bamboo-green or bluish-brown body, but whatever the tint, a powerful silver-white beam of light moves across its half-round or cabochon-cut surface when stimulated by even the slightest movement.

Known as a "stone gourmet's delight", this gem was believed by the ancients to guard against physical danger and the devil's assault against the soul. Its main characteristic, a bright ribbon of light, occurs through reflection of light from fine, paralleled fibres or hollow crystal tubes which the growing crystal encased when forming. Cat's Eyes are generally thought to be the most beautiful of the "ray" gems and (unfortunately for those born under Gemini Two) are priced accordingly.

CHRYSOBERYL

If a person in this group would prefer a transparent crystal, then the same variety of mineral to which the Cat's Eye belongs, known as the Chrysoberyl, will provide a brightness superior to most other gemstones. Seventeenth and eighteenth century Spanish and Portuguese jewellers favoured the Brazilian pale-yellow type, but Gemini could have a rare colourless stone from Burma, or choose from yellow, brown, light-green, mid-green or deep bottle-green stones from, among other places, Burma, Madagascar, Zimbabwe, Russia or Sri Lanka.

The name Chrysoberyl comes from the Greek word for "gold". It has a superior brilliance, a hardness count of 8,5, and contains the metallic elements aluminium and beryllium and, sometimes, a trace of iron, all links with planet Mercury. Its body weight and rarer elements correspond, with Uranus, the mutable globe in this area of the zodiac.

First Half Gemini Talisman

MOSS AGATE and MOCHA STONES

Through the ages, men thought they identified, in the markings in Moss Agate and Mocha Stones, species of imprisoned moss, leaves and hairy plants. But what scientists not so long ago were still labelling as fossil remains was nature's blueprint for future foliage, for these two stones came into being long before Earth's present vegetation began to form.

Moss Agate and Mocha Stones are now known to be a quartz mineral compound comprising amorphous crystalline grains impregnated by natural, metallic fluids rich in iron and manganese. The interwoven patterns occurred when watery substances injected themselves or filtered into the cellular structure of the quartz. The iron and manganese fluids are commonly called "green earth" and are formed in the cooling process of molten volcanic rock. Moss Agate has dark-green and blackish-green designs imitative of ferns and moss, while Mocha Stones have red, brown or black tree and plant patterns.

The Mocha variety was originally found near an Arabian seaport somewhere in the vicinity of Mocha and Moss Agate was first discovered in western India, the area which supplied some of the best specimens even today, including one of the largest examples weighing in at over thirteen and a half kilograms, or approximately thirty pounds. America's Rocky Mountains have an abundance of Moss Agate, the stream beds there yielding fine quality material.

When still thought of as stone incorporating fossils, Moss Agate was the chief talisman for farmers and agriculturalists, its main use being as an aid to water divining. At that time it was placed under the rule of planet Venus, as were all semitransparent minerals with fossil-like inclusions, in tribute to Venus the goddess of fertility. Now both Moss Agate and Mocha Stones are seen as perfect parallels with planet Mercury (Gemini's ruler) and Venus (mutable planet in this area of the zodiac), particularly the former, since Mercury, scorched by the Sun, is so largely composed of metallic elements.

UVAROVITE GARNET
This special member of the garnet family is another talisman for first set Geminis. Its colours range from transparent emerald to dark emerald-green. Primarily a calcium iron crystal, Uvarovite is a new gem recycled by Mother Nature from "old rocks" buried deep in Earth's crust aeons ago.

Second Half Gemini Talisman

TRANSVAAL JADE
Grossularia, the Latin word for "Gooseberry", is where the second set Gemini talisman derives its proper, geological name, but the gemstone is better known as Transvaal Jade.

People who think of Garnets as clear, red stones are in for a surprise, as Transvaal Jade is a Garnet which is opaque and, at its best, bright green, but it simulates Mercury's blazing day by fluorescing dazzling orange-yellow under X-ray. Because all members of the Garnet family originated millions of years ago, subjected in the depths of the earth to the vaporization and recycling brought about by volcanic action, they all contain a little of most metals and are weather resistant. But in each type of Garnet one or two metallic elements predominate, and in the case of Transvaal Jade they are the white metals, calcium and aluminium. chromium, a brilliant, white metal of industrial importance, has properties which impart hardness to iron and steel, and this element is responsible for the talisman's green hue. A pink version is coloured by Manganese, a pinky-grey metal which is also used for toughening steel. Transvaal Jade always contains some iron, but some varieties have black flecks contributed by a magnetic mineral called magnetite. The less vibrant examples of Transvaal Jade come from Burma, Canada and Scotland, but the brightest and best quality occurs in Africa, whence eggs and wonderful Jade carvings of creatures and human heads can be obtained, as well as the occasional bit of jewellery.

Mercury is the globe with the largest metallic core in our solar system, and in this area of the zodiac Geminians' mutable planet is Uranus, the big, green planet well-endowed with metallic elements.

Varieties of the transparent Grossular Garnet family are alternative choices for Geminians of this set: for instance, the gem quality green crystal type to which vanadium provides its tint, the yellow variety, which fluoresces orange and the clear white type, a lovely gem but hard to obtain.

First Half Gemini Bedside Rock

STAUROLITE
This stone derives its name from the Greek word staurus, meaning "cross", and is naturally cruciform, with a notable iron content which makes it an obvious match for planet Mercury and a resilience which suits Venus. In colour it is usually a vibrant red or grey-brown but very occasionally transparent Staurolite crystals are found which, when cut and polished, resemble "table wine garnets". In laboratory tests some varieties of the gem fuse, changing under stress into a black, magnetic glass a recognized feature on planet Mercury's surface.

The ancient Britons called these gems "fairy stones" and used them in magical rites. The early Christians knew them as "cross stones" and wore them as charms, while myths tell "Staurolite stars" fell from heaven.

VERDITE

A second bedside rock for Geminians first half is Verdite, which hails from the Transvaal. A noted fertility stone, it was administered in powdered form by witch doctors to barren women. This brilliant, opaque and ornamental member of the serpentine family stands apart from its cousins by virtue of an added ingredient the glorious, green fuchsite mica, much utilized in the electrical industry. The metallic elements magnesium and iron are usually present in Verdite, which occurs in small and largish boulders, so making it a popular stone for carving. Lions, frogs, hippopotami, owls and all sorts of other animals are carved by African craftsmen and sold commercially.

Second Half Gemini Bedside Rock

RUBELLITE in LEPIDOLITE

Formed in excessively hot, pressurized conditions, this small piece of fluffy iridescence comes in a variety of hues rose-red, pink-violet, violet-grey, lilac, grey, and yellow-white colourings which it owes to industrially important metallic chemicals. Lithium, used in batteries, medicine and ceramics, is one; aluminium is another.

Then there is mica, which is used as a thermal insulator, and last but not least, potassium. Rubellite comprises many metallic and non-metallic elements and when found in gem quality is a prized crystal. The metallic elements in both Rubellite and Lepidolite ensure correspondence of these minerals with planet Mercury, while their light bodyweight and water content supply the link with Uranus.

Rubellite in Lepidolite occurs in pegmatites, which are veins of mixed minerals formed in the final stages of volcanic cooling.

GEODE

This miniature cave, also called the Potato Stone is a second bedside rock for part two Geminians. The Geode is the product of an old volcanic bubble and is more usually of roundish proportions.

The best specimens have an outside crust of solid Agate, and its centre is beautified by lacy Rock Crystal, Amethyst or Opal, a conjunction brought about by the watery, mineral rich fluids which percolated into the cavity or hole left by the bubble which occurred in the lava when it was steaming hot.

Frequently a crystal of calcite or other lovely minerals are found clinging to the inside walls. When first discovered the outside of most Geodes is coated with a fine film of "Green Earth", or Delessite, caused by iron and magnesium rich fluids running and squeezing their way through all the cracks and splits which were not filled with the more solid minerals.

Rock shops generally sell Geodes in half pieces (either matching pairs or singles), but Geminis must have both halves, as their emblem is the Twins. Some inventive jewellers set mini Geodes in silver and gold to be worn as cufflinks, earrings, pendants and pins. The main sources of Geode supply are Brazil, Mexico and South America. The part two Gemini mutable planet (Uranus) balances the water content of the Geode.

First Half Cancer Precious Crystal

MOONSTONE ADULARIA

This is arguably the most precious variety of Moonstone, Adularia echoes the Moon's pearly sheen. It has a soft, luminescent glow in striking contrast to the flared radiance of most precious stones. When cut in domed shapes (as it must be) a hovering line of light dances across its surface giving the illusion of being above the crystal, rather than coming from the fine, fibrous particles within. Named after its place of discovery in Adula, Switzerland, the gorgeous Adularia is nature's purest version of the simple field rock known as feldspar.

This pale blue-mauve gemstone was once thought to have medicinal powers which triumphed over epilepsy and was considered a cure for love sick women. Another ancient belief was that if an Adularia was held in the mouth it would cause the memory to quicken. Beads of Adularia were carried in the pocket to ensure potent good fortune and Gypsy races believed that during our Moon's waning period the Adularia was the best stone to use in foretelling future events.

Moonstone is sensitive to pressure and is formed at low temperatures making it an ideal match for the Cancerian first half mutable planet (Pluto) and its satellite (Charon), since both are on the outer limits of our solar system, while its composition tallies with the most prolific minerals found on our Moon, which is the Cancerian ruling body. Australia, Burma, Brazil, India, Sri Lanka and Tanzania are the most important sources of Adularia.

CAT'S EYE SCAPOLITE

Another precious crystal for first half Cancerians is Cat's Eye Scapolite, which occurs in the romantic shades of transparent to translucent pearly pink, violet, yellow-pink, yellow and white. More often used for carving small animals and rarely cut as a gemstone, it was only discovered in 1913 in Upper Burma. Scapolite contains aluminium, calcium and sodium. The last two of these, being water calcium and sodium. The last two of these, being water enticed, correlate with the Moon by virtue of its effect on Earth's water. Aluminium relates to the moon because it remains untarnished by air (an element absent on that satellite). When cut to be set in jewellery Cat's Eye Scapolite is always cut cabochon (half round) and occurs in Madagascar and Tasmania as well as those countries already mentioned.

Second Half Cancer Precious Gem

WATER OPAL
Of the beautiful Opal, Pliny the Elder ecstatically wrote: "It is made up of all the glories of the most precious gems and to describe it is a matter of inexpressible difficulty". Even more could this be said of its variant, the Water Opal, in whose crystal clear depths the colours dance through the spectrum like bubbles riding on a gambolling dolphin. Its basic tints of electric blue and grass-green intermingle with violet flames, behind which flares a pink trail reminiscent of camp fires in the continent mainly associated with this stone, that is, Australia. The Greek compiler Onomacritus, writing four hundred years before Pliny, conceived the Opal as having the tenderness and colour of a beautiful child's love. That too could be said of the Water Opal.

Because of its unique combination of pattern and hue, an Opal can never be duplicated. Geologically, it is classed as quartz, the world's most abundant mineral, and indeed Opal and quartz varieties occur together and their chemical composition is almost identical. But here the likeness ends, for quartz has a three dimensional character while Opal is a glass like material composed of spheres so small as to be invisible to the naked eye. These spheres, or cells of silica, to produce precious Opal, must be of fairly regular size, stacked into closely packed planes to give first class quality and yet it is not the spheres themselves which produce the Opal's unique and exciting colour loveliness but the refraction of light on the material packed between them.

Top quality Water Opal comes from an area in South Australia called Andamooka.

WHITE OPAL
Another choice for second set Cancerians is White Opal, particularly with asterism. The rarest white Opals have what looks like a hovering star on

their surface. This phenomenon, known as asterism, is caused by fault areas or breaks in the regular pattern system of the cells.

As Opals contain more water than other gems, and accordingly will shrink and expand with changes of temperature, they must be set with longer claws than any other gemstone or otherwise held in for safety. Their high water content makes them parallel to the moon and to the mutable planet (Neptune) now established scientifically as having the same density as water, in fact more often believed to be a great ball of water.

First Half Cancer Talisman

PEARL

Cancerians are lucky to be able to claim as their talisman a jewel with such a long, well charted and distinguished history. Four thousand years ago a word denoting "Pearl" was recorded in a Chinese dictionary. Caskets dating from Ptolemaic times have been found with Pearls still inside them. In Byzantium Pearls were used to adorn crucifixes and prayer books and, on one occasion, a box containing a relic of (possibly) the True Cross; and they featured just as significantly in the religious history of Christian Rome.

Pearls have been hoarded by pirates, dived for in the South Seas, and treasured by many princes, among them England's Henry VIII and Elizabeth I, as well as by the tragic young Lady Jane Grey, queen for nine days, who wore a single Pearl drop on a cross up to the eve of her premature death. Pearls, in fact, have been a sign of distinction both sacred and profane. Does not the Book of Revelation inform us that each of the gates of the Heavenly City is crowned by a Pearl?

Federico Fellini said of the Pearl "All art is autobiographical; the pearl is the oyster's autobiography".

Being formed in water, the Pearl is an apt talisman for first Cancerians whose ruler, the Moon helped by our Sun, regulates the waters of Earth, and it also parallels Charon, the main satellite of Pluto, these Cancerians' mutable body.

Mother-of-Pearl and Snail Shells are other talismans for people in this area of the zodiac.

ROSE QUARTZ

This beauty is the true mineral talisman for Cancerians for Pearls, being organically formed, fall into a different category called a Mineraloid.

Rose Quartz is thought to owe its tint to the metallic element titanium, of which the Moon has a plentiful store. Like the Moon, this stone gives off light almost as generously as it receives it. In laboratory tests Rose Quartz shows traces of lime, water and manganese, elements all suitably gentle for the lunar world. Its mid-rose can fade to pale pink on exposure to extreme heat, but the former colours will often be restored if the stone is thoroughly soaked in fresh, clean water.

PINK QUARTZ

Gem quality Rose Quartz is far less common than most other variations of quartz and only top grade has the necessary gemstone clarity. Transparent Rose Quartz is a collectors' item and is simply named Pink Quartz. But some consider the loveliest "gemmy" Rose Quartz features a four pointed star, which moves around its surface according to the play of light.

Second Half Cancer Talisman

RED CORAL

The Greeks believed that sea nymphs stole Medusa's severed head and that the drops of blood seeded Red Coral. The Romans thought that if their youngsters wore twigs of vivid Coral round their necks they would be safe from danger. Indeed, some Italians even today wear Coral for protection against the Evil Eye. They also prescribe it as a cure for women afflicted with sterility.

The Gauls ornamented their weapons of war with the brightest Coral twigs available and Coral was once worn by Chinese Mandarins to signify their high position in government service.

Geologically speaking, the Cancerian talisman is a hard substance comprised of the lime secreted by whole tribes of marine animals for purposes of shelter. A coral reef is simply a mass of such protective structures, the ocean's answer to a housing estate.

First recorded in 1712 as a plant growing at the bottom of the sea with neither seed nor bloom, and embellished with pores like stars, this gemstone is still fashionable as a gift for newborn babies, having once been considered the cure par excellence for teething troubles and bad tummies in growing children.

Indian Astrologers rated this sea flower highly, commending it in all its shades to anyone cursed with a badly aspected Saturn. They also, wrongly, considered Red Coral to be the appropriate stone for Arians, whereas in fact it is not Mars but the Moon which must be matched with this watery gem of organic origin.

Neptune, however, gets a look in too, exerting its influence by virtue of being the only planet to have the same density as water.

First Half Cancer Bedside Rock

ARAGONITE and CALCITE
Calcium minerals of ethereal fragility should grace a first set Cancerian's home as his or her bedside rock, and Aragonite and Calcite of the land variety, formed in dry lake beds or in hot springs, are the two first choices. A lot of Calcite was originally Aragonite, which turns into Calcite under pressure of its own weight. Coral, for instance, is Aragonite on the top and Calcite at the base. Weighing a little more than Calcite because of its water content, Aragonite changes to Calcite or crumbles when exposed to a hot flame.

Although both Aragonite and Calcite are normally translucent, there is an absolutely clear variety of Calcite called Iceland Spar which, when placed over a line drawn on paper, will produce a double image, due to the splitting of the light into two rays.

A particularly attractive type of Calcite is Flos Ferri, a luminous, snowy and tree-like variety with branches often sprinkled with Iron fragments which cause a pinkish, though patchy, coloration.

Other impurities may lend tints of grey, blue, green, violet or yellow. Nailhead, another variety, resembles a bunch of nails as its name suggests, and Dogtooth Calcite, equally obviously, has the appearance of canine teeth.

Calcite is the basis for marble, chalk and limestone, and is a common constituent of fossil shells.

BARNACLES
Other bedside rocks for Cancerians of this set include any colour Coral or even a cluster of barnacles, which sometimes have a surprise fan of Coral hiding in a cup.

Our Moon is very obviously the celestial ruler of these minerals formed in water orientated, gentle conditions which equally suit the planet Pluto.

Second Half Cancer Bedside Rock

DESERT ROSE

We must thank the dusty Sahara for the loveliest form of this charming flower of the desert, which is formed through the percolating action of salt water evaporating from almost dry lakes. The water's movement picks up time eroded granules of sand, coats them with a mineral substance and rolls them up with similar grains which cling to each other to form tiny plates of matter projecting exterior shelves or fine wings. As the percolating water and weather conditions continue their work, these materials group together and the result is a Desert Rose. Obviously this stone contains quite a lot of water which evaporates in heat, when lo and behold! this poetic looking jewel turns into prosaic powder and becomes ... plaster of Paris! The Bedouin believed that the Desert Rose was created from the tears of their womenfolk mourning for lost warriors but that was a long time ago. Desert Rose belongs to the gypsum family of minerals and can be grey, buff, reddish, pale-yellowish and brown. It is found in most desert regions in most countries.

SELENITE

As a bonus for second half Cancerians, an alternative bedside rock is another precious crystal called Selenite, which is fragile and must be cherished. Selenite is transparent, tinted grey, yellow or brownish and always exquisite. Like the Desert Rose it should never be washed in soapy water, which wrecks the lustre and leaves an unattractive opalescent film. Nor indeed should any form of gypsum be soaked in liquids. Instead, and only if it really needs cleaning, sweep the stone with a soft makeup brush or in clear water and dry quickly.

WATER NODULE

Properly called "Anhydrous" the intriguing Water Nodule is yet another bedside rock for second half Cancerians. This amazing creation started life in a cavity left by a volcanic bubble or a decomposed shellfish. In time this void became encrusted with the form of quartz known as Agate and inside this, in a bath of trapped, mineral rich water, grew the rock crystals. If a window (thin slice) of the Nodule is removed, the prehistoric water can be seen swishing around its hiding place and its weight felt when held. Brazil and the Western coast of America yield most Water Nodules.

First Half Leo Precious Crystal

YELLOW DIAMOND

This stone can be cut in countless styles from the modern round "brilliant" with 58 facets and the appearance of a spider's web when viewed from above to the 25 faceted "full Dutch rose". A Diamond is a pure crystal of carbon which those in the know believe started life deep in the earth many thousands of years ago. The carbon, dislodged from its ledge by volcanic disturbances, mingled with molten rock and made its way under pressure along cracks and fissures towards Earth's surface. Then more volcanic action probably occurred and the whole process repeated itself: break, fold, remelt and rise. The carbon finally transformed into a Diamond and settled in a rocky mix of soil called "Blue Earth", along with Pyrope Garnets, Olivines, shiny flakes of Mica and a few other gems formed under similar pressure and heat.

No wonder Diamond is the hardest, natural substance known to man, with a top count of ten to match the Sun's given number. Its name is derived from the Greek word adamas meaning "Invincible" or "Unbreakable", its structure is ultra-complex, and its atomic composition is held together by powerful bonding.

This gem is appropriate as first half Leo's precious crystal because Jupiter, the mutable influence on the sign at this point, seems, when viewed from Earth, to give off a yellow light. In the opinion of gemmologists the yellow Diamond is coloured by nitrogen impurity, which according to Scientists was gifted to our solar system by the incarnation of a once massive Star over ten times the size of our Sun more than a few billion years ago.

Kahlil Gibran said of the Diamond "Perhaps time's definition of coal is the diamond".

Second Half Leo Precious Crystal

WHITE (CLEAR) DIAMOND

Sometimes this flawless gem is referred to as "of the first water", meaning a Diamond of the purest kind. Traded by Indian merchants in the fourth century, it was called by them "a fragment of eternity", and from Indian mythology comes the legend of the Koh-I-Noor, which came to mankind on the forehead of the child Karna, son of the Sun and of a princess of the reigning family. Legend decreed that only a god or woman would be exempt from punishment and injury as a consequence of possessing this stone, and tragedy indeed stalked "the Mountain of Light" where it was kept before being seized and, in 1850, presented to Queen Victoria.

Since then it has adorned the crown of state worn by three other royal ladies Queen Alexandra, Queen Mary and the present Queen Mother. But, significantly, Britain's four most recent kings have all chosen not to wear it, so perhaps its terrors still hold. The Mountain of Light is now captive in the Tower of London.

The ancients believed that the White Diamond would protect them from harm anyone plotting against the owner of such a stone would have his evil designs catapulted back at him.

For unhappy Leos with lunatic tendencies, the traditional cure was an elixir of water, alcohol and Diamond dust this, however, is supposed to have brought about the untimely end of Emperor Frederick the Second.

This Diamond is well chosen because it is the Sun's own crystal having no affinity with water, and also because Mars, the mutable planet in this area of the zodiac, has been observed to have its soil coated with a thin layer of white.

First Half Leo Talisman

ZIRCON
The gem loving Greeks were so besotted by this stone that they named it after a favourite flower, the Hyacinth, while the Persians called it Zargun, meaning "all shades of yellow".

For centuries, deep in the Cambodian jungles, where most of the ravishing specimens occur, the natives heat treated the more prolific orange-brown Zircon until its colour changed to a glorious sky-blue, a process which is carried on today in Thailand. In either shade, its brilliance is often equal to that of a Diamond.

To Roman Catholics this stone once signified humility, while Hindus associated it with the Sacred Kalpa Tree. In ancient lore it was thought of as a guard against poison, Its allocation to Leo comes through Jupiter, the mutable body for Leos in the first half, with which it is thought to share certain scientific properties.

This gemstone is variously named, according to its tints. Zircon itself denotes green; the yellow variety is called Jargon, the orange Jacinth, the brown Malacom, and the clear, or white, is Matura, name of the famous temple site.

PHENACITE

In 1833 geologists discovered a stone which has become a second talisman for part one Leos, namely Phenacite. Originally mistaken for Rock Crystal, it is harder and heavier than that mineral, with a brilliance and play of light approaching that of the diamond.

Taking its name from phenas, the Greek word for a deceiver, Phenacite comes in shades of pale rose, wine-yellow and clear white.

It is found in Brazil, Mexico, Namibia, Zimbabwe, Russia, America, Switzerland and Tanzania, and contains the rare metallic element beryllium.

Second Half Leo Talisman

HELIODOR

For second set Leos, there is a talisman of golden-hued Heliodor from South West Africa.

This crystal belongs with the beryl family as does the Emerald and Aquamarine, but neither of those two could be coupled with the Sun as only the Heliodor is thought by scientists to be radioactive.

The Heliodor is conceived through and born in extreme pressure and high temperatures. It has a light bodyweight and an uncommonly high melting point.

The intensity of its hue is thought to be caused by Iron, the same metallic element that is responsible for the rusty-pink Martian soil (Mars being the mutable planet for second set Leo).

SPHENE

Another Talisman for second half Leos is the very lovely yellow or green Sphene. The Sun's pure white light comprises the full spectrum of the rainbow and in correspondence Sphene contains titanium, a metal which lends the full spectrum to other metals when applied as a surface coating. Titanium is also a metal of unsurpassed toughness and will not melt in the most elevated temperatures.

For the mutable planet, Sphene contains iron. At gem quality it also possesses qualities of light fit for a Sun ruled individual, while corresponding suitably with the surface of Mars.

If your jeweller can't supply this glorious gemstone, it would be well worth a trip to Switzerland, America, Brazil or Mexico, where it mainly occurs.

First Half Leo Bedside Rock

VANADINITE
Sun ruled Leos in the first group, with Jupiter as a mutable globe, have this brilliant orange-red or dazzling yellow-brown mineral as their very out of the ordinary bedside rock.

Belonging to the lead family of minerals and rich in vanadium, a grey metallic element used for strengthening steel, Vanadinite comprises unusual, complex chemicals and only begins melting in exaggerated temperatures.

Our Sun is a heavenly furnace of radiation, and Jupiter, albeit to a lesser degree, generates that same energy. When ice mantling the body of Io (Jupiter's principal moon) melted, its water vaporized into space and ultimately produced the golden haloes potent with radiation which even now continue to crown it, while its red and yellow colouring results from active volcanoes. Nature presents Vanadinite in all tints of amber, yellow, orange-red and ruby-red, not a hue out of place as a match for either the celestial sovereign or the mutable body. Gloriously pretty, tougher than steel, and sometimes holding minute amounts of arsenic, Vanadinite crystals usually grow on dark, weathered-looking rock, luxuriously filling crevices and coating the outside with smaller, lighter coloured and sunset toned crystals.

MUSCOVITE
A second rock for first half Leos is Muscovite, which contains mica. An occasional Diamond may be found where mica resides because together they were formed in and migrated from deeper earth, travelling along nooks and crannies until close to the surface. Usually Muscovite is flaky. Sometimes, however, it develops in long, flat sheaves resembling a row of silver backed books.

Muscovite derives its name from "Muscovy" (the old name for Russia) which led to the same word being employed to denote other temperature resistant products such as furnace doors and windows. Now Muscovite is used as an electrical insulator and a host of other things including artificial Christmas "snow". This pearly, shimmering mineral also contains aluminium and iron, both elements emanating from the Sun. Placed against the light, Muscovite shows up as a six pointed star and appears in translucent shades of grey, yellow, brownish, green and white. This part one Leonine bedside rock is an abundant mineral, with America, Canada, India and Russia being its primary producers.

Second Half Leo Bedside Rock

SULPHUR
Known in Biblical times as brimstone, Sulphur is usually found perched on a dark, parent mineral and is generally formed in translucent, box like crystals of bright yellow, some measuring several centimetres across. When a sulphur crystal is held in the warm palm it will expand, and when rubbed will produce a negative charge. Sometimes Sulphur occurs in column form, or in tiny, powdery lumps.

It is not always pure and added chemicals will give the basically yellow mineral greenish or amber tones when lit from behind. A nest of Sulphur crystals becomes a gorgeous mass of luminosity, a ravishing centrepiece for any Leo home where it should be kept in a glass cabinet and never washed.

Homer refers to Sulphur as incense, probably owing to confusion with roll sulphur, which is obtained by melting and casting unrefined forms of Sulphur into thin sticks which burn with a blue flame. Roll sulphur was used for many centuries as a purging agent after illnesses, as a means of cleaning out a dwelling infested with bugs, and in the hope of driving away demons. It was also applied to insect bites. Today Sulphur is a major constituent in gunpowder, matches, fireworks, fertilizers and fungicides and has an annual production of over 24 million tons worldwide. America (one state alone produces three million tons a year), Canada, France, Italy, Japan, Mexico and Russia are among the suppliers.

For the Sun, Sulphur forms through hydrogen based chemical reactions and in conjunction with Mars (mutable planet).

VOLCANIC BOMBS
Other bedside rocks for second half Leos are stones known as "Volcanic Bombs".

These resemble small, blackish pears and, while not pretty, are certainly fascinating. Measuring only a few millimetres in diameter, Volcanic Bombs originate as molten rock spewed out from a volcano. While still fluid (or plastic) these pellets spun in flight, and in the process gradually solidified into spindle like, solid minerals.

Another miracle of nature In the world of minerals.

First Half Virgo Precious Gem

BLACK OPAL
Until recently the only Black Opals in the world came from a nine square mile area in New South Wales, Australia, called Lightning Ridge. Some top grade stones have now been discovered in Java Indonesia, where they often cost less because their potential market value is less well understood. The Indonesian "Java Black", with its flashing, iridescent "fire" displays a stunning range of colours covering the whole spectrum and set off against a jet-black background is a particularly appealing gem and more than suitable for this area of the zodiac.

The subtle stacking of a once liquid mineral gel to form layers of uniform, spherical cells accounts for the depth and vitality of this exquisite gem, with its rainbow like colours formed by a refraction of white light.

The only Black Opals in history are those the Romans had an insatiable desire for. We think they came from Ethiopia or Hungary and are believed to have been poor quality White Opals given dark backgrounds artificially having sugar or honey burnt into them. It is important that Virgoan people understand that a top calibre, solid Black Opal is meant, not a doublet or triplet, pretty as these may be. Triplet is a thin slice of Opal glued to a dark background and topped with a transparent dome. The "doublet" is the same, minus the clear crown, although in rare cases it can be a slice of Opal capped with another, clearer material, or a natural doublet of the "Boulder Opal" variety.

The ancients believed the Opal was the mineral bridge between heaven and earth, for which reason they sometimes called it "The Eye of the Universe". Even more significantly it was, and is, "The Stone of Hope"

PIETERSITE
Here is another precious crystal for first half Virgoans. This quartz variety gemstone is a recently discovered stunner occurring in two different countries — Africa and China. Both varieties are named after

Sid Pieters who discovered the gemstone in 1962 while prospecting farmland in Namibia. Chinese Pietersite was apparently discovered in 1993 but wasn't marketed till 1997. Even though these two forms look similar they are somewhat different in composition, the Chinese being magnesium rich and a brand new mineral while the African variety is mainly crocidolite.

Whether African or Chinese, Pietersite owes its glory to the many fibrous bands of blue, gold and/or red tiger eye type fibres and to our planets geological processes which put the original mineral under heavy stress, reheated folded it over and over again, braking and fracturing it again and again then when the game was over re-cemented the battered pieces together with quartz. Gemstones that undergo this process are referred to as brecciated, creating a finished product with multiple colours, and patterns of chaotic swirls, swathes and fibrous segments in various blues from baby to royal, a range of gold to make a wealthy monarch's mouth water and reds from almost cardinal to brown-gold, which may be together or alone. The rarest shades in Pietersite are blues followed by the reds.

Pietersite must always be cut cabochon (half round) with a curved surface or beads to show its most mysterious feature – a sheen which can be likened to the illuminated light from a spool of silk. Gemmologists call this ribbon of light "chatoyancy".

Lucky first half Virgos.

Second Half Virgo Precious Crystal

IOLITE
This crystal's composition of two white and two dark metallic elements corresponds with the dark side of Mercury, which popular astrology says rules the Virgo personality, and equally with the sun bleached side of that planet.

Deriving its name from the Greek word meaning "violet", Iolite's display of different tints when viewed from different angles also earned it a nickname "dichroic". Most gem quality Iolite grows in empty cavities originally made by gas bubbles in hot lava flows. Matching Mercury's intensely hot position and its mutable planet (Venus), Iolite is formed under pressure and in elevated temperatures, where concentrated steam and rare metallic chemicals force their way through lava already cooling to the last solidifying stage in the centre mass. There, in empty spaces, some of the mineral rich liquid hardens into large, perfect Iolite crystals, containing varied mixtures of magnesium, aluminium, iron and manganese.

In times past Iolite was known as "The Water Sapphire". It is iron that gives it its prevailing blue-violet shade, although unusually lovely specimens from Sri Lanka show interesting red hues, caused by added iron mineral scales within the body of the stone, which is then called bloodshot Iolite.

ALAMANDINE GARNET

Called Carbuncle when cut cabochon (half round), this gem is another precious crystal for second half Virgos. All Garnets have the same basic composition, formed at elevated temperatures, and all are rich in metals, though Garnets differ with each variety. The Alamandine is predominantly iron and aluminium composition and is possibly the most famous member of the Garnet family. The ancient Greeks, wizards with the drill and cutting wheel, worked on it to good effect as a fashionable stone, and their artistry lives on in an Alamandine carved about the middle of the sixth century BC. Carved in exquisite detail, a man wearing a cap, draped in a cloak and seated on a rock offering a cup to an eagle as large as himself. An arched, leafed tree encircles both and a line denotes the flat earth.

Crusaders carried Carbuncles as a protective agent against battle wounds. Just as "working Diamonds" are used in the manufacture of machinery, so imperfect Garnets are sometimes found in stones used as building blocks and foundations of buildings.

NEW MEXICO RUBY

Correctly a Red Garnet, also called the Arizona Ruby, sits well in this area of the zodiac. New Mexico Ruby was once gathered by the Navajo Indians from ant hills and scorpions' nests. Some creatures have excellent gemstone taste.

First Half Virgo Talisman

LABRADORITE

Due to the presence within this mineral of countless minute Iron plates, Labradorite shimmers in iridescent shades of peacock-blue, green, gold and greenish-yellow. Sometimes a pinky-red or purple specimen peeps shyly from its hiding place. Like a dragonfly's wings and with true Mercurian swiftness the colours appear, and then vanish, this optical effect being achieved, in the main, by interference of light in Labradorite's physical structure.

The background tint of this, the loveliest variety of feldspar (Swedish for field rock), is often deep-grey, while a more ethereal type is a transparent pale grey, but whatever version Labradorite presents itself in, it is Mercury ruled (like the people in this area of the zodiac) with Saturnian undertones, Saturn being the mutable planet for first half Virgoans.

Used through the ages for cameos and carvings, Labradorite and its sister stone Spectrolite are nowadays mostly cut flat for mounting in rings, or in spherical shapes for beads. But nothing delights connoisseurs of this mineral's gentle grace so much as a simple string of tumbled, drilled, Labradorite pieces strung to be worn as a necklace and big, fat beads are simply divine.

It should be mentioned here that a pure, crystal variety Labradorite has recently been discovered in Australia, but lacks all the beauty and fascination of the non-gem quality stone.

The mausoleum constructed in Moscow in the 1930s in order to house the body of Lenin is built of red Ukrainian granite and Labradorite tons and tons of it, probably from pits in the Urals. The stone itself is named after the country in which it was first discovered, namely Labrador.

SPESSARTINE GARNET
Another talisman suitable for Virgos of the first half is the Spessartine Garnet. Jewellers use five members of this family in the course of their work, corresponding to the number (5) allotted to planet Mercury by the science of numerology. Its hardness and metallic constituents make this a definite Virgo talisman. It occurs in Africa, America, Brazil and Sri Lanka.

Second Half Virgo Talisman

TIGER EYE
Resembling the gleaming eye of a tiger in the night, this stone has a golden streak of light which stretches full width across its curved and polished surface, giving it a shifting lustre. Fashioned in beads, or carved it presents parallel, pale, silk-like ribbons of colour alongside deeper tinted velvety bands, wheeling and reversing its colour order with each movement. An iridescent combination of yellow-brown and chocolate-

brown is the shade generally associated with the Virgo talisman, yet Tiger Eye can display variegated greens alongside bronze-red or it can have lemon-tinted lines revolving round (and beside) dark-blue.

Its geological name is Crocidolite, which also denotes the fibrous asbestos mineral which, infiltrating its basic quartz body, can give it an indigo blue tint. Less glamorously, Crocidolite is used for brake linings, boiler coverings, fireproof fabrics and insulation. There lies the correspondence to Mercury (Virgoan ruling planet) and Venus (mutable body). By natural process in Earth's crust, Crocidolite changes composition (not form) and usually assumes a yellow-brown tint, which makes it the more commonly seen yellow Tiger Eye, but sometimes a part way mark is reached in the change process and a residual portion of the original blue product produces green Tiger Eye, or "Zebra" to the trade. If there has been no change to the Crocidolite, the gemstone remains dark-blue and then it is termed "Hawk Eye". The red Tiger Eye is another matter altogether as this shade comes from reheating, which can happen naturally in the earth or artificially at the hands of man. Tiger Eye contains a trace of iron and was thought by the ancients to be a guard against the Evil Eye.

VESUVIAN LAVA
Blue tinted Vesuvian Lava can hardly be called a gem, but is certainly a sterling second talisman for second set Virgoans. This natural, transparent beauty looks more than terrific when shaped and polished. When volcanic eruptions occur they cause fusion of minerals and after the molten mass has set, some areas glitter with a myriad of crystals, while others are dull. Most lava is unworkable by man, but the Vesuvian variety has most of the qualities essentially needed by craftsmen, plus an amazing tint and known history.

First Half Virgo Bedside Rock

SPECULAR HEMATITE
This glittering, black stone is one of the chief iron ores, which gives correspondence to Mercury's enormous metallic core and rock composition, while its colour links it to Saturn (the mutable globe in this area of the zodiac).

Hematite is an abundant mineral which often occurs in small crystals which, eventually, other minerals grow round and enclose. At other times it sprinkles itself on an already developed, separate mineral. Either way it then acts as a colouring agent to otherwise dull material. Although its own shade is a dark steel grey, if it is scored on a ceramic tile the resulting streak is red, hence its alternative (but seldom used) name, "Bloodstone".

Hematite can be a blaze of crystalline radiance, or come in thin plates grouped in rosettes in specimens from Alpine areas. The type of Hematite used in jewellery develops a bulbous, kidney structure known as "Kidney Ore". Cameos, beads, ring stones and cufflinks in Hematite are a "must" for the fashion conscious.

MAGNETITE

A second bedside rock for Virgoans of the first half is Magnetite, another important iron ore. This also is an abundant and widespread high temperature mineral which, when occurring in sulphide veins, is usually magnetic, and was used to make early compasses, when splinters of the mineral would be placed in buckets of water and painted with points marked north, south, east and west. For this reason seamen once wore iron crosses as a talisman.

Although this form of Magnetite guided many sea going vessels to safety, we read in "Tales from the Arabian Nights" of passing ships' planks being wrenched from galleons by the force of the attraction which mountains of Magnetite had for the nails!

The magnetic qualities of Magnetite, also called "Lodestone" are extensively used in industry and for the purpose of attaining polarity in alternative medicine. Of this mineral a scholar once said: "Being carried about, the Lodestone should be wrapped in red cloth and stored in a dry place so as to retain its virtue of curing cramp and gout. The Lodestone will also make a man gracious in conversation".

More often Magnetite occurs in a dull, dark lump but sometimes it adds beauty to violet Amethyst, Rock Crystal and Mica.

Occasionally Magnetite's iron content, or some of it, is replaced by magnesium, aluminium and/or chromium, but it is still a Virgoan mineral, since all the replacement elements are metallic and suited to a sun-boiled ruling planet. Magnetite has a hardness count of 5.5, which is Mercury's own number.

Second Half Virgo Bedside Rock

METEORITE

Corresponding with Mercury's dense, sun baked surface, a Meteorite has a hard crust where many chemicals have become fused and clotted by heat and pressure. Science categorizes these as "Stony", "Stony Irons" and "Iron". The second set Virgoan's bedside rock, then, is the remains of a large mass of primitive matter from the Solar System generally thought to have originated in the asteroid belt between Mars and Jupiter. When flung out of orbit the material would have been automatically drawn by gravitation towards the Sun, and by chance or pull reached our atmosphere, where it became white hot and usually exploded. Those fragments reaching the Earth are known as Meteorites.

A dagger hewn from the Virgoan bedside rock was found in Tutankhamen's tomb; and once, some years ago and also in Egypt, an Iron Meteorite killed a dog — a most unfortunate happening. In general, however, these objects have done little harm. Indeed, most are so tiny that nobody ever finds them.

OBSIDIAN
Another bedside rock for Virgoans second half is Obsidian, once more, appropriately, registering a hardness of five. In fact, Obsidian is not strictly speaking a mineral but natural glass once spewed from an erupting volcano. Favoured by ancient Mexican cultures, this material, which is usually dense black or dark brown, can also contains white and grey markings which have given rise to such appropriately descriptive names as "Snowflake", "Flowering", and "Apache Tears". Another variety, called Mountain Mahogany, has orange-red and brown bands, caused by cavities present at its formation. Mexicans once thought these tinted bands neutralized negative magic.

Green Obsidian flies under the flag of Bottlestone and is equally suitable for Mercury's children.

First Half Libra Precious Crystal

SPINEL
This chameleon among jewels has a wider range of tints than any other variety and is rarer than Ruby or Sapphire, with which it is often found. Unlike them, it plummeted in popularity about a century ago for a variety of reasons, all of them unjust. Until that time, its history was dazzling. The Black Prince wore a Spinel at the Battle of Crécy. That same gem now glows alongside the world's second largest Diamond in the English crown of state. The British royal family also own an uncut Spinel known as the Timor Ruby a stone rendered unique by the fact that the six previous owners have their names drilled into its surface.

More romantically and sadly, a Spinel danced at the high point of the last Tsarina's pretty crown.

Spinels come in several colours and for Librans of the first half the best, in reverse order, are: the clear variety or transparent white; the blue, containing zinc; and the dark-green type known as Ceyloite containing iron and a trace of chromium. This last is to be preferred above the rest because it pleases not only planet Venus, Libra's ruler, but also Uranus, the mutable planet.

Composed of the metallic elements magnesium and aluminium, Spinels of different varieties come from Afghanistan, Burma, Sri Lanka and Thailand. The gem's hardness is considerable at 7.5 to 8.

WHITE TOPAZ
As a second precious crystal Librans in this area should choose a White Topaz. Occurring in acid induced rocks, this gem is usually found in Australia, Brazil, Japan, Zimbabwe and the Urals.

KYANITE
A third crystal of great beauty is gem quality Kyanite, the purest of all forms of bedside rock adopted for Librans.

Second Half Libra Precious Crystal

BLUE SAPPHIRE
From the Middle Ages onwards the Greek name Sapphirus, meaning "blue", was recognized as referring to the Blue Sapphire, a crystal of gem quality belonging to the corundum variety. Since then all tints except red and orange are referred to a Sapphire, but when we use that name we generally mean blue and that is the precious crystal for second half Librans.

The Sapphire has a basically aluminium composition and its colouring pigments are iron and titanium. It is a hard gem at a count of nine, is not attacked by acids and remains solid even when exposed to elevated temperatures. It is a worthy Earth mineral partner for the metallic worlds of Venus (ruling planet) and Mercury (mutable), both of which are exposed to the unimaginable heat of their close neighbour, the Sun and acids. The blue and blackish tints are allotted on the grounds that most astrologers agree that Librans are influenced by the nights of their celestial monarchs, but these individuals may choose one of the brownish-blue or greenish-blue shades.

Probably the most desired, as well as the rarest, of the blue Sapphire's tints is the intense cornflower colour with its velvety translucence. Called the "Kashmir", this occurs in Australia, Burma and Sri Lanka, but earlier it came from the mountainous Kashmir region of India, a deposit now sadly worked out.

STAR SAPPHIRE
Librans who find the Kashmir unobtainable or above their means should take a look at the Star Sapphire.

They may find they forget the Kashmir when they watch in fascination their ruling planet's effigy mirrored in this wonderful six rayed star.

A fine Star Sapphire is easy to define. It should have good colour (though starstones are generally paler than clear crystals) the star well centred on the stone and have straight, strong rays. "The Star of India", at 536 carats, is the largest cut blue stone in existence, while the largest Black Star Sapphire is the "Midnight Star" weighing 116 carats. The hypnotic black bodied Starstone is also correct for this area of the zodiac. It occurs mainly in Australia.

The Starstone must be cut cabochon (half round) in order to fully display its six rayed star, sometimes caused by inclusions of rutile (needle like crystals) which run in three directions crossing at a common point.

Rutile is a separate mineral which the growing Sapphire crystal trapped as it developed.

In conjunction with Venus and Mercury, rutile is used in industry as a source of titanium.

SILLIMANITE
This seldom mentioned, and definitely not in jewellery circles because great specimens are more often grabbed by collectors, also sits well with Librans of the second half as it is conceived in elevated temperatures, which make it uncommonly resistant to chemicals, heat and stress. The Sillimanite crystal most suitable here appears, at first glance, to be violet-blue, but when viewed from a different angle changes to pale yellowish-grey.

First Half Libra Talisman

DIOPTASE
From the Tsumeb Diamond mines in South West Africa, and the oxidation zones of copper deposits, comes a glittering cluster of hypnotic green

crystals more vibrant than any Emerald. This is Dioptase. Yet though matching the brightness of its ruling planet's glimmer from Earth, this transparent gem has not yet emerged as suitable for cutting. An inherent brittleness has disqualified it to date, but pendants, earrings, cufflinks and bracelets are fashioned by leaving the gleaming Dioptase in its original uncut state and placing, or electroforming, metal on its base and sides. The result may be thought of as a gold or silver mount holding elfin dreams. Dioptase is right for this area of the zodiac, being rich in copper and usually found in association with sulphur, a main constituent of Venusian rain. It matches Uranus, the mutable planet for Librans of the first half, because of its colour.

TSAVORITE

A fashionable second talisman for Librans in the first half is Tsavorite. Belonging to the garnet family, this transparent, emerald green to yellow-green gemstone was found in Kenya and introduced to the market by Tiffany & Co in 1974

Second Half Libra Talisman

IMPERIAL GREEN JADEITE

Brightest of green is one of the most sought after shades of the highly venerated Jadeite mineral and also one of the hardest to find. There are many other colours white, red, rust, yellow and all shades of violet but emerald green is chosen for this area of the zodiac because that tint is due to chromium, which when added to iron and steel imparts hardness and tenacity, qualities needed for an Earth mineral parallel to both Venus (ruling planet) and the mutable body, Mercury.

The Chinese call Jadeite "Yu Shih" meaning the Yu stone. They believe it contains all five virtues needed for a happy and civilized existence; charity, courage, modesty, justice and wisdom. In times past the Chinese Emperor wore Jadeite sandals and his officials had badges of office of the same material.

Chinese who practice Feng Shui consider bright to medium green one of the major colours for encouraging the energies of good health, family ties, all partnerships and prosperity.

To this day great Jadeite boulders embedded in orange clay are cracked open by heat caused through purposely lit fires. Then, after being wedged apart with chisels, they are cut with thin, steel saws held tight on bamboo bows by man power.

First Half Libra Bedside Rock

KYANITE

Formed in stressful circumstances and containing aluminium, Kyanite is the perfect example of symmetrical elegance, and the bedside rock for first half Librans. Habitually reminiscent of greyish-blue sky, its finely furrowed, flat blades stretch tautly, reaching as far as its chemicals will allow, a soft luminosity glowing from its grey-blue depths showing lights of patchy white, muted green and pale mustard.

Kyanite also occurs in rosettes, which still show its pearly lustre and shading to good advantage. It is remarkably heat resistant and is almost completely immune to the forces of other chemicals (such as acids).

When heated to 1,300 degrees Celsius, it not only decomposes into the aluminium type product known as Mullite but also into silica rich glass.

Kyanite matches the opposing traits of Venus and Uranus with contradictions of its own. Venus spins close to the Sun and is torrid, while chilly Uranus trudges slowly on the outer limits of the solar system. Kyanite similarly shows a Jekyll and Hyde character by being much softer lengthways than it is across. The Greeks spotted this and called the stone "Distbene" meaning dual strength. The name itself is from another Greek word and refers to its overall colour, that is, "blue". It is nowadays obtainable in most countries in rock form, with St Gothard (Switzerland) and Arizona (USA) yielding fabulous gem quality crystals – which clever Librans, incidentally, could wear as a precious gem.

WAVELLITE

Nature wasn't in a hurry when it designed Wavellite, another bedside rock for first half Librans. Containing aluminium and iron, the crystals of this mineral are best described as white and brownish-yellow needles with striated faces, which can be stout or long. But more usually Wavellite forms in masses of radiating fibres which start from the same common point and span outwards, making flatfish spheres up to half an inch in diameter reminiscent of silk wound tightly on a circular piece of cardboard. A mathematician among minerals, it occurs in the county of Cornwall in England and at Holly Springs, Pennsylvania, in the USA.

Second Half Libra Bedside Rock

ADAMITE on LIMONITE

For a model of their bedside rock, second set Librans should take a dark-brown pudding basin, chop half the sides away so as to leave the base intact, and let it find its own standing position. Next they should throw spoonfuls of pinky-violet water ice into the vessel, letting the globular masses fall where they will. Then they should take thin slices of melon and place them on one side of the bowl's interior and sprinkle the lot with green icing sugar. That completed, they should stand back and look at their creation with half shut eyes. What they will see will be Adamite on Limonite.

Water ice is reminiscent of Adamite, a translucent copper, zinc and cobalt mineral. Similar to nickel in many ways, cobalt is a silvery-white metal used to make a deep-blue paint pigment. copper is a major metallic substance used in the electrical and pharmaceutical industries, and zinc is employed in many fields necessary for man's comfort and pleasure, among them dye making. Limonite contains much iron, its existence resulting from other iron minerals which have been altered by weather conditions. It either forms in "icicle" structures, as squashed spheres, or in long, furrowed, flattened pieces. Most often these occurrences are shiny, but they can also be dull. Lovely specimens of Adamite on Limonite come from Mopimi in Mexico, Cornwall in England and from Saxony, Russia and America.

ILMENITE

Second half Librans can use a component of their other bedside rock, Ilmenite, to make white smoke for sky writing, yet this stone itself is black. It is usually glossy, contains iron, sometimes more metallic elements, and is an important source of titanium. It occurs in flakes and grains, in broad, flat crystals or in a chunk. Heavy beach sands often contain the granular type, notably at Travencore, a seventeen mile beach in India, and at beaches in Australia and America. Inland deposits occur in Norway and Quebec, so fun loving Librans of the second set can simply have a bucket of black sand as their bedside rock.

First Half Scorpio Precious Crystal

RUBY

In the beginning, according to ancient Burmese legend, there was a great serpent which laid three eggs. The first produced the King of Pagan, the second the Emperor of China, and the third a miraculous seed which sprouted Burmese Rubies. These last were thought to guarantee invincibility in battle if the owner of the stone inserted it into his flesh. A similar belief in the Ruby as a protective gem was held by the Ceylonese, who thought it formed itself from the Buddha's tears. In the Bible a Ruby is placed at God's command on the throat of Aaron, the elder brother of Moses, and is designated the most precious of the twelve gems first created in the world. In the 14th century it was apparently believed that the Ruby should be worn on the left hand side to secure its protective properties, which included turning black to warn the wearer of imminent danger and regaining its vibrant hue when he or she was out of harm's way. Interestingly, a Ruby of exquisite quality worn by Catherine of Aragon, Henry VIII's first wife, was reported to have lost its lustre and inner fire when she lay on her deathbed in 1536.

First grade Rubies, generally known as "Pigeon's Blood", carry a hefty price tag which would sink a comparable Diamond to the bottom of the deepest ocean. The most important sources are Burma, Sri Lanka, Tanzania and Thailand, the best deposit being in the Magok, or Mogok, Valley of Upper Burma. For centuries women and children have crawled along the narrow pits, shafts and tunnels which run at a depth of several yards under the surface of this valley to bring up specimens which, when sorted, yield only one per cent gem quality. Large stones are rare, but the work brings its reward because it also produces a proportion of first grade, "Pigeon's Blood" stones, of a rich deep-red touched with blue.

Sri Lanka produces a less valuable gem with tints varying from light red to raspberry, some of which are found by panning the river sands and gravel. Recently found Tanzanian Rubies show a distinctive hue ranging from purple to brown-red, while those from Thailand re brown-red. Ruby deposits cover many parts of the world, but most are unsuitable for jewellery as they are opaque or of poor colour. These are powdered and used as an industrially important abrasive known as emery.

The mineral variety Corundum to which Ruby belongs, is the hardest naturally occurring material next to the Diamond which sits well with planet Neptune, the mutable mass for this area of the zodiac and itself possibly prolific in Diamonds.

The Ruby corresponds with Pluto and Mars colour shift from red to green when certain laboratory tests are applied, and that it comprises chromium and iron and much aluminium in its basic formula. The Ruby's hardness count of 9 corresponds with Mars.

Ruby derives its name from the Latin rubens meaning "red". Foreign inclusions in a Ruby fail to diminish its value, first because they indicate its source area and second, because inclusions usually point to the fact that the gemstone is natural and not laboratory grown.

STAR RUBY

The Star Ruby, also suitable for first half Scorpios, has the same composition as a plain Ruby, with the addition of a multitude of foreign, hair-like crystals which introduce a silky sheen. When the stone is cut cabochon (half round), these crystals, growing in three different directions, produce a six rayed star which hovers over the surface when the gem is moved. This very desirable stone shows a more prominent asterism if the Ruby's basic body colour is very rich red or medium pink.

BENITOITE

If another precious crystal is desired, try Benitoite, a rare titanium mineral found in San Benito, California, USA. Discovered about 1907 by Mr. Hawkins and T. Edwin Sanders, this normally deepish-blue gem is similar to a Sapphire, but excels it in brilliance. Not long ago a glorious pink was reported. At a count of 6 Benitoite can be recommended as very usable "dress" wear.

Second Half Scorpio Precious Crystal

RHODOCROSITE

The second half Scorpio precious crystal began its career just before the Second World War when a forgotten mine, once worked by ancient Mexicans for silver and copper during the 18th century, was reopened. Now "Inca Rose" and "Rosinca" are understandably popular for the pink delight which is properly called Rhodocrosite. This stone comprises calcium, magnesium and iron, is formed in gentle circumstances, and is hard enough to wear and enjoy as a dress jewel. Rhodocrosite equates with Pluto, Mars and the Moon by its toning, elements and hardness.

A location in South Africa's Kalahari Desert produces top grade Rhodocrosite shades ranging from clear and bright sunset-pink to varied shades of rose, but Rhodocrosite can have a greenish tinge through added impurities. Although the original Mexican mine has failed to yield gem material, but it does supply the world with the very lovely semi-precious kind, which is characterized by lacy cream ribbons on its bright yet soft-pink background. In fact this semi-precious variety is popping up all over the world in North America, India, Hungary, Romania and Saxony.

SRI LANKAN ALEXANDRITE

A second precious crystal for Scorpios of this set is the Sri Lankan Alexandrite, which is really a colour change Sapphire of slaty blue-green (in sunlight) to purple (under artificial light). Iron and other metallic elements including vanadium are for Mars and the Moon, while the colours are for Pluto. Buyers should be warned always to obtain a note of guarantee supporting this gem's authenticity, for synthetic versions of it are frequent.

First Half Scorpio Talisman

BLUE JOHN

Nero is said to have handed over the modern equivalent of £120,000 sterling for a vase made of it; Pliny the Elder sang its praises; the Pompeii excavations revealed two Blue John urns, proof that the Romans not only discovered and mined this mineral 2,000 years ago in their outlandish province of Britain, but also cherished it. Today wine goblets have retailed in Harrods of London for up to £2,500 sterling and Elizabeth 11 personally owns at least one modern Blue John chalice. Blue John occurs in only one place, a hill situated about a mile from Castleton in the county of Derbyshire, England. This stone, the world's most exclusive fluorite, is distinguished from others by its undulating dark-blue and purple-red bands on a white or yellow-white background, making circular, lacy patterns round a central focal point in colours matching both Pluto and its moon, Charon.

Fossils of marine life which swam in underground streams some 330 million years ago, and pockets of green oil (thought to be derived from extinct ocean vegetation), are found where Blue John has developed, giving it a tie with the watery planet Neptune, the mutable globe in this area. The secretive character of Scorpio's heavenly ruler and the sumptuous Blue John run parallel, as the prized ornamental bands of the stone have long been a source of mystery as to their cause. Could it be iron, asphalt, bitumen or irradiation from uranium? Nobody is absolutely certain. Even the origin of the talisman's name is a mystery. Was it from France, where masterpieces were fashioned from it? The French could have called it bleu-jaune (blue-yellow). Or did the British lead miners name it Blue John to distinguish it from their own working material, nicknamed "Black Jack"? In size matching tiny Pluto, Blue John is naturally formed in small, round nodules and gentle conditions. Superb selections of inexpensive jewellery in silver and gold mounts are available in this material, as are collector eggs, bowls, urns and clocks.

Second Half Scorpio Talisman

AMETHYST
Caused by radiation effects on iron, the colour of Amethyst matches many stabs of colour on the Plutonian surface. In addition to that, it has usually formed in the remains of old lava bubbles with an outside coating of a super-rich iron substance. Iron is the metal which colours the rusty-pink Martian soil and that planet has a sub influence on all Scorpios.

Although most quartz, the family to which Amethyst belongs, corresponds to Saturn, planet Pluto is of equally light bodyweight and far enough from the Sun not to deny the presence of water albeit frozen. In Amethyst, added flecks of iron and golden rutile (foreign hairy crystals) are occasionally present, making an extra piece of magic in parallel. Few of these specimens hit the market, unfortunately, but when they do they are collectors' items. Earlier associations of this stone include Saturn (its vinous tint connecting it with Bacchus), Neptune (the Romans dedicated it to Neptune's month, February), Taurus (Venus), Jupiter and the Sun. Amethyst quartz was also confused with the Oriental Amethyst which is in fact a Sapphire.

One of the stories linking Amethyst with Bacchus is that he frightened an innocent maid who changed into a rock crystal through fear of him. The remorseful god sighed and as his wine soaked breath touched the miserable girl her veins ran purple with the tint of the grape. From then on the gemstone showed pity to those over indulging in wine and was said to prevent drunkenness.

So the ancients quaffed from Amethyst goblets, hoping to remain sober and avoid the morning after effect.

Amethyst was a popular choice in Roman times when engraving was in vogue, made possible by new instruments such as drills and turning wheels. So Mark Antony's handsome features can still be gazed upon today, causing us to understand why he won an Egyptian queen's heart.

First Half Scorpio Bedside Rock

STIBNITE
The shadowy world of Pluto attracts Stibnite, a brittle, bluish-silver to lead-grey mineral of excessive vulnerability and some malleability,

its personality expressed in straight radiating needles or flat rods, sometimes with criss cross lines which are usually grouped in parallel.

Stibnite occurs in small specimens matching the petite planet Pluto, is visually pleasing and occasionally exhibits surface iridescence. When heated in charcoal it shows its dislike of high temperatures by leaving as a residue a crumbly, white encrustation. White is the colour of Pluto's moon, Charon, and the intense cold of this globe suits Stibnite's softness, which is measured at 2 out of 10 on the hardness scale. Gentle Mars, a sub-influence for first half Scorpios, and Neptune, their mutable planet, both have a low temperature and lead placid lives. Mars is a planet in which the soil is rich in metallic elements.

Stibnite derives its name from the Latin stibnium, meaning antimony a tin white, brittle metal. About five thousand years ago it was used as eye shadow perhaps the first luxury use of a product of Earth.

CROCOITE
For Scorpios who prefer glitter in their bedside rock Crocoite boasts shiny, clear crystals of hyacinth-red usually displayed on brown parent rock, allowing Crocoite, proud of its high born character, full scope for showing off. Its colours correspond with Mars and Neptune by virtue of the fact that in one laboratory test the red crystals turn green and, in the course of another, turn dark before reverting to their red brilliancy. Containing chromium, Crocoite yields in Tasmania, America, Brazil, the Philippines, Hungary, Romania and Siberia, and develops in the oxidized zone of lead deposits.

Second Half Scorpio Bedside Rock

OKENITE
Open the palm of your hand and imagine a small cave resting on it. Peer into its depths and see minute and shimmering Rock Crystals hanging at various lengths from the ceiling with more scattering the floor, these last straining to grow just a little bit higher.

Strewn at random over the starry carpeting imagine balls of pale green mimosa (wattle to Australians and New Zealanders) coated in glittering, seed Rock Crystals, their confusion suggesting the aftermath of a goblin fight.

Then imagine these green balls rolling as you move your hand, and as the light plays on the seed crystals. Just inside and against the outside of the small cave are fluffy, white trees and bushes, with no branches and, in the case of the trees, no trunk. Each tree is just a mass of long, straight hairs, their pompom appearance caused by hairy crystals starting from a common centre point, their miniscule weight pressing them slightly flat at the base.

You are looking at Okenite, a calcium mineral with high water content and an even higher fragility rating, one push and Okenite is gone forever! The shapes, whiteness and enormous size of this mineral correspond with Pluto's moon, for its delicate body is only able to survive if placed far from the heat of the Sun.

For Neptune and Mars the correspondence is with Prehnite, of pale green "Mimosa" appearance, calcium mineral which differs from Okenite in having added aluminium and less water. Prehnite is an ethereal gemstone when tumbled, cut and polished, and often has a pearly lustre.

Though not always easy to find, Prehnite, in the form of beads, pendants and cufflinks, is well worth searching.

Quartz, the most prolific, and probably also the most appreciated, of all varieties of minerals, is formed in gentle circumstances and suitably matches all three worlds involved.

This additional choice is much discussed elsewhere in this book, particularly in the healing section, and second half Scorpios are exceptionally lucky in this wonderfully useful and attractive bedside rock.

First Half Sagittarius Precious Crystal

TOURMALINE
There is only one precious crystal tempestuous enough to correspond with the wild world of Jupiter and that is the Tourmaline. The multi coloured variety known as Melonstone is allocated to first half Sagittarians, as usually it has a strawberry core surrounded by a blueish-green band, or a green-blue inside and an outer layer of pink. The pink is important as first half Sagittarians have the rusty-pink Mars as their mutable planet and the metallic elements causing the tint are formed in correspondingly cool temperatures. Although the green parallels with both Mars and Jupiter, in reality Tourmaline of any colour is correct for those ruled by this planet, in which many precious metallic elements are thought to be swirling about.

No other family of gemstones has the richness in colour variation of the Tourmaline, for the composition of each stone differs from that of the next and each tint depends on the dominant metallic element present when the crystal was formed. Like its ruling planet, the Tourmaline is extremely complex and often holds aluminium, boron, potassium, magnesium, iron, sodium and lithium in varying quantities in the one crystal, a point amusingly underlined by the English art critic John Ruskin in his book The Ethics of the Dust (1866), where he wrote: "And on the whole, the complex and often holds aluminium, boron, potassium, magnesium, iron, sodium and lithium in varying quantities in the one crystal, a point amusingly underlined by the English art critic John Ruskin in his book The Ethics of the Dust (1866), where he wrote: "And on the whole, the chemistry of it is more like a mediaeval doctor's prescription than the making of a respectable mineral". Indeed, the only regular feature of the Tourmaline is its basic structure, the variations thereafter are myriad.

The Tourmaline's unique positive and negative electrical properties gave it its early name of "The Mineral Magnet". Warmth also activates it, as a group of Dutch schoolchildren discovered in 1703 while playing in the Sun with what they thought were worthless stones. In fact these were coloured Tourmalines which had been given to the children by gem traders and which attracted dried leaves and twigs. Adults then took up the game, placing Tourmaline gemstones near the fire or rubbing them with their hands, whereupon they were found to entice ash at one end while repelling it at the other. This caused the Tourmaline to be nicknamed "Aschentrekers", meaning "drawer of ash".

The Tourmaline probably derived its proper name from the Tamil word Tormalli, meaning "Something little out of the earth".

Most Tourmalines are small but exceptions to this are the famous "Brazilian Rocket", measuring 109 cm (43 in), and the nest of variegated crystals as large as a man's head found in Burma and given by the King of Ava to the Count de Bouron. The separate crystals making up this cluster are almost as thick as a pinky finger and each starts at the base of the stone as a dark shade, becoming more luminous towards the extremity.

Although most of the surface is golden-brown, the mass, as a whole, is a pale violet-red. The King of Ava's extravagant gift now lives in the British Museum. The collector can find Tourmalines in Australia, America, Brazil, India, Russia, Zimbabwe and elsewhere.

PHOSPHOPHYLLITE

A second precious crystal for first half Sagittarians is Phosphophylite. This transparent mineral with the very difficult to pronounce, was named in Bolivia where it was found.

Phosphophyllite has a divine and delicate, turquoise tint and can be cut, polished and handled, but should be treated as a collector's item because it has a low hardness of 3.5, so it is best kept in a glass cabinet. When expertly cut Phosphophyllite echoes Jupiter's steady light as seen from afar, and one of its principal components, zinc (the other main ones are iron and manganese), matches Jupiter's white southern zone. Here it is worth mentioning that Amber, a Sagittarian talisman, with a hardness of 2.5-3, has endured for centuries after having been handled, worn — and sat upon. Not that your sit on Phosphophyllite!

Second Half Sagittarius Precious Crystal

TOURMALINE

Already matching Jupiter, this stone is also in parallel to the Sun, which is the mutable body for second half Sagittarians, by virtue of its light bodyweight and astonishing energy.

The most suitable colours or predominance of colours in this powerful crystal for Sagittarians of the second set are the yellow-greens and the blue-greens, but as Tourmalines in one or even two colours are relatively rare, additional tints or even quite different ones are acceptable. In matching the Tourmaline and its celestial counterparts the key factors are the stone's compositional elements, its density and its energy output.

To connoisseurs, the most alluring quality of a Tourmaline is its butterfly personality. Green will show anything from yellow to greenish-blue, red displays varied pinks, dark red and brown have mingled tints and the clear stone has shadings of rust and green glinting from some spot within its body. The violets merge with turquoise; yellow can be dark, light, or even orange. Sections of cut Tourmaline exhibit contrasting shades on opposite sides. In most Tourmalines, in short, the rainbow seems to be throwing a party.

The Tourmaline should be called "The Gem of Youth" as it has almost always come to fame through children. For example, on an autumn day in 1820, two schoolboys from Mount Mica in Maine, USA, spotted a glittering mass of brilliant green crystals by the roots of a tree. From there the stone came to the notice of Parisian jewellers who used it extensively, although even now the Tourmaline is too "new" to be used by the smartest shops for regular window displays.

Over the centuries this harlequin mineral has been confused with other precious crystals. Thus a "Hen's Egg" Tourmaline was originally thought to be a Ruby of remarkable light, and a stone of this sort is housed in the treasure room at the Kremlin today. It was first presented to Kaiser Rudolph II (died 1612) y his sister; from him it passed to the Swedish Crown; and from there it became the property of Catherine the Great in 1777.

Tourmaline is found in many countries but an accessible place for finding one of your own is the island of Elba, which produces some of the loveliest in the world.

First Half Sagittarius Talisman

AMBER

One thing can be said with confidence about Amber; it is unlikely to exist on any planet except Earth unless there is (yet to be discovered) another Earth-like planet in the habitual zone of its day-time star which once grew trees that produced like resin. For Amber is not a mineral (though it can be cut and polished like one) but a fossil of vegetable origin which came into existence between 30-110 million years ago in the form of resin from some deciduous trees and various conifers.

Amber is correctly called a Mineraloid. a honeyed crypt for all manner of prehistoric objects from orchids, feathers, drops of water and spiders' webs to ants, fleas, moths, hatching eggs and basking lizards. A particularly bizarre specimen, now in the possession of an American natural history museum, is a lump of Amber containing three sets of copulating flies a sort of Pompeii without the people. Formed of carbon, hydrogen and oxygen, Amber is soluble in alcohol, scratches easily and has a negative electrical charge when friction is applied, hence its ancient name of Electron, the Greek for "electric".

Amber from Sicily often glows internally with rich-green and brown-red tints. That from the Dominican Republic does the same, if less vividly, but occasionally specimens display a bright royal blue which shows when placed in direct lighting. The softer, opaque, butter and honey-coloured Amber comes mostly from the Baltic area.

Amber was prized by prehistoric cultures, doubtless because it was easy to work and light to carry. It also appealed to them as Sun worshippers.

Attempts have been made to identify it as a "Peace Stone" but, oddly enough, it has usually become most popular in societies in the throes of political upheaval.

Because of its low melting point one of the lowest of all gemstones Amber is suitably placed with Mars, the mutable planet in this area of the zodiac, which is covered with a constant ground frost.

EILAT STONE
Eilat is a second Talisman for Sagittarians in this set. Also known as King Solomon's Stone, Eilat is the national gemstone of Israel, named after its most southern city located on the north end of the Red Sea. As though mirroring the ocean, first grade Eilat presents in deep, bright shades of blue, turquoise and green because this famous stone is really a rock comprising a unique combination of Chrysocolla, Turquoise, Malachite, Azurite, Copper and Dioptase. As yet there is no access to the Israeli Eilat mine but near the location where it occurs is a stunning geological and historically-rich park where one can see remains of an ancient copper mining industry, including workshops, furnaces, tunnels and shafts, shrines, mining camps and rock drawings mostly dated around 12-13th century BC. This heritage park is situated where it is said the world's legendary copper mines of King Solomon were and Eilat is certainly rich in that mineral. It is hard to track the actual occurrence localities of Eilat sold in Israel, but it is common knowledge that most is imported from foreign mines, possibly Whim Creek/Western Australia and reworked copper mines in South America, Chili or/and Peru.

Eilat is also formed in a gorgeous pink variety.

Second Half Sagittarius Talisman

TURQUOISE
Once the most sought after gemstone of antiquity, Turquoise represented not only beauty to the Egyptians, but perfume as well, for this jewel was originally fashioned into the shape of the leaves of the sweet smelling lotus. Those early inhabitants of the Nile Valley concerned themselves very much with gardens. In their daily prayers they asked to be allowed to return from the "Land of the Dead" to sit under the blue lotus tree, eat its fruit and bask in its sweet and heady scent. Party guests wore garlands of lotus, boatmen wore a single bloom, and bowls of lotus flowers decorated the poorest homes and grandest palaces, while lines of single petals and buds were sculptured and painted in tombs.

The Egyptians' desire to give permanent form to all things beautiful led them to trade with their neighbours for Turquoise, and to develop the art of cloisonné jewellery originally fashioned in Ur. Making this jewellery was an exacting and exhausting task. First, fine sheets of beaten gold had to be cut to a required shape. Then wires were soldered round the detailed design. Finally, the resulting hollows were filled with Turquoise strips, imitating the long, curved petals of the lotus. The forget-me-not, another much admired flower, was imitated in the same way, using the left-over Turquoise pieces. To add the final touches after all the strips of Turquoise had been slotted into place, the surface of the jewel was brushed with tinted and powdered limestone and heated by flame until the gold and the gemstone were fused. Shoulder buttons, clasps, pendants, crowns and many other pieces of beautiful cloisonné artwork survive in Egypt to this day.

Turquoise was also jewel royal to the kings of Persia, where the gemstone was thought to protect horses and their riders and featured accordingly in pieces designed for both. This ubiquitous talisman came to Europe from Persia via Turkey, ubiquitous talisman came to Europe from Persia via Turkey, hence its name. Wearers still use it as a guard against the evil eye, and to dream of it is said to foretell a new and lasting friendship.

American Indians thought the stone made a man warlike, and implacable towards his enemies. Thus the well-equipped brave would carry with him on a war party corn, sweet corn, beans, dried meat, a bear claw and a chunk of Turquoise.

Turquoise contains water, Iron, copper and Aluminium, an appropriate combination for Jupiter. It is of medium hardness, light in weight and largely resistant even to a strong flame (though heat turns its colour brownish) a durability which matches the Sun, the mutable celestial body in this area of the zodiac.

Turquoise for world-wide supply comes mostly from North America, but the buyer must make sure to obtain a certificate of guarantee if a fine stone is required, for the average specimen is an imperfect soft stone hardened up and improved by means of wax impregnation and tinting fossil teeth and bones, coloured by components of iron, are often cut and polished, reaching the market as Bone Turquoise. These of course must also be distinguished from the genuine stone.

HAUYNE
A second talisman for people whose birthday falls under the domain of Jupiter is Hauyne. This pretty and very wearable gemstone resembles a slightly opaque Aquamarine and occurs regularly around the world.

German Rhineland Hauyne, glowing orange under ultra violet lighting, matches Jupiter's clouds and Io, its largest moon. Hauyne is not as well-known as one might expect. Its translucent beauty comes from a mixture of elements in its composition sodium, aluminium and calcium which matches it with Jupiter as does also its light bodyweight.

First Half Sagittarius Bedside Rock

AURICHALCITE
Specimens of this stone, formed in tufted nests of straight, needle like crystals which correspond with their ruling planet, make a delightful bedside rock for first half Sagittarians. Like Jupiter, Aurichalcite has a light bodyweight, and reflects that planet too in its composition of zinc and copper, the former white and volatile, the latter malleable, enduring, and reddish. With its delicate, transparent blue or green tints it is as stunning as its celestial sovereign, whether it has formed in solitude, or with others, or on a dark parent rock.

CHRYSOCOLLA
A second bedside rock for first half Sagittarians is Chrysocolla, a mountain-green or sky-blue opaque mineral with an enamel like lustre which can be found in Australia, America, Bavaria, Chile, the Congo, England and Siberia. Though of varying hardness, it is an unusual and durable jewellery material, showing both its vibrant colours, green and blue in the same piece, or even in the tiniest bead. Some truly gorgeous specimens contain Opal and Rock Crystal; others are overall turquoise in appearance; others again, depending on the impurities, can have brown or black markings as well.

Chrysocolla is essentially a copper element mineral, but containing also variable amounts of silica and with many other metallic and non-metallic elements present as inclusions. It occurs in the county of Cornwall in England; in Adelaide, South Australia; and in Siberia, Chile, the USA and Katanga.

Second Half Sagittarius Bedside Rock

BORNITE & CHALCOPYERITE
Both Jupiter's clouds and Io's volcanoes are honoured in these two stones. Bornite's red-bronze surface leaves a yellow deposit of sulphur

when heated in the laboratory and is a valuable ore of copper laced with elements of iron. Chalcopyrite is simpler though more brassy in appearance. Whether occurring separately or as a duo, both these stones form in big, gaudy, opaque pyramid shaped crystals, though sometimes triangular crystals appear and both stones can occur in microscopically small crystals on a separate, dark rock.

Bornite's "eye-of-the-feather" iridescence has given it the nickname of Peacock Ore, but neither stone is ordinarily used as a gem material. Treasure each in its natural state. The Sun, which is the mutable body for part two Sagittarians, is as well pleased to be matched with these two flamboyant stones as are Jupiter and Io. They come from most parts of the world including, in particular, Australia, Japan, Korea, Chile, Britain, Germany and Norway.

THUNDER EGG

As an alternative, second part Sagittarians can try the well named Thunder Egg. The origin of these stones is still a mystery to geologists, though it was probably volcanic action. Some, on the outside, resemble concrete hot cross buns. They are much fancied by collectors. Good stones, when cut in half, show a four or five pointed star pattern,

with the tops touching the outer edges. The centre of the stone itself can have a hollowed out form, filled with clear Rock Crystal, opaque grey and red-brown quartz, or precious Opal. America yields some splendid specimens of this stone, which also occurs in profusion in Australia, notably in the states of Queensland and Tasmania. Warring gods in Aboriginal myth threw these stones as missiles, a practice no longer to be recommended, however tempting.

First Half Capricorn Precious Crystal

TOPAZ

"The golden Topaz reminds us of autumn leaves, and so is the birthstone for November". Such ignorant remarks have dogged the study of astrological gems and been the cause of much confusion. This particular observation would be less obviously ridiculous if autumn in all countries fell in the same months, or if natal gemstones differed from place to place or from one side of the world to the other. In fact they do not. Your gem is the same, whether you live in Sydney or Timbuktu.

First half Capricorns score any colour Topaz as their precious crystal. Nicknamed "Diamond slave" because its larger specimens often replace

Diamonds for purposes of display, the colourless Brazilian Topaz has a pure, fierce brilliance typical of the whole family, even the highly coloured varieties. It was perhaps this characteristic which encouraged the age-old belief that the pious could read prayer books in the darkness of night by the brilliant light of Topaz and perhaps also the reason why knights on crusade were given a Topaz by their lady loves before setting out.

Containing aluminium, Topaz is almost unique in being one of the few first rate crystals to contain fluorine, a non-metallic element of considerable industrial importance. This chemical, plus a small amount of water and its consequent beautiful range of hues including blue, green, pink, yellow, brown and white, correspond with planet Saturn, and its hardness count of eight gives this stone the same digit assigned to Saturn by the science of numerology.

For Venus, the mutable planet in this area of the zodiac with sulphuric rain in its atmosphere, Topaz is also a match, since it decomposes only slightly when contaminated by sulphuric acid; also it is conceived in elevated temperatures.

According to fable, the Topaz was discovered and named by some shipwrecked sailors awaiting rescue. The island on which they were stranded was difficult to locate as it was constantly surrounded by mist and fog. The sailors called both the gem and the island "Topazos", meaning "lost and found".

The Royal crown of Portugal has a very grand Topaz weighing in at 1,680 carats. It displays magnificent transparency.

Many stones however are wrongly sold as Topaz, including Yellow Citrine, the bedside rock for first half Capricorns. The blue-green variety is often confused with Aquamarine, and the white with Rock Crystal, white Sapphire and the white Diamond, the Topaz being rarer than all of them. Superior examples of Topaz are not easy to come by, nor are large or pink toned specimens.

Modern stones sold as Rose Topaz are merely natural yellow stones artificially heated.

Topaz is of wide occurrence and can be found particularly in Australia, Brazil, Burma, Sri Lanka, Russia, Mexico, Nigeria and the USA.

CHONDROLITE
This is another of the rare fluorine gems, and a second precious crystal for first group Capricorns and is mostly thought of merely as an unusual mineral for a collector's box. It deserves more extensive use, however,

for its deep red crystals are of great beauty and lustre, and its hardness count of six out of ten makes it perfectly possible to fashion this stone for dress wear.

Red variety Chondrolite comes from the Tilly Foster mine in Brewster, Putnam County, New York, but not to be despised are the rich yet soft honey-yellows found in Kafvelorp, Sweden.

Second Half Capricorn Precious Crystal

TANZANITE
A cornflower blue gem with violet lights flashing from its depths, Tanzanite, discovered in Tanzania as recently as 1967, is becoming well through advertising campaigns.

Of the lighter body weight group, which corresponds with planet Saturn, and just over medium hardness, Tanzanite holds a reasonable amount of water along with calcium and aluminium. Its blue colour is thought to be due to a trace of vanadium, a silver-white metallic element used in the manufacture of special steels, but this stunning colour is generally not natural. The stone is heated in gemmological ovens to change the original less attractive colour, a process which does not invalidate its position as a Capricorn precious crystal. Tanzanite is a delicate gemstone owing not to its medium hardness but it's unfortunate habit of breaking along its cleavage if treated roughly, knocked or worn while working so, unless set with higher-than-the-stone protective surrounds and only worn in a genteel environment, it should not be set in a ring or cufflinks, but rather as a pendant, broach, pin or earrings.

OPAL PINEAPPLE
Another precious gem for second set Capricorns is the Opal Pineapple. Contrary to what you may think, this is not a crystallized fruit but an Opal filled Glauberite crystal resembling a pineapple which started forming about 70 million years ago. These collector pieces are only found in White Cliffs Opal fields located 295 kilometres northeast of Broken Hill/NSW/Australia.

An Aboriginal dreamtime story tells us that Opal Pineapples formed from the Rainbow Serpent's droppings as she rested on her journey while wakening the world from its deep sleep at the beginning of time.

The Opal's fast flashing, changeable colour patterns belong to Mercury, the swiftest world in our part of the Milky Way and mutable planet in this part of the zodiac. Its featherweight body corresponds with the lightest planet in the Solar System, which in no way compromises Opal's high water content, since Saturn is cushioned in space far from the Sun.

For Capricorns, the tints of their Opal Pineapple are important, since their celestial ruler's body is yellow, shaded with indigo, blue and violet. Its flashes of other tints are appropriate too, as the planet's circuiting hoops are multi-coloured. The background colour, however, must be dark.

Of all Opal Pineapple specimens found, only about two per cent display top grade Opal. A lesson in life could be learned from precious Opals as their characteristic tints and designs come from structure mistakes and changed paths.

First Half Capricorn Talisman

JET

The most frequent word used in the English language to describe something ravishingly dark is "Jet". Tennyson described a maiden's locks as jet black and Shakespeare referred to Jet as a jewel. This lustrous and velvety mineraloid accords well with Capricorns of the first set, for its tint blends in with the deeper shadows seen on their celestial sovereign, Saturn, and its light construction and body weight are equally appropriate. In parallel with the mutable planet, Venus, Jet needs tremendous pressure when forming. The world's finest quality Jet comes from Yorkshire in England and is not in plentiful supply.

At a period roughly assumed to be 1800 BC, Northern British early Bronze Age jewellers were fashioning great lunar collars with zigzag patterns of up to fifty jet beads to each necklace. These collars often accompanied their wearers to the grave, and although the surviving pieces preclude analysis of their detailed designs, it is clear that the patterns were made by hand gouging. Each piece had triangular terminals and toggles, spacers of different shapes, and elongated "beans" with multiple holes. In later times the devout carried prayer counters, and the Hopi Indians and other tribes of the Western United States of America fashioned fetishes and beads from this dark beauty. Jet was favoured in the seventeenth century for memorial purposes and in the nineteenth century, on the death of Queen Victoria's beloved Prince Albert, Jet was worn at court for the next twenty five years. Prussian peasants still carve boxes, baubles and toys from Jet, which they call "Black Amber".

Although Jet is very slightly harder and heavier than Amber, the two gems show similarities. Both release their own pungent aroma when burnt, both crack if not cherished, both explode under high friction or when subjected to violent temperature changes, both have electrical properties when rubbed, and both originated from prehistoric trees and are thus not proper minerals. Unlike Amber, which is resin, Jet is ancient wood which was compressed under great pressure after being subjected to chemical action in stagnant water. It is much more difficult to obtain than Amber, and there is less of it in the world.

The lustre of Jet can be destroyed by perfume and body acids but is sometimes restored by a brisk rub on a soft cloth impregnated with beeswax.

LAZULITE
Capricorns in this set have another talisman, Lazulite a superb, ornamental stone which should be much more widely used than it is. Containing elements of iron, aluminium and magnesium, sky-blue to azure blue Lazulite has a hardness of just below 6 and is a main constituent of Lapis Lazuli, the second half Capricorn talisman. Wonderful specimens of Lazulite are found in America, Austria, Brazil and Sweden. It corresponds with planet Saturn in all ways and is a match for Venus by virtue of its metallic elements.

Second Half Capricorn Talisman

LAPIS LAZULI
In an isolated area at a site where thousands once lived, and twelve miles from the banks of the Euphrates, excited archaeologists a century ago identified the King of Kish (sometimes called "Me-Salim"), resting in a suit of exquisite wafer thin gold armour. Suspended from his shoulder was a gold filigreed sheaf worked as finely as a spider's web and containing a ceremonial dagger, its hilt carved from a solid piece of Lapis Lazuli. Between 1922 and 1034 British archaeologist Leonard Woolley and his team excavated the Royal Cemetery of Ur". Here they discovered the intact tomb of the Akkadian Queen Pu-abum still clad in her best coat of woven gold thread, nine long Lapis Lazuli and Carnelian necklaces, and a mixed stone choker of Lapis and Carnelian beads spaced with gold motifs. Adding height to her small figure (just over five feet tall) was an enormous black wig entwined with gold ribbon and topped by three open, bright yellow-gold flowers attached to a triple fingered comb. Crowning all this were wreaths of sheet-gold beech leaves embellished

with Lapis Lazuli. Her two gigantic, double-hooped gold earrings must have jingled against the finery as she was laid in peace, guarded in death by four male soldiers and 68 women attendants ritually slain. They too wore jewellery to die for featuring Lapis Lazuli beads.

Among other artifacts were a lyre adorned with a gold Lapis Lazuli encrusted bearded bull's head; a profusion of gold tableware and Lapis bowls; a chariot adorned with lioness' heads, and an abundance of Lapis, and gold jewellery, and a talisman depicting fish and land creatures.

So second half Capricorns inherit the most coveted rock since at least 3500 BC. The poor of that time, who could not afford this precious stone, came to the conclusion that Lapis Lazuli inspired devout contemplation, since the Priest-Astronomers also wore it. But in truth the rich blue jewel with silver and gold tinted flecks represented the night sky and the far off dwelling place of the gods, Enlil and Anu, believed to inhabit the Sirius System known to Ethiopians as "The Lapis Lazuli House". Not much further on in time the peasants of the Nile, no more able to afford Lapis Lazuli than their earlier counterparts along the Euphrates, believed it counterbalanced the ill effects of incest, for how else, they must have argued, could the incestuous Pharaohs, who used these jewels as a permanent adornment, retain their sanity?

Despite the stone's slightly unstable composition, commercial Lapis weighs in at about the same each time and has a hardness rating of about 6. It was early found in the mountainous north eastern region of Afghanistan, which Marco Polo visited in 1271 to view it in its natural surroundings. The region still supplies a fine quality. Iran, formerly Persia, yields the best, but political reasons make it impossible to obtain this at present. Lapis occurs in Chile, Russia, America, Canada, Burma, Angola and Pakistan.

In colour, hardness and its constituent elements, Lapis Lazuli corresponds admirably to Saturn, the Capricornian ruling planet and mutable body, while its metallic elements are ideal for Venus.

First Half Capricorn Bedside Rock

STICHTITE
Robert Sticht, an Australian, discovered the first set Capricornian bedside rock in Tasmania in 1910. Lilac hued Stichtite is opaque, has a waxy finish and is sometimes veined in dark, slaty green. A magnesium and chromium mineral which often contains iron, Stichtite can be cut and

polished. Though too young to have a romantic past, it provides choice specimens which are fast appearing in collector's showcases. Canada logged a Stichtite finding in 1918, as, more recently, did South Africa and Algeria. Stichtite's tint, weight and water content are well paralleled with the Saturnian world, and its metallic elements are ideal for first set Capricorns' mutable planet, Venus.

BROWN QUARTZ

Members of the Quartz family, in which the violence of Venus, all heat and pressure and change, and the docility of Saturn are happily reconciled, provide alternative choices of bedside rock for Capricorns of the first set. Properly called Morion, Brown Quartz can be as light as a whisper and as dark as a moonless night both in the same stone. Its transparency, whatever its shade, contrasts with the virtual opacity of Smokey Quartz, a similar mineral also once extensively quarried in the Cairngorm Mountains of the Highlands of Scotland.

Many a Highland laddie wore a "Cairngorm" in his kilt, and many a Highland lassie wore a similar stone in her sash.

Now the supply from that region has begun to run short, so Citrine and Amethyst from Brazil have arrived to fill the breach. (They have similarly replaced the exhausted supplies of Kerry Diamonds from Ireland.) Orange-gold Citrine owes its tints to a trace of iron in its composition and to the process of natural reheating in the Earth's crust.

But it too is now becoming rare and its position in the market place has been taken by burnt Amethyst. Fortunately for Capricorns, reheating suits their horoscope, so this orange-hued stone is a more than acceptable match.

Constructing a stone of double or triple tints, composed of a combination of Citrine and Amethyst, or of Morion, Citrine and Amethyst, is a new and developing art, although occasionally multi-coloured Quartz occurs in nature.

Second Half Capricorn Bedside Rock

ROCK CRYSTAL

Rock Crystal, the perfect form of quartz, is more associated with magic than any other stone. The ancient Greeks believed it to be an invention of the gods, since they found it first in a cave in Thessaly near the foot of Mount Olympus, legendary entrance to Heaven. They thought of it as water frozen perpetually by the Immortals and called it Krystallos.

The first foundation of the Heavenly City, revealed by St John the Divine, was of Jasper, another variety of quartz; and of course crystal balls have been used for centuries by soothsayers and fortune tellers, genuine and false.

Rock Crystal forms in David and Goliath sizes. Some grow to the height of a small telegraph pole, others remain as minute as a speck of dust. A beach of ivory coloured sand is about 99 per cent Rock Crystals, and if it wasn't for flint, in which Rock Crystals are also present, Man would hardly have emerged to become the dominant species on Earth. The most prolific of our minerals, Rock Crystal has a unique atomic structure which allows it to grow in exact mirror images. It began as a deposit from mineral rich water journeying through cracks and cavities in cooled lava, or as quartz ingredients floating above others to form the top-most level in veins of many minerals. There its glittering purity added lustre to all the rest.

RUTILATED QUARTZ

For the jewellery loving or egg and sphere collecting Capricorn, "Maiden's Hair" or Flèche d'Amour" (Arrow of Love) is a compelling second choice. Its criss crossing golden lines suggest the energy emitted by Saturn while its light recalls the brightness of planet Mercury. Properly named Rutilated Quartz, "Venus Hair" is actually clear Rock Crystal with fine, hair-like "needles" of golden and reddish hue, formed of metallic titanium, that fiery mineral, patterning it from within. Germany is probably the best source of supply for this not easily available jewel.

First Half Aquarius Precious Crystal

PERIDOT

Have you ever heard of a stone with an identity problem? No? Then meet the Peridot. Sought after as early as 1500 BC, it figures in the Bible disguised as a Chrysolite, or so many people believe. Nowadays, of course, green Spinels are sold as Chrysolites, a Russian green Garnet is retailed as a Peridot and the Peridot itself is known in some countries as the Evening Emerald. Oh, and this stone is also known as The Serpent Isle Crystal, or alternatively as the Zibirat, owing to the fact that the island on which it was found, Zibirat, now St John's, in the Red Sea, is, or was, snake infested. Is everything quite clear?

Yet first half Aquarians are lucky in their precious crystal, which belongs to the olivine family and displays a charming range of greens, from the palest yellow-green, through bottle green to the dramatic deep, velvety olive, the most sought after by collectors as well as the most appropriate for those born under this sign. This type has yellow lights blazing from its depths. It is completely transparent with a slightly oily surface. Its light bodyweight and lack of density suit Uranus, its ruling planet, as does the fact that it only melts at high temperatures. Its constituent elements of iron and magnesium harmonize with Mercury.

The Pharaohs considered the Peridot to be the property of their gods and slew the slaves who guarded these stones on Zibirat on completion of their duties. In Christian times the Crusaders plundered these stones, giving them to churches which still have a large treasury of them. Australia, Burma, Brazil, Hawaii, Mexico, Norway, South Africa and St John's are the chief sources.

BRAZILIANITE
Another precious crystal for first set Aquarians is Brazilianite (from Brazil and the USA), a bright yellow to yellowish-green gem discovered in 1944. It has aluminium in its composition, is very light, and occurs in rather large crystals in correspondence to its celestial sovereigns.

Brazilianite's colour and hardness (5 out of 10 on the scale) make a good match for Mercury.

Second Half Aquarius Precious Crystal

DIOPSIDE
Some seven thousand years ago a mine was worked in the Badakshan district of the mountainous north east area of Afghanistan. Its treasure was a beauteous rock with tints varying from greenish-blue to rich purple-blue called Lapis Lazuli, but the crystal Diopside, a constituent of Lapis, remained hidden for much longer. Occurring pure and unaccompanied in fine gem material In Siberia and the Diamond mines of Burma, this stone only started to make a real impact on the world when absolutely top grade specimens appeared in association with Rubies in the Hunza Valley of Pakistan.

As a planetary correspondence, perfect Diopside is formed has little stress and elevated temperatures, allowing the growth of a flawless gemstone from condensed vapour of reheated fluids. But true to its Aquarian character, the Uranus cum Saturnian mineral waited for its supreme moment. Then, in 1964, the most resplendent Diopside of all materialized, displaying a four rayed hovering star with two sharp and two muted lines, hanging suspended over an almost opaque black-green to brownish-black body.

Possibly the only top grade magnetic gemstone, Star Diopside contains needle like crystals of an extra iron mineral, making it fractionally heavier than pure Diopside and a fraction harder.

Star Diopside has hit the market without revealing its birthplace, which learned Gemmologists locate most probably in Southern India. Italy produces a plain, sombre green crystal Diopside. So do Austria, Sri Lanka and Brazil. Yellowish brown comes from Canada, bright green from America and Russia. Violet Diopside comes from Piedmont in Italy and is often called Violane.

Diopside's light bodyweight parallels with both Uranus and Saturn, with a slight change of stoutness depending on the amount of iron present. With magnesium, calcium, and sometimes chrome, as well as iron in its composition, it also accords well with the metal rich planet Venus.

TUGTUPITE
Aquarians of the second group have another precious crystal in gem quality Tugtupite, which derives its name from tugtup meaning "Reindeer". This pink stone was logged as recently as 1960, after having been found lodged in a semi-precious mineral exclusive to itself, and used extensively in Greenland for ornamentation purposes. Of good dress wear hardness, the "Reindeer Stone" is also found in the USSR.

First Half Aquarius Talisman

AVENTURINE
Russian craftsman Carl Fabergé devoted many hours of skill to the resplendent Aventurine and in the English royal collection many treasures also exist — notably a bowl with silver mounts, a goblet embellished with red gold and Moonstones, a box decorated with a combination of Rose (cut) Diamonds, Olivines and gold, a sparrow with Rose (cut) Diamond eyes and a lovable farmyard pig with Ruby eyes all carved from various shades of this stone, which has also been favoured by craftsmen in China, from ancient times until today.

Green, pink and sunset tinted Aventurine is a unique member of the quartz family and owes its gold spangled countenance to featherweight flakes of mica in its body.

Mica, with its shiny surface and heat resistant qualities, is an excellent match for both Mercury and Saturn, while its bodyweight and remarkable complexity of composition make it a parallel for Uranus.

ONYX

A second talisman for first half Aquarians is Onyx, a light weight quartz variety mineral with black, white and bluish-grey bands, corresponding with the black Uranian rings and the lighter Saturnian bands.

Aquarians are in good company with such a talisman, for this was the material used by the craftsmen of ancient Rome when they wished to display their skills with the drill and cutting wheel. Using the layers of banded Onyx, they sculpted three dimensional cameos on such subjects as "Victory", usually depicted as a winged maiden with floating hair borne along in a horse drawn chariot. The manes of the thundering steeds, the chariot wheels, and the locks and tresses of the girl were carved in Onyx of different shades, miraculously capturing the melodramatic scene in terms of the basic elements of the Solar System.

Second Half Aquarius Talisman

JADE

Certain Indians once considered that two good slaves were worth one pure Jade axe head, prized for its toughness and shine. Earlier still, in a country now known as Sing kiang, peasants shortened their miserable lives stoking furnaces by day and extinguishing them by night in order to crack open great boulders of Jade and Jadeite.

All night their calloused and blistered hands chiselled and hammered the minerals until chunks were broken off. The precious cargo was then loaded and transported by camel train to its destination further east. There it was carved for the use of the Emperor who wore Jade sandals and in death had a wardrobe of Jade.

In 1983 a Chinese archaeological dig unearthed evidence to prove that in the second century AD the Chinese Emperor Wen Di, ruler of the area now known as Canton, dressed in a Jade suit. Thirty Jade discs, each more than twelve inches in diameter, had been placed below and above the body and the tomb itself contained over a thousand Jade articles, including a horn shaped cup made of Jade and forty three ritual swords carved with dragon and tiger effigies.

This was a typical imperial tomb of the period.

Today descendants of those poverty stricken slaves have small Jade carvings adorning their own mantelpieces and more often than not wear Jade charms. But the quarries of Burma are exhausted of Jade proper (only Jadeite remains) and sixty to seventy per cent of the world's Jade supply now comes from the mountains of North West British Columbia, where well paid crews blast with dynamite and cut the boulders with diamond tipped, diesel powered saws.

Motor vehicles transport the Jade to Vancouver and from there it is usually shipped to China where it is carved and sold as "Chinese Jade". This British Columbian Jade is reputedly the best in the world. It is tough, gloriously translucent, and cool, gentle to the touch and easy on the eye, and comes in shades of green from medium to almost black.

Unfortunately, however, supplies are running out it is estimated that they will have no more than twenty five to thirty years to run if demand carries on at its present level.

That said Australian Black Jade is a very high quality Nephrite Jade discovered recently on a farm in the town of Cowell in South Australia. Australian Black Jade is very strong, takes on a high polish and is difficult to carve so it is more usually fashioned using drills and wheels then polished. There are reports of Australian Black Jade selling for as much as $US2, 500.00 per Kg.

Nephrite Jade's extra-strong, fibrous and interwoven crystal structure and bodyweight give it correspondence with Uranus, Saturn and Venus. Its name derives from the Spanish "piedra de ijada" meaning loin-stone, as Jade was given credence as a remedy for kidney ailments.

The term Nephrite came from "lapis nephriticus" another of Jade's early names because of its healing effect on the kidneys.

In 1981 Jade carvings were presented to the Western political leaders at the Economic Summit meeting as a token of unity.

There was an eagle for President Reagan of America, a bear for Germany's Chancellor Helmut Schmidt and a Canadian goose for Britain's Prime Minister Margaret Thatcher. Davis Wong was the artist.

CASITERITE
A second talisman for Aquarians of the second set is gem quality Casiterite.

Heavyweight planet Mercury will be well paralleled by its ultrahigh density, strong light absorbency and tints of yellow, buff and buff grey, while Saturn will respond to the colours, which are the basic shades of its body without its shadows. The hardness count and water content are also appropriate for Saturn and even more so for Uranus, the ruling world of this area of the zodiac.

When Casiterite is not in its perfect crystal form, the non-gem quality is the chief ore of tin, found in many countries and occurring most often in Bolivia, China, Indonesia, Malaysia and Russia.

First Half Aquarius Bedside Rock

WULFENITE

In this area of the zodiac the most influential bodies are Uranus and Saturn, both of them being big, gaseous balloons of sparse mass and light bodyweight, while Mercury, the mutable lobe, is by contrast small and heavily compressed, comprising all, or almost all, the metallic elements in existence. Gold, red and green are the predominant shades of these galactic firmaments, and Wulfenite, with its splendid hues, unusually low hardness count, metallic elements, colour shifts in laboratory testing, and metallic yield when heated, corresponds to them perfectly.

The metal ylelded is lead (a Mercury parallel), but sometimes nature contrives to substitute products more suitable for the planets Uranus and Saturn. But whatever the changes, a silvery white metallic substance called molybdenum always remains. This is alloyed with steel for the manufacture of high speed tools which themselves correspond to the planets Mercury and Saturn (Mercury for its swiftness, toughness and metallic elements, Saturn for its zooming, ice composed ring system). Correspondence with Uranus emerges through the laboratory test when the Wulfenite goes through colour shifts of black, flecks of green and black, yellowish-green and dark green, all Uranian shades.

Wulfenite is named after Father F. Wulfen, the Mineralogist who discovered it, and who in 1875 described it and furnished coloured pictures of its crystals. Since then even more magnificent specimens of transparent red, gold and orange have been located in America, while elsewhere olive green and honey tints have surfaced. Characteristically Wulfenite's crystals are seldom concentrated, matching (by density) its celestial sovereigns.

Second Half Aquarius Bedside Rock

CHAROITE

The eye takes in a sumptuous version of what looks like purple Lapis Lazuli, causing the beholder born under other signs to wish that he or she were an Aquarian of the second set, and thus entitled to this bedside rock. Charoite does not come in shiny crystals or on an innocent bed of snowy quartz. It is an opaque, lilac streaked mineral comprising calcium and potassium; not much in heavy metallic elements here, thus ensuring correspondence with Uranus and Saturn. To parallel Venus, Charoite comprises some metallic chemicals and its cellular structure is often fused. A mini mystery about this wonderful mineral is, how did such an awe inspiring, rich and hypnotic creation manage to hide in the banks of the Charo River in Vatutsk, USSR, until the late 1970s?

Charoite is an expensive stone and not easy to come by. It is also less easy to buy in its rough state than fashioned into eggs or the occasional piece of jewellery (and too often, alas, Charoite jewellery is set with a woeful lack of expertise). The time of this monarch of the mineral kingdom is yet to come. When it does, Charoite will assuredly take its place beside the famous Lapis Lazuli.

TORBENITE
As a second bedside rock for second half Aquarians, try a modern sculpture of naturally formed Torbernite crystals from the county of Cornwall in England. The square of Torbernite, transparent to translucent in appearance, and emerald green to yellow-green in colour, sits gleaming in thin, brittle plates of opaque, scaly stone. Torbernite is associated with uranium minerals and is distinguished by radioactivity.

First Half Pisces Precious Crystal

DIAMOND
Those ruled by the sign of the Fish are in a special situation. Three moons influence them: Triton (moon of Neptune); Io (moon of Jupiter); and the moon of our Earth. All are strong characters and demand possibly the services not merely of one gemstone but of two. The blue Diamond is a must for Neptune, a planet well supplied with Diamonds, as has been mentioned, and wrapped round with a covering of water and gases which, seen from afar, transmit a glorious and very definite mid, blue colour. Triton, too, produces this appealing shade and is also likely to have hatched crops of Diamonds, by reason of the fact that its escaping internal heat would more likely have caused methane gas clouds to break down to carbon.

AQUAMARINE
Another precious gemstone for first half Piceans is Aquamarine which tallies with all three moons and with the planet Neptune itself,

thanks to its composition of aluminium, lithium, silica, water, soda and beryllium. Triton, with its lunar type crust and density, its Earth-type atmosphere, and its limpid Neptunian depths especially calls for this stone. So first half Pisceans are lucky indeed in having two such beautiful gems.

Aquamarine has a hardness of 7 on the scale (just over Neptune's own number) and often occurs in giant crystals appropriate to the size of both its planetary monarchs. Ancient soothsayers scrutinized its lucid depths. Simple folk thought these stones were formed from the solidified tears of sea sirens, who kept them in cabinets on the ocean bed. In Renaissance England no lady in love with a sailor would let him leave her without his blue amulet. Nowadays the Aquamarine is found chiefly in America, Brazil, India, Burma, Madagascar, Tanzania, Zimbabwe, Norway, Russia and Ireland.

Second Half Pisces Precious Crystal

KUNZITE
Discovered in America about 1900 and named after the noted Mineralogist Dr. G. F. Kunz, pink-lilac to dark lilac-rose Kunzite draws admiration by its flawless transparency and high lustre.

It has great sensitivity and is uniquely phosphorescent. When subjected to X-ray it glows with a strong yellow-red or orange colour which tones in with the cloud colouring and major moon of the Piscean sub influence (Jupiter), then turns blue-green, the associated tint of both Jupiter and Neptune. On reheating, the triumphant sorcerer hidden in this lovely gem's depths returns to its original hue, matching Jupiter's rouged areas and Pluto's lighter regions.

Kunzite shows yet another loyalty to its celestial sovereigns by displaying visible flares of a blue tinged green when viewed from a side angle.

For Neptune and Pluto it contains a smidgeon of water; and like both these and Jupiter it contains that rare element, the soft and silvery lithium as well as the most abundant of Earth's minerals, the rust resisting aluminium.

Kunzite has a hardness of about 7 (Neptune's number also), and a specific gravity measurement of about 3 (Jupiter's number). In imitation of its mighty rulers, it grows crystals of enormous dimensions; one is on record as measuring 42ft x 6ft x 2ft and weighing in at 65 tons!

HIDDENITE
Wherever the stunning Kunzite occurs, so does another Piscean precious crystal, Hiddenite. Named after A. E. Hidden, the superintendent of the mine where it was discovered in 1879, this stone is generally identified with Kunzite in its body and composition but has a trace of added chromium, grows in smaller crystals, and has a weaker fluorescence.

Hiddenite is often called the "Lithia Emerald".

EUCLASE
Transparent Euclase is another choice for Pisceans in this grouping, a rare crystal of fragile appearance in tints of soft or greenish blue, or else colourless. Not frequently found and even less frequently cut for jewellery owing to its unsuitable structure, this brightly lustred gem has the bewitching charm of an Aquamarine.

Euclase contains aluminium and the rare metallic element beryllium. In correspondence with its heavenly monarchs, and like Kunzite and Hiddenite, it has Neptune's 7 for hardness, a bodyweight of just over Jupiter's number 3 and a proportion of water.

Euclase occurs in Austria, Bavaria, Brazil, India, Russia, Tanzania and Zaire.

First Half Pisces Talisman

SMITHSONITE
This stone holds the soft tranquillity of the Moon, the mutable celestial body in this area of the zodiac. It contains calcium and magnesium, both silvery white; cadmium which is bluish-white and so soft it can be cut with a knife; cobalt; copper; and sometimes a little iron all elements which harmonize with the Piscean ruler, Neptune, its sub influence, Jupiter, and the Moon. Significantly, too, it is an important ore of zinc, without doubt the artist's metal and for that reason right for this sunsign which natives love to surround themselves with beauty.

Nicknamed "Dry Bone" owing to its cellular structure, Smithsonite is also marketed under the name Bonamite and is a comparative newcomer to the market. It is found in America, Britain, East and South West Africa, Greece, New Mexico, Sardinia and Spain. Smithsonite is for those who prefer chic to overstatement. It has an exquisite range of gentle tints passing from grey-blue to medium green and soft yellow, all corresponding with Neptune, Jupiter and the Moon.

SATINSPAR

A particularly fine second talisman for first half Pisceans is Satinspar, a translucent to opaque mineral reminiscent of milk coloured raw silk. Corresponding colour wise with the stark southern zone of Jupiter, all but one of Neptune's many moons and indeed with our own Moon, this gem belongs to the gypsum clan, a group of stones which are often formed from chemical action between shells and sulphuric acid released on the decay of other minerals (usually those containing iron). By the same token Satinspar parallels elements found on Triton. It occurs where volcanic vapours have shown reaction to limestone or in the basins of dried out lakes, rivers or other waters, here paralleling our Moon, the mutable mass for this area of the zodiac. This pearly white gem, composed of long, hair like crystals solidly attached to each other, contains water and calcium, two more reasons for it to be happy with the cooler, outer planets and quite wrong for any explosive correspondence with the Sun.

Second Half Pisces Talisman

CHRYSOPRASE

This ancient "Symbol of Reward" (whether of good or bad deeds) was placed in graves in pre Iron Age Japan and by the side of the deified cat and the lion headed goddess Baste in ancient Egypt. It was worn by Roman thieves to achieve invisibility, by Alexander the Great in his girdle, and by Jewish High Priests in their breastplates, besides being nominated as one of the twelve precious gems in the Holy City. Though there seems to be no real clue as to where the ancients mined this flawless beauty, it is known that the Romans called it Phrase, meaning leek-green, and that the Greek name Chrysos Prasious translates as "golden leek". Its stunningly rich tints also made it exceptionally popular in the early Victorian era in England until the jet black of mourning swept all away on the untimely death of Prince Albert.

In cheerful shades of apple to lime green, the best Chrysoprase occurs in the town of Marlborough Creek in Queensland, Australia, and comes in almost as fine quality and profusion from California, Brazil, Russia and Tanzania. Coloured by nickel, it belongs to the chalcedony family, a variety of quartz formed of microscopically small crystals. The Piscean talisman corresponds with Neptune and Jupiter by its light bodyweight and basic colouring. Pluto, the mutable planet in this area of the zodiac, is also happy with its composition.

BLUE LACE AGATE

A second talisman for second half Pisceans is Blue Lace Agate. Marketed in the form of semi-precious jewellery, ashtrays, eggs and solitaire sets, this is a soft, sky-blue, opaque gemstone. It flaunts its innocence in translucent, white lacy patterns, and is altogether a delight.

First Half Pisces Bedside Rock

OPALISED FOSSIL

An Opalised Fossil is a cast left by a disintegrated object which has part filled with quartz crystals and later acquired Opal for added glory. It is found in the hot desert areas of Australia, once a network of rivulets in which flourished marine creatures similar to our oysters and mussels. When the water receded, trapped creatures dug themselves into the silt, their remains eventually becoming so many empty chambers scattered about in dry land. A few yielded precious Opals but most were mere fossil shaped shells, with a thin surface layer of Opal, the interiors filled with opaque, greyish white stone. Opalised Fossils come from the tapering, pointed bones of extinct cuttlefish called Belamnites or from sea snails, which seem oblivious to their metamorphoses but live on in movement of colour and have incomparable beauty in this final, precious form.

Opalised Fire Cones from America's Virgin Valley and Fossil Wood is another variation, a magnificent example of ingenuity, with dreamy tints of Opal dancing along ridges left behind by the departed product. Opal Fossil forms have been chosen for first set Pisceans because they have a double water influence: their ruling planet, Neptune, has the same density as water, while their mutable mass, the Moon, controls (with the sun) the swell and depletion of water we call tides. Opal holds more water than any other mineral from one to twenty two per cent in the dull valueless kinds and from six to ten per cent in the more precious varieties. Most Opal holds a trace of iron, and minerals with this element have been found on our Moon and are definitely present on Triton. For Jupiter, a Piscean sub influence, Opal is appropriate because of its body weight and the energy it gives out through colour and pattern changes.

Second Half Bedside Rock

FLUORITE

Fluorite usually has a basic white body, but can be angelically coloured in the softest shades of pink, green, amethyst, yellow and blue. Occasionally deeper tints make a showing, but even these gleam with a saintly translucence in keeping with the mineral's innocent character. Frequently occurring and obtainable almost anywhere, Fluorite is an ideal match for the Piscean ruling planet, being formed, like all members of the calcium group, in cool, watery places.

Fluorite is often found in limestone caverns and as natural cement in sandstone. Its crystals usually grow in cubes and, when hardest and of best quality, are cut as gemstones. To Western connoisseurs, the alluring sunset-pink from Switzerland probably takes top marks for unsurpassed good looks, though the Chinese favour the blue tones when carving the magnificent pieces which seem, through their inner strength, to draw the viewer into their very depths. Under ultraviolet lighting Fluorite gives a glorious glow hence the term "Fluorescence".

APOPHYLITE

Yet another ethereal bedside rock for second set Pisceans is water related calcium mineral. This pearlised, milky glory sometimes has suggestions of rust, yellow, green or grey in its cleavages, thus acquiring the appearance of a great white cloud floating above a fairy-tale castle. This stone does not have crystals suitable for cutting yet its crystals are often cut for collectors and cherished. The delicate, cloud like version of Apophylite occurs mainly in India, but another magnificent Apophylite bedside rock comes from Mexico, which yields an amethyst variety touched with pink. In whatever form, it is rarely opaque but rather translucent to transparent.

Both Fluorite and Apophylite are adversely affected by heat, which makes a suitable parallel for planet Pluto. For Jupiter both are equally appropriate through their colours, extensive occurrence, and water content.

A final note for those born under Pisces: all Piscean birthstones can be set with Diamonds, which appear to proliferate on their ruling planet.

Asteroid Belt Minerals and Gemstones

For those who feel an association with the Asteroid Belt between Mars and Jupiter wear carry or have in your vicinity one or more of these carbon rich, stony, and metallic associated minerals...

- Chrysoprase
- Diamonds
- Labradorite
- Meteorites
- Peridot
- Quartz,
- Serpentine
- Tourmalines,
- Zircons

PART THREE

General Knowledge

Jeweller

A specialist who designs jewellery, shapes and assembles metals and other materials, secures gemstones in settings, engraves articles, repairs and remodels jewellery, and sells direct to the public or/and to the retail market. Unless much extra study has been undertaken jewellers, in general, have little gemstone or mineral knowledge.

Gemmology and Geology

These are separate, further studies of the same basic study— mineralogy.

Geologist

A Geologist is a specialist who deals with the history of our planet as recorded in rocks, mainly for geological engineering, mining engineering and geophysics.

Gemmologist

A Gemmologist is a specialist study in the science of gemstones, ornamental materials and their synthetics, and evaluates their qualities. Both gemmologists and geologists agree that;

Mineral

This is a natural occurring geological, solid substance that has a defined chemical composition and a highly ordered atomic and crystalline structure.

Mineraloid

This does not have a crystalline structure. Amber, Jet, Obsidian, Pearl, and Coral are mineraloids which began their life in the vegetable kingdom and have no crystal structure. Opal and natural glass such as Obsidian are of pure mineral origin, but are mineraloids because they too have no crystal structure.

Stone

This is generally a name referring to a small piece of mineral.

Rock

Often a name used loosely but in truth it is an aggregate (combination, mixture) of separate minerals and/or mineraloids and does not always have one specific chemical composition, the most famous being Lapis Lazuli.

Crystal
A clear mineral more often associated with quartz rock crystal, but most gemstones are either a crystals of their family of minerals or are composed of sub microscopic crystals en mass. Generally colourless crystals are examples of pure chemical composition of its mineral family, while coloured crystals derive from impurities and/or irradiation after their formation.

Gemstone
This is more usually a mineral with a high price tag. Properly a Gemstone is a piece of top grade mineral which has been carved, cut and polished or tumbled. However fine quality mineraloids such as Lapis Lazuli, Amber, Jet and Pearls are considered gems (more usually) after they have been set in jewellery or carved. All gemstones have characteristics which contribute to their price and rarity known in the trade as the "four Cs": carat (weight), clarity, colour or lack of colour and cut.

Mohs scale of hardness
Devised by German Mineralogist Frederick Mohs (1773-1839) the Mohs scale determines the relative hardness of one solid substance in relation to others. Because Mohs scale is a relative scale the difference in hardness between the Sapphire (9) and a Diamond (10) can be far greater that the hardness between Amber (2.5-3) and that of Jet (3-4) and that of fluorspar (4). Mohs scale is based on the fact that solid materials of lower numbers will be scratched by those of higher numbers. Following is a fascinating list of just a few minerals, gemstones and common items showing their place on the Mohs scale of hardness.

1 . . . . graphite and talc the latter is an important industrial mineral.
2 . . . . gypsum, used in carvings and as plaster of paris.
2.5 . . . . . . fingernail, Amber and Pearl.
2, 5-3 . . . . native gold, silver and aluminium.
3 . . . . calcite is in limestone, marble, marine shells and bronze.
3-4 . . . . . . Jet and Malachite both used for gemstones and carving.
4 . . . . fluorspar is the principle source of fluorine and fluorite.
5 . . . . apatite is a gemstones and a component of tooth enamel.
5-5.5 . . . . Lapis Lazuli, Hematite, Obsidian, most knife blades.
5.5-6 . . . . Turquoise, Magnetite (major magnetic iron ore.
6 . . . . feldspar, titanium, Opal (variable to 6.5).
6.5 . . . . . . steel, iron pyrites, Tanzanite, most glass.
6.5-7 . . . . Kunzite, Peridot, casiterite (principle ore of tin).

7 . . . . quartz family, made-made crystal glass, black Opal.
7-7.5. . . . . most Garnets, Tourmaline, Zircon.
8 . . . . Topaz, Spinel, Emerald, Aquamarine.
8.5. . . . . . Alexandrite, Chrysoberyl, Chromium, cubic zirconia.
9 . . . . corundum, Ruby, Sapphire.
10. . . . . . . Diamond.
10+. . . . . . nano Diamond produced by graphite compression.

Popular Gemstone Facts

Alexandrite
A mineral belonging to the chrysoberyl family with a stunning and extraordinary colour-change, the most sought after Alexandrite showing emerald-green in daylight changing to purple-red under incandescent lights. Yet this fascinating gemstone is still mesmerising in its more often seen muted green or bluish-green in daylight, turning to a soft shade of red, purple-red or raspberry-red at night. Along with this unique optical quality and extreme hardness Alexandrite has become one of the rarest and possibly the most sought after of all precious crystals. There are other gemstones which colour-change but they lack the hardness and rich beauty of the Alexandrite.

The first recorded Alexandrite was discovered under the roots of a stunted tree by a farmer who lived in Russia's Ural Mountains on the birthday of Czar Alexander II. Unfortunately the farmer's name was not recorded.

Russian mines do not yield many gems these days, but lovely specimens have been located in Brazil, Madagascar, and Zimbabwe. The Indian regions of Orissa have fine crystals, but are generally in the half carat or smaller, a size too small to show the precious colour-change to advantage.

Amber
Fossilized resin which was released either after an injury or after a radical climate change by trees which lived 30-110 million years. Scholars speculate reddish Amber came from deciduous trees, such as the cherry and plum, while yellow tones were the produce of various conifers. Most of these trees are now extinct, but the (still growing) Australian Bull Kauri, the North African Cedar, and the Canadian Larch may also have produced this miracle of nature.

Entomologists have a field day when studying pre-historic life forms in Amber because the original, sticky material made a honeyed crypt for spiders, their webs and captured victims, ants and moths. In 2008 scientists from the Natural History Museum in London announced the discovery of the oldest known fossil of a gecko found embalmed and perfectly preserved in Amber from 97 million to 110 million years ago. This gecko is considered a juvenile who, if it had not run into the slow flowing, scented mass of resin would have grown into a large adult possibly up to a foot long. But this little being's karma was to be entombed forever, its fragile remains and last exhaled breath a tiny bubble for all to behold.

A famous entomologist—Charles Darwin—would most certainly have spent many happy hours with a microscope and ancient life forms in Amber.

The science of botany has also been enriched by entombed orchids, drops of water, pieces of bark and other vegetation. Amber can be transparent, translucent or opaque, is coloured brownish, yellow, white, reddish and blackish with some rare specimens showing muted green and royal to purplish-blue lights which are thought to be fumes from captured plant life.

Amber displays electrical properties when rubbed and if an unset piece is put into salt water it will float. Before modern tools were available Amber, being one of the softest and lightest gemstones, was fashioned for jewellery, and carved into bowls and thrones. Early traders used Amber as currency.

Amber is often found washed up on the shores of the Baltic and North Seas, is mined in America, Canada, Burma, Chili, Cicely, Germany, Greenland, Italy, Lebanon, Mexico and the Dominican Republic. Most red Amber sold in bric-a-brac and antique shops is not Amber but early plastic. Historically Amber has had many names, some of them being Blue Mud, Burning Stone, Dragon's Blood, Freya's Tears, Hardened Honey, Nordic Gold, Perfumed Crystal, Petrified Light, Sea Gold, Sea Stone, Soul of the Tiger, Sun Bead, Sun Stone, Tears of the Sun, Tiger's Tears, and. Tiger's Soul.

The Roman Emperor Nero described his beautiful wife—Poppaea—as having amber-coloured hair which started a fashion in Rome during which Roman ladies bleached their hair. In later years pipes, cigar and cigarette holders were fashioned from molten Amber in the belief Amber would not transmit infection.

Amber is not a mineral it is a Mineraloid because it is of vegetable origin and does not have a crystal structure.

Amethyst

A quartz mineral boasting colour extravagance in purples through violets. This relatively inexpensive gemstone has historically obtained a prominent position in the coffers of royalty, churches, religious groups, and mythology. The ancient Greeks believed it prevented drunkenness; the name Amethyst deriving from the Greek "amethystos" meaning not intoxicated. Moses described it as a symbol of the spirit of his god, it features in ornaments of the Roman Catholic Church, and has long been the stone of bishops and cardinals. In Tibet the Amethyst was dedicated to Buddha, Aztec graves contained Amethyst and the Russian Empress Catherine the Great sent thousands of miners into the Urals to look for it.

Amethyst has everything in common with other quartz in its hardness of 7, its light refraction and weight, but its structure is different. Amethyst is stratified which results in varying colour intensity in the same gemstone. This is why large, cut Amethyst gems usually show more than one shade of violet. Amethyst crystals often show two colours — purple and yellow — known as Ametrine, those from Bolivia showing the most stunning combinations. Amethyst is mostly found lining caves and boulders. A particularly large boulder discovered in 1900 in Brazil measured 10 x 5 x 3 metres (33 x 16 x 10 ft.) and weighed an estimated 8 tonnes! It contained dark violet Amethysts, many as large as a man's fist and one weighing 200 kilograms. Much Amethyst for sale is found in Brazil, Uruguay and Madagascar, but Australia, Canada, Germany, Russia, Sri Lanka, Tibet, South America also yield great specimens.

Aquamarine

This is one of the most loved gemstones. Despite its lower price range, Aquamarine is almost as popular as the more expensive classics, which are Emerald, Sapphire and Ruby. Aquamarine is related to the Emerald as they both belonging to the beryl family of minerals.

The blue of Aquamarine is a divine reflection of our planet's sky and reminds one of water. The rare, intense blue Aquamarines from the Santa Maria de Itabira mine in Brazil, are called "Santa Maria" while the Mozambique Aquamarine is called the "Santa Maria Africana'. One beautiful Aquamarine was named after the Brazilian beauty queen of 1954 "Martha Rocha". Mythology would have us believe Mermaids have treasure chests of this beauty which may be why the Aquamarine has always been known as a lucky talisman for sailors. The Aquamarine's name is derived from the Latin "aqua" meaning water and "mare" meaning sea. Aquamarine is a gemstone of great qualities, those being extreme clarity, wonderful hardness and for its soft, but magnificent shine.

Beryl

A mineral family of historically famous gemstones which many jewellers use for their divine colours and hardness.

As with most gems the pure colour of the Beryl crystal is colourless (clear white), the coloured varieties occurring through impurities.

The Beryl group include the limpid beauty of the Aquamarine, the Imperial Emerald and some very rare gems which are often only seen in Gemmological museums or in a collector's pride. Beryls are found in America, Afghanistan, Austria, Australia, Brazil, Bulgaria, Cambodia, Canada, China, Colombia, Egypt, Ethiopia, France, Germany, India, Italy, Kazakhstan, Madagascar, Mozambique, Namibia, Pakistan, Russia, Somalia, South Africa, Spain, Switzerland, Zambia and Zimbabwe. Beryl gemstones have individual names which are as follows;

Aquamarine—sky-blue to blue-green, but if treated by radiation or heat it will more likely be either a darker or dark blue;

Dark Blue Beryl known as Maxixe in the trade is a naturally occurring, lovely gem which fades when it is exposed to heat or strong light is usually bought for a collectors box rather than to be set in jewellery;

Emerald—green Beryl. See write-up under Emerald in this section;

Goshenite—being colourless is pure Beryl;

Green Beryl—all pale shades of green except bright emerald;

Heliodor—golden to greenish-yellow;

Morganite is rarer than its very famous sister the Aquamarine, and is also known as the Pink Emerald. Morganite varies in colours from pink to rose, peach and salmon;

Red Beryl—is also known as Bixite and the Red Emerald. This is the rarest of the Beryl group. Due its rarity, Bixite is a favoured collector's item and attracts high value; hence it is rarely seen set in jewellery or for sale.

Chrysoprase

This mineral with its translucent, apple-green colour and fine texture is the rarest and therefore the most valuable of the chalcedony group of gem quartz. Its colours range through greens to a yellowy leek-green hence its name from the Greek "chryso" meaning gold and "prason" meaning leek. Chrysoprase was first mentioned in 3AD, but was not commercially mined before 1740 in Poland.

This beauteous mineral was dedicated to the Egyptian cat and lion headed goddess Baste, so her subjects wore beaded necklaces of Chrysoprase coupled to Lapis.

Cleopatra wore it to retain her youth, the Roman scholar Pliny wrote about its inner glow, and his countrymen believed the wearer of Chrysoprase had the power to communicate with lizards, Greeks carved cameos from it, and it was the mineral symbol of reward in ancient Japan. Frederick the Great of Prussia commissioned two, solid Chrysoprase tables 2 feet wide, 3 feet long, and 2 inches thick! Alexander the Great openly called Chrysoprase his "Victory Stone", he wore one on his belt (along with an Opal) during his eleven year winning streak. Today Chinese carvers claim the finest Chrysoprase for their exquisite talents. Fine quality is found in Queensland and Western Australia, and good deposits occur in America, Brazil, Germany, Russia, America and Brazil.

A mineral sold as Chrysoprase is coloured pale yellow to soft-green showing brown web-like patterns and is not translucent. It is not the same chemical composition and has none of its fineness or monetary value.

Diamond
A sensational gemstone because it has the ability to split white light into individual wave lengths (light dispersion) which we see in multi-colours and call "fire". The Diamond is the hardest, natural gemstone known which ensures high resistance to scratching and has the ability to withstand breakage from forceful impact. Diamond derives its name from the ancient Greek "adámas" meaning unbreakable.

The colour of a Diamond depends on either an impurity or a structural defect. Pure Diamonds are clear and colourless, while yellows and browns are caused by a nitrogen impurity and boron is responsible for blue; green is caused through irradiation, while pink, champagne, cognac, and red Diamonds are thought to occur by structural deformation. Black Diamonds are not black, but appear so because they contain numerous dark inclusions. Pink Diamonds are the rarest, and have been known to fetch up to US$1 million per carat.

The Argyle Diamond Mine in Australia is the world's foremost source of pink. This mine has been operating since 1983 and is 100 per cent owned by Rio Tinto, the leading company in the British Crown's global raw materials cartel in which (arguably) the wealthiest woman in the world, queen Elizabeth 11, is the largest non-institutional shareholder. Argyle mine has produced over 670 million carats of rough Diamonds and generated more than US$6 billion in revenue, but it goes without words that little of this money enriches Australia.

In industry, specialised Diamond applications exist or are being developed. Blue Diamonds are natural semiconductors, in contrast to most Diamonds, which are excellent electrical insulators. Diamond is a crystal of carbon atoms, and it is the only gemstone whose surface cannot be wet by water.

Diamonds are not rare; they haven't been since huge deposits were found in South Africa over a hundred years ago. So why are they so expensive? For a thousand years, a Jewish business has owned and controlled the Diamond market almost exclusively. Eighty per cent of the world's Diamond market is controlled by De Beers, who in turn, are controlled by the Oppenheimer family. De Beers has a brutal monopoly on the Diamond industry and is active in every category of industrial Diamond mining, open-pit, underground, large scale alluvial, coastal and deep sea. In Namibia a vast area is isolated where no one is allowed to enter because it is so rich in Diamonds you can literally pick them up off the ground! Our planet has millions of Diamonds and so do De Beers who have warehouses full of them, so many that the vast majority are made into cutting tools which include surgical knives.

The retail value of Diamonds is regulated by the supply of "rough" De Beers allow on the market, not because the gemstone is rare. The popularity of Diamonds as a trophy is the direct result of one of the most successful marketing campaigns in history. "A Diamond is forever" "A symbol of love" and "A family jewel", price tag $999999999999999 was named by the Advertising Age magazine as the best advertising slogan of the twentieth century. The original custom of giving a ring as an engagement gift can be traced to the ancient Greeks and Romans, but it wasn't until De Beers decided to make a fortune from beauty and romance that the "tradition" of the Diamond engagement ring was invented.

To many thinking people, the appalling human rights abuses associated with much Diamond mining operations and the public knowledge that Diamonds have been used to finance some of Africa's most murderous wars and civil conflicts, along with the devastation of (one example only) a fragile habitat approximately the size of 2,000 football fields, makes Diamonds less appealing as a jewel emblem of eternal love.

Greed has violated this beautiful gem.

Emerald
A mineral of rare beauty which should be treated with kid gloves because its resistance to breakage is generally poor. Emeralds are

the most important gemstone in the beryl family. Records show that it was known and sold in markets in Babylon as early as 4000BC, while modern history of the Emerald begins in Egypt where they were mined before 2,000BC in the desert south of Cairo. Because Cleopatra adored this gem the ancient mine was renamed "Cleopatra's mine". Emeralds have always been coveted by the wealthy. History has it that the Incas worshipped the Emerald, Rome's Nero supposedly watched gladiator fights through a large transparent Emerald, and it has been rumoured that King Arthur's Holy Grail was fashioned from an Emerald. The rarest Emerald exhibits a 6 pointed star pattern formed from spokes of carbon impurities within the crystal. Emeralds range in colours ranging from yellow-green to blue-green, but only gems that are medium to dark in tone are considered precious, the brightest greens are called "Imperial Emeralds". Pale green gems are known as Green Beryls. The original source of the word/name Emerald is probably either a Hebrew word meaning green or the Sanskrit word "marakata" meaning green. Colombia, Brazil, and Zambia mine most commercial Emeralds while Pakistan and Zimbabwe, mine smaller amounts.

Garnet

The name given to a group of gemstones popular since the Bronze Age. There are six common species; all recognised by their individual chemical compositions — Pyrope, Alamandine, Grossular, Uvarovite, Grossular and Andatite. Garnets are found in myriad colours including red, yellow, orange, green, brown, blue, purple, black, grey, wine, pink and colourless. The rarest Garnet displays a colour-change from blue-green in daylight to purple in incandescent light, but this Garnet does not give competition to the Alexandrite which displays similar colours because Garnets are dense while the Alexandrite is bright and clear with ethereal light.

Another collector's Garnet is the bright green Uvarovite usually found in small crystals in Russia and Finland, while another green Garnet is Tsavorite from Kenya, named and launched by Tiffany & Co in 1974.

The most popular variety of this mineral to the general public is arguably ruby-red from Bohemia.

Jade

There are two minerals legitimately called Jade, Nephrite Jade and Jadeite, but many countries and nationalities call any and all opaque or translucent green stones "Jade". Nephrite is derived from the Greek word "nephros" meaning kidney and Jade from the Spanish word "lapis ijada" meaning loin stone because the Spanish believed Jade cured kidney stones. Nephrite Jade is the only stone named after its healing properties. Nephrite Jade artifacts ranging from indoor decorative items to Jade burial suits, ceremonial axes, bridal carriages and jewellery have been unearthed from prehistoric and historic China, European countries, New Zealand, British Columbia, Mexico and South America. Nephrite Jade's structure is composed of interwoven, fibrous crystals making it very tough, therefore it is not carved, but ground into shape then polished. British Columbia Jade is considered extremely fine quality, while Australian Black Jade is a collector's mineral. Nephrite Jade occurs in a range of colours from translucent white to light yellow, opaque white to light brown, grey, and black as well as many shades of green.

Jadeite

This mineral is commonly called Jade. In pure form is white, but the most popular and sought after colours are bright apple-green, lavenders and violets, with pink, orange, brown and black also in great demand. The Chinese claim Jadeite as their own, but this translucent stone has been imported from Burma to China since the mid eighteenth century.

Burmese Jade (Jadeite) is well known as being the finest quality Jadeite in the world for depth of colour, intensity, charity and translucency which all affect the price. True Jadeite is found in Burma, California, Guatemala, Russia, Japan, Hawaii, and Switzerland. It forms in stones and boulders).

Jet

This dark beauty has been called Black and Dark Brown Amber because they are both of vegetable origin, both belong to the mineraloid group, neither have a crystal structure, both are featherweight and soft to carve and both induce an electric charge when rubbed. But that is where the likeness ends because unlike Amber which is ancient, fossilised resin, Jet is the end product of wood that has been immersed in stagnant water for millions of years, compressed under pressure from earth, and then fossilized. Jet found at Whitby in Yorkshire/England is of early Jurassic age, approximately 182 million years old. It is related to coal which is evident by smell when heated and burnt.

The oldest Jet jewellery was found in Asturias, Spain, dating from 17,000 BC. Jet was used extensively in mourning jewellery in Victorian times probably due to its dark colour and the fact that Queen Victoria continuously wore black after her husband's death. Jet was the favoured jewellery of the Roaring Twenties, when fashionable women danced the

Charleston wearing long, multiple strands of beads swinging from throat to below the waist.

Jet has been mined since 1400BC and carved Jet artifacts have been found in prehistoric burial mounds. In the 16th century Jet was used to create rosary beads for monks, and Pueblo Indians buried Jet with their dead to protect them in the afterlife.

The finest Jet comes from England, but good specimens are also found in the United States, Poland, France, Germany, Spain, India and Russia.

Jet derives its name from the French word for the same material "jaiet".

Jet sometimes contains inclusions of pyrite, which may create a metallic lustre when polished. Because Jet is organic, it can dry out, causing the surface to crack, so, if you are fortunate and own Jet jewellery, when not in use wrap it in silk, and store in a dark nook.

Kunzite
This mineral was discovered about 100 years ago and has been named after a famous Gemmologist and Jeweller George Frederick Kunz.

This seductive mineral at its best shows intense pink to violet pink lights which can carry through to most delicate of pink/mauve shades, and all Kunzite has high brilliance. There is no such thing as an unattractive Kunzite gemstone, but whatever the colour Kunzite is sensitive to sunlight and has a tendency to fade. For that reason, Kunzite jewellery should never be worn while sunbathing, picnicking or on the beach and is a touch fragile so it should sensibly be set as a brooch, earrings, as a pendant or if set in a ring should only be worn on dress occasions when there is little chance of knocking this heavenly gemstone.

Kunzite deposits in Afghanistan show wonderful shades of deep pink through to violet, and lovely gems have been found in Brazil, Canada, Madagascar, Sweden, and the United States.

Labradorite
Belonging to the feldspar group of minerals, Labradorite displays colours and patterns equal to those of iridescent butterfly wings and teases the eye with a continual interplay of coloured lights. This translucent, grey bodied gemstone has connections beyond our planet because Labradorite has been found in some Meteorites.

According to Eskimo legend, the Northern Lights (aurora borealis) were once imprisoned in the rocks along the coast of Labrador. A wandering Eskimo warrior found them and was able to free most of the lights with a mighty blow of his spear. But some lights were trapped forever in the divine Labradorite.

Modern specimens of Labradorite were originally discovered on St. Paul Island, Labrador, Canada in 1770 hence its name.

Lapis Lazuli

Considered the royalty of minerals, this opaque, royal blue rock that rightfully deserves its title "Rock of Ages." Lapis was, throughout pre and written history, the gemstone of the gods. It was the chosen rock of Enlil and Anu, the two great gods of Mesopotamia, with a solid connection to the Sirius System and keystone to higher knowledge. In the fourth millennium BC the legendary city of Ur plied a keen Lapis Lazuli trade, the material coming from deposits in Afghanistan and probably Persia.

The original ten commandments of the bible were originally believed to have been engraved in slabs of Lapis, it was featured in the dress jewellery of Pharaohs, and their priests used Lapis as an inscription stone for various passages from the Book of the Dead. In Indian legend the approach to the sacred place of Bacchus supposedly had a flight of steps carved from Lapis boulders. Excavations have given clear indications that the deep blue stone was treasured thousands of years ago among the people of Mesopotamia, Egypt, Persia, Greece and Rome. Lapis is a mineraloid because it is a rock comprising many minerals mainly Lazurite, Hauynite, Sodalite, Noselite, Calcite, Diopside and Augite with evidence of gold being found in ancient artifacts.

This most glorious of gemstones was once called Sapphirus, but that was before the blue Sapphire crystal was found. Apparently man mistakenly thought the Sapphire was a clear crystal of Sapphirus, which meant the opaque rock was renamed Lapis Lazuli, "lapis" being the Latin word for stone, and "azula" which comes from the Arabic meaning blue, or from the Persian "lazhward" meaning blue. Just as it was at least 5,000 years ago, first grade Lapis still yields from the steep Hindu Kush in the north east of Afghanistan.

Lapis also yields in Russia, the Andes, Italy, Mongolia, America and Canada, Myanmar and Pakistan.

The differing shades of blue to grey to greenish, purplish and white greatly affect the retail price, the most expensive dependent entirely on intensity of the colour blue. Before 1834, Old masters of the art world used ground Lapis mixed with binding agents to produce electric-quality royal blue because ultra-marine was impossible to produce synthetically before then. Today Lapis pigment is mainly used in restoration work.

Moonstone

This mineral owes its name to its mystical shimmer which resembles moonlight. It was cherished by Romans and Greeks who associated Moonstone with lunar gods and goddesses. It has been reported that even today Arab women sew Moonstones into their garments as a fertility totem.

Moonstone belongs to the mineral group feldspar, one of the most abundant minerals on our planet. Deposits of Moonstone occur in Australia, the Austrian Alps, Mexico, Madagascar, Burma, Norway, Poland, Sri Lanka and America.

Moonstone was extremely popular about a hundred years ago at the time of Art Nouveau. It adorns a large number of jewellery creations of the French goldsmith René Lalique and his contemporaries.

In their uncut state Moonstones are dull and boring and are not shown to advantage until a cutter has performed his/her art. The most sought after Moonstone is almost transparent with a bluish shimmer, although the pale champagne, green, brown, orange, smoky, black and reddish are also popular.

Moonstone should be handled with care, for it is sensitive to wear being fairly soft. Some Moonstones present with a four rayed star which normally occur in honey colour, peach and greenish varieties.

Opal

The national gem of Australia, which produces 90% of the world's Opal supply, though varieties of precious Opal also occur in many other parts of the world including Ethiopia, Indonesia and Mexico. Mines are believed to have once existed in parts of Africa because artifacts from a cave in Kenya dated from around 4,000 years BC have recently come to light.

Opal is the gemstone most representative of life on our planet because it is a silica gemstone. Silica is a form of silicon, the most abundant element on Earth's crust after oxygen, found in every cell and organ in our bodies which helps our tendons, tissues, hair, nails, bones and cartilage. Without silica we are not and neither are all other members of our beloved animal kingdom.

Opal is unique among gemstones because no two Opals are the same, not even if they are cut from the same specimen or split. The colours and infinite patterns of Opal are not caused through a crystal structure (the arrangement of atoms, ions or molecules in a crystal) or mineral content but through the packing of layers of very small spheres of silica which have grown around a central nucleus. Because Opal does not have a crystal structure it is classed as a mineraloid, making it obvious that "Crystal Opal" is a name given to the transparent to translucent Opal to boast sales to crystal buffs.

Colours in Opals are determined by the size of the spheres, the patterns in Opals caused through light interplay between the spheres.

Opal colours range from clear through white, grey, slate, red, orange, yellow, green to olive, blue, magenta, rose, pink, slate, olive, brown, and black. Harlequin Opal is the most precious of patterns displaying a mosaic, broad pattern of close set colours. Black opals are regarded as the most expensive, with the most valuable displaying a harlequin.

The ancient Greeks called Opal Opallios, the Romans called it Opalus and dubbed it the "Stone of Justice" and in Sanskrit it was Upala. Is it remarkable that all three names mean "Precious Stone"?

Pearl
The only gem made by a living animal. If natural Pearls are of organic origin created when a parasite invades the home or body of a shellfish. The uncomfortable oyster, mussel or clam secretes a fluid and painstakingly coats the irritant, and because the foreign object doesn't go away, the unhappy creature keeps secreting and coating, layer upon layer until a Pearl is formed. All Pearls are created like this whether they are wild or cultured.

Because Pearls are not formed by chemical actions and lack a crystal structure they fall into the mineraloid group which means they are not classed as minerals.

Natural Pearls are a rarity and if one is found by divers it would be snapped up by collectors who are willing to pay any outrageous price, otherwise the astute eye can find natural Pearls set in estate sales jewellery. In 2007, a double strand of 68 Pearls known as the "Baroda Pearls" was auctioned at Christie's/London for £7 million.

Cultured pearls are still real Pearls, grown organically the same way as natural Pearls but the irritant is administered by man not nature. A foreign form called a nucleus is implanted into the sexual organ of a saltwater mollusc or into an existing pearl sac in the mantle of a freshwater mussel. Oysters are one giant gonad. A worker opens the shell, cuts the living creature's sex gland, then inserts either a bead and/ or a piece of flesh (which eventually rots resulting in a "seedless Pearl") from another shellfish into the incisions then close the shell. Next the shell housing the anguished sea creature is attached to a frame and lowered into water so that it may continue a tortured life as a Pearl slave, constantly trying to ease its man administered discomfort by secreting a fluid called "nacre", coating the invasive items with layer upon layer until it creates a Pearl.

Fresh water mussels suffer 12 to 16 cuts and insertions, whereas saltwater creatures usually have less, but regardless of how many cuts and insertions an animal has, every Pearl has caused a living organism grief, to live one hell of an unnatural life and then have an untimely death, ceremonially thrown on a heap with other rotting innocents for the sake of human greed and conceit.

China claims it had natural Freshwater Pearls about 4,000 years ago. India's god Krishna is associated with Pearls while their ancient epic poem, the Ramayana, describes a necklace of 27 pearls, each up to 11mm. 2,400years ago a Persian Queen was buried with a Pearl necklace comprising 3 rows of 72 pearls each, while a bracelet and necklace set dating back 2,000 years was in a Native American burial mound near Wapallo/Iowa. Greece, the Philippines and Ceylon also have a long history with Pearls.

One can tell an imitation by rubbing a Pearl gently on one's teeth. Fake Pearls are smooth, while the layers of nacre on real Pearls feel gritty like fine sandpaper.

Peridot.
Legend has it that Peridot was Cleopatra's favourite gemstone, and can be found in Egyptian jewellery from the early 2nd millennium BC. The stones used at that time came from a deposit on a small volcanic island in the Red Sea, some 45 miles off the Egyptian coast at Aswan. Peridot is treasured in Hawaii as the goddess Pele's tears and the ancient Romans adored its radiant green, because it keeps it intensity in artificial light. Peridot is also found in Europe in medieval, European churches where it adorns many a treasure, and the shrines in Cologne Cathedral.

Peridot is one of the few gemstones that occur in only one colour. It is always green, however that green can vary from yellow-green to olive to brownish-green, the most valuable being dark, velvet-green which shoots yellow light from its depths. There is always an oil-like sheen to the cut stone.

Extra-terrestrial Peridot crystals have been identified in Meteorites, on our Moon, on Mars and in the dust and core of comets as well as on an asteroid. One such Meteorite was offered for auction at Bonhams (British auction house) in 2008 with a requested price of £3 million.

Peridot is also found embedded in lava. Gem quality Peridot yields in Mogok, Myanmar, Pakistan, Minas Gerais, Brazil, Eifel, Germany, Chihuahua, Mexico, Ethiopia, Australia, America, and Hawaii. Peridot is the gem quality crystal of a mineral called olivine which itself is composed of two minerals fayalite and forsterite. The name Olivine is from the Latin "oliva" in reference to the mineral's colour. Some scholars say Peridot is from a thirteenth century English word "peridote" meaning bright button or bright spot.

Ruby
A red, but not hot red variety of the mineral family corundum. Throughout gem history, Ruby has been considered one of the most valuable gemstones because it has everything a precious stone should have glorious colour, excellent hardness and outstanding brilliance. The most famous pair of shoes in Hollywood was named after this gemstone, Dorothy's Ruby slippers in Wizard of Oz.

The name Ruby comes from the Latin "ruber" meaning red, even though Rubies are found in a wide range of reds, pinkish, and purplish-brownish but the finest colour is Pigeon Blood found in Burmese mines.

All natural rubies have imperfections, including colour impurities and inclusions of rutile needles known as silk. A clear or almost clear stone will command a premium, while a ruby with no needle like inclusions usually indicates the stone is synthetic.

Today Rubies are more usually heat treated to enhance the stone. Some Rubies show a 3 or 6 point star which occurs when light is reflected off the inclusions and this is one example where inclusions increase the value of a gemstone.

The occasional Ruby has been known to show colour changes.

In ancient and medieval period the Mogok mines were controlled by Burmese kings therefore all stones were part of royal treasury. Rubies also occur in Australia, Tanzania, Madagascar, Vietnam, Nepal, Tajikistan, and Pakistan America, Greenland, Kenya, and Mozambique.

Sapphire
This gemstone derives its name from the Greek "sappheiros" meaning blue stone and, as this beguiling gemstone belongs to the corundum family of minerals, it is sister to the Ruby. Sapphires have been named the flower garden of gems because they occur in purple, violet, clear white, orange, brown, green, darkest of blue, black and a combination of multi colours in one stone, although a pink Sapphire changes its name to Ruby as the colour deepens. The most converted colour has always been

the brightest of mid to royal blue. Often called the Ceylonese Sapphire because that colour first occurred in Ceylon, it commands the highest price, though from a collector's view the orange Padmaraga (sometimes written Padparadja) romps home easily in second place. Star Sapphires are awe inspiring.

Because of their remarkable hardness Sapphires, whose colour is not precious, are used in many non-ornamental applications including infrared optical components and fine surgical blades.

Sapphires are mined primary from underground workings in Burma, Madacaska, Sri Lanka, Australia, America, Thailand, India, Pakistan, Tanzania, Africa and China.

Russia's Catherine the Great favoured a Sapphire which weighed a massive 337 ct, and Queen Marie Antoinette wore a seven piece jewellery set containing approximately 29 sapphires, of which 18 are stones of perhaps 20 carat or more.

The largest cut Sapphire in the world is known as Queen Marie of Romania's Sapphire, at 478 carats and blazes with sensational blue. According to lab reports it is completely untreated and is of Sri Lankan origin. King Ferdinand of Romania purchased it in 1921 for his wife Queen Marie, who was a granddaughter of both queen Victoria of England and Czar Alexander II of Russia. That Sapphire is now on permanent display in the Diamond Fund Exhibition, within the Kremlin Armoury Museum in Moscow.

Spinel
Sadly the Spinel is relatively unknown to the public, though Spinel does occur naturally and should be sought after as this is surely one of the most alluring and rarest gemstones. It is a favourite gem of collectors and connoisseurs on account of its brilliance, hardness and wide range of spectacular colours.

Natural Spinel occurs in virtually every possible colour and coloured Spinels on show together displays a gem tapestry from the mineral kingdom. Historically famous for glorious, rich reds, Spinel can be found in shades of pink and violet, green, deep purple, and orange. Recently, in Burma, a Spinel was discovered boasting one of the most spectacular gemstone colours ever seen, a vivid hot pink with a hint of orange. In addition to Burma, Spinels are mined in Sri Lanka, Tanzania, and Tadzhikistan, part of the former Soviet Union.

Until the 18th century Spinels and Rubies were both called Rubies. It was easy to assume they were the same gemstone because they are both red, both hard, and occur together in the same deposits. Then modern science stepped in and discovered the ultra-glorious, rich red stone had a different chemical composition and crystal formation to the softer red stone. Following that, the name "Ruby" applied to the softer red stone belonging to the corundum group of minerals and the even more divine red stone was named Spinel and Balas Ruby.

But now we know that in Burma, as early as 1587, Spinel was recognised as a separate gem species, it's just that the rest of the world didn't. Many Spinels are among the most famous gemstones, but they were named before the two gems, Ruby and Spinel, were recognised as different minerals. Among them are the "Black Prince's Ruby" and the "Timor Ruby", both in the British Crown Jewel collection, and the "Cote de Bretagne" formerly from the French Crown jewels. The Samarian Spinel weighing 500 carats (100 g), is reportedly the largest Spinel in the world.

Spinels were set in jewellery by the ancient Romans and mining for Spinel was first seen in Afghanistan about the ear 750 AD.

Now, treasured for its own sake the Spinel is prevented from achieving popularity as the very precious gemstone it is because fine Spinels are now rarer than the Rubies they are mined with.

Finally, many "birthstones" sold in jewellery shops are coloured, synthetic Spinels or stones of other mineral groups flying under the name "Spinel" and very few sales people working in jewellery shops know that natural Spinels exist.

Tanzanite
Discovered in 1967 and named after Tanzania, the country in which it was discovered Tanzanite is noted for its alternating colours of cornflower-blue to violet and burgundy depending on lighting conditions and the angle at which it is viewed. But it should be noted that with exception of the first stones found close to our planet's surface, these colours are not natural.

Natural Tanzanite is more usually reddish-brown, so it is universally heat treated in a gemmological oven or furnace with temperatures between 500 and 700 degrees Celsius to produce its range of stunning colours.

Tanzanite yields mostly in the foothills of Mount Kilimanjaro. It is a stone which should sensibly be only worn as a pendant, a brooch, or as earrings because it is softer than other gemstones and has an unfortunate habit of breaking in its natural cleavage line if knocked or treated roughly.

Because of its fragile nature, if it wasn't for heavy advertising campaigns which have resulted in public demand, it is unlikely Tanzanite would ever have been set in finger jewellery.

In 2002, the American Gem Trade Association added Tanzanite to December to boosts sales of the stone, but of course the choice in the calendar (near Christmas) was solely for retail purpose. If corresponded to the character of a solar system world Tanzanite couples with Saturn, not Jupiter. Tanzanite belongs to the zoisite family of minerals. Green Zoisite exists, but is never called Tanzanite.

Topaz

A mineral with many ancient names, Topaz was once famous as a "Diamond Slave" so called because jewellers displayed them instead of Diamonds. Topaz comes in larger crystals and has brilliant lights flashing from its depths if cut to show them. Another name is Brazilian Sapphire, but today these names are seldom used. Bohemian Topaz, Madeira Topaz, Golden Topaz, Occidental Topaz, Spanish Topaz, Indian Topaz are names still in use, though not officially correct or recognised. Mystic Topaz is colourless Topaz which has been artificially coated giving it a rainbow effect. The name Imperial Topaz was originally given to Pink Topaz mined in the Ural Mountains in 19th century Russia, where they were restricted to the royal family of the Czar. Today Imperial Topaz can be yellow, pink and pink-orange while Precious Topaz is bright orange. The name Topaz comes from the Sanskrit meaning fire.

Most Topaz is wine, pale yellow, soft grey, reddish-orange, greenish or blue brown. Naturally occurring blue topaz is rare. Typically, colourless, grey or pale yellow and pale blue material is heat treated and irradiated to produce a darker blue.

Natural crystals can occur in enormous sizes, one weighed in at 1000 carats. However, cut stones of the prized, Imperial Topaz in colours of orange, pink and red, are not common. Fine pinks and reds above 5 carats and pure orange above 20 carats are also rare.

Topaz occurs in localities around the world—Australia, America, Afghanistan, Brazil, Italy, Japan, Nigeria, Sri Lanka, Sweden, Russia, Burma, Pakistan, America and Mexico. Topaz is one of the hard gemstones, but does not appreciate rough treatment due its crystal structure.

Tourmaline

A mineral family with gemstones boasting an incomparable variety of colours and colour combinations in the same stone.

According to Egyptian legend, when the Tourmaline was on its long journey from Earth's core to Earth's crust it passed a rainbow which gave its colours to the precious stone. Crystals of only one, single colour are fairly rare and often a stone which appears to have one colour will display other colours when seen from different angles, or the original colour will appear richer.

Tourmalines were first noticed when the Dutch brought rough, unpolished crystals to Europe. Dutch children used to play with them while their families were trading other goods. The children heated the crystals then scattered them on the earth. This created an electrical charge which attracted ashes and short straws to the positive end, while the negative charge repelled. The traders used a heated Tourmaline to draw the ash from their pipes, so the common name for Tourmaline in Holland was Aschentrekker meaning "ash attractor". Tourmaline also becomes charged under pressure, the polarity changing when pressure is removed, then Tourmaline begins to oscillate, similar to quartz crystal only much stronger. These qualities were put to use during and after the Second World War in sub-marine instrumentation and other war uses.

Tourmaline wasn't used for jewellery until German immigration to Brazil caused gem quality stones to be brought to the notice of stone cutters in Germany's Idar-Oberstein (a major gem fashioning centre).

Colours in this Pandora's box of gemstones ranges from black to dazzling bright pink, through blues and greens, brown to yellows, oranges to the brightest and most dazzling red.

Catherine II of Russia was the proud owner of a 255 carat, red, grape-shaped tourmaline pendant. Rare colour change Tourmalines have been found showing different variants depending on day or artificial light, then there are the crystals with two colours a pink centre with green surrounds known as Water Melon Tourmaline, and others which show the features of a cat's eye. Tourmaline knows no boundaries when it comes to the colours, colour combinations and varieties. All Tourmalines have wonderful hardness, have excellent wearing qualities, are a delight to look after, and have chemical/structural properties which make almost every Tourmaline unique. The name Tourmaline comes from the Singhalese "turamali" meaning stone with mixed colours.

Non gemmy Tourmalines yield almost all over the world, but fine colours and gem quality are not frequently found. For this reason, the price range of Tourmaline is almost as broad as that of its colour range.

Major deposits are in Brazil, Sri Lanka and south and southwest Africa.

Turquoise

One of the few opaque minerals considered precious, and the only mineral to have a colour named after it. Turquoise occurs in different shades of blue, blue-green or green, can be plain or have dark markings through it.

The word Turquoise dates back to the 17th century, when trading routes passed through Turkey, so the stone was named Turquies in reference to Turkey. Turquoise has been highly regarded in many powerful civilizations including the Persian and Chinese. Turquoise was the gemstone of the ancient Egyptian goddess Hathor, who personified the principals of love, beauty, motherhood and joy, and it was and still is the mineral emblem of North American Indians and of Mexico.

Navajo Turquoise from the American Southwest, especially Arizona contains black or brown patterns throughout, which in many people's opinions does not take away from its loveliness, but the precious jewellery trade prefers a solid coloured stone without veins, the most sought after being a deep turquoise or sky-blue known under two names, Robin's Egg or Persian Blue, the latter because this colour is found only in Persia.

Turquoise deposits of Iran, Sinai and China yields stunning specimens. Afghanistan, American, Chile, Mexico, Russian Turquoise are of a decidedly inferior quality but still appealing. Australian Turquoise is lovely with gorgeous, solid nuggets having been found in the Northern Territory, Victoria and NSW but the yield is not plentiful.

To retain the colour of pure Turquoise it should be cleaned at least once a year with ammonia diluted with water. This restores its original colour which otherwise tends to green with age. Turquoise should never be stored with other jewellery, but wrapped in a soft, non-greasy cloth then stored in a dark place.

Turquoise is abundant on our planet, but most of it has a fragile character which easily breaks or crumbles. Thus most Turquoise on the market has been stabilised using various glues and/or plastics to improve its workability and durability such as dyeing, waxing, and oiling, plastic impregnation and epoxy filling. Much copycat Turquoise material is sold as real Turquoise. They are more usually called Bone Turquoise, Fossil Turquoise, Occidental Turquoise (Much Occidental Turquoise is fossilized bone or teeth perhaps coloured by copper salts) and dyed Howlite.

A mineral often mistaken for Turquoise is the intriguing, opaque Eilat Stone—a greenish-blue mixture of Chrysocolla, Turquoise and other copper minerals such as Malachite from the copper mines near Eilat, Israel. Eilat is often called the national gemstone of Israel

Zircon

Zircon has lustre and fire and is more like a Diamond than any other gemstone; so many experienced jewellers have mistaken a Zircon for a Diamond. But this beauty has been cheated of its rightful place as one of our loveliest minerals due to the similarity of its name of the laboratory grown, artificial Diamond called Cubic Zirconia.

Notable occurrence of natural Zircon have been found in America, Australia, Cambodia, Canada, Norway, Pakistan, Russia and Thailand, perhaps the most glorious colour being a striking blue, not seen in any other gemstone, which is found in deposits at Ratanakiri in Cambodia.

Zircon also occurs in shades of pale blue, bluish-green, black, brown, champagne, coffee, colourless (clear), golden-yellow, green, red and violet.

When browns and are heat treated they colour change to exceptionally lovely blue and golden shades and being quite a hard stone Zircon has great durability.

Zircon is mentioned numerous times in the Bible under its original names of Jacinth and Ligure as stones of fire given to Moses (Ezekiel 28:13-16), set in Aaron's breastplate (Exodus 28:15-30) and set as one of the foundation stones in the wall of Jerusalem (Revelations 21:19). Hindu poets tell of a glowing tree covered in gemstone fruit with leaves of this green gemstone.

Scientists have named a fragment of Zircon as the oldest object on Earth at 4.404 billion years old after its discovery in Western Australia.

Zircon is a heavy gemstone so carat for carat it will look smaller than other gemstones.

This is a gemstone you probably won't find in your average rock shop because firstly, the public and many rock and/or jewellery shop owners are either not aware of its existence or may have, as already mentioned, confused the natural crystal with the artificial Diamond Cubic Zirconia.

However, Zircons are available and to the lover of gemstones, it is well worth the search and find.

Zircon is special because it is a glorious gemstone, and not common-place.

The name probably comes from the Persian word "zargun" which means gold-coloured. Today the Zircon is usually referred to by its colour as part of its names, such as Cognac Zircon or Green Zircon with the exception of those found at Ratanakiri in Cambodia. They are Ratanakiri Zircon.

Quartz

The most abundant and widely distributed mineral found at Earth's surface. It is present and plentiful in all parts of the world, is found in all rock types, as sand grains, as crystals in rocks, and in veins that cut through all rock types, sometimes bearing gold or other precious metals and precious gems.

The word Quartz is derived from the German word "quarz". Other sources attribute the word's origin to the Saxon word "Querkluftertz", meaning cross vein ore. Quartz is the most common material identified as the mystical material Maban or Mabain, from which the Clever Women and Men of Indigenous Australian Aborigines reputedly derive their magical powers.

The Irish word for Quartz is "grian cloch" which means stone of the sun. The word crystal comes from the Greek word "κρύσταλλος" meaning ice because it was then found near glaciers in the Alps and was thought to be frozen water.

Quartz is found regularly in European cemeteries in a burial context.

Quartz Crystals typically grow in hot watery solutions. The ideal crystal shape is a six sided prism terminating with six sided pyramids at each end.

Herkimer Diamond Quartz Crystals are harder than regular Quartz, are brighter and are doubly terminated, clear crystals, some showing a slightly yellow appearance.

Popular Quartz Gemstones are;

Amethyst — palest mauve to deepest purple clear Quartz;

Ametrine — a clear, bi-colour Amethyst and Citrine with zones of purple and yellow;

Cairngorm — a deep, rich, yellow-brown to greyish-brown, clear Quartz which took its name from the Scottish mountain range in which it was found;

Citrine — yellow to golden clear Quartz. Citrine is Amethyst which has been heated or irradiated by nature after the crystal formed as

Amethyst. Because Citrine is scarce, most Citrine on the market today is laboratory-treated Amethyst;

Morion — brown, clear Quartz;

Pink Quartz is gem quality Rose Quartz and surely one of the most beautiful gemstones. It is clear, coloured pink with sunset overtones and has a mysterious, almost translucent glow. Pink Quartz is a collector's gemstone;

Rose Quartz — powder-pink to soft-pink. Generally milky in appearance, Rose Quartz can have included rutile crystals which show as a six ray star;

Smokey Quartz — dark to mid-brown/greyish-brown, can be almost clear to opaque;

Tourmalinated Quartz — clear Quartz which formed around needles of Black Tourmaline.

The Agate Family is Quartz defined by having a pattern to its colours. Varieties are sometimes opaque, but are usually translucent, and occasionally transparent;

Banded Agates display rich, bands of colours, but many on sale have been either dyed or heat treated to enrich;

Moss Agate contains mineral inclusions which look like plants;

Lace Agate displays delicate, old world lace designs generally in blues and browns;

Fire Agate a stone covered with grape-like shapes showing iridescent colours of red, gold and green, with the occasional violet-blue;

Chalcedony is a form of Quartz whose natural crystals are too small to see without high magnification. In common practice, only the translucent, single colour types are called Chalcedony. Most popular members of this variety are;

Aventurine — soft blue-green with inclusions of Mica which shimmers;

Blue Chalcedony — mid-blue which often varies in colour, because it can have an overtone of grey or pink, the latter giving it a lavender hue. Blue Chalcedony is an ethereal gemstone which often shows a moonlight shimmer;

Black Onyx naturally occurs in thin bands. Most Black Onyx sold in shops is dyed;

Carnelian ranges in colour from yellow-orange to reddish-orange, to orangey-brown, and can vary from semi-opaque to highly translucent;

Chrysocolla Chalcedony is a rare gemstone is often called Gem Silica, is blue to turquoise in colour;

Chrysoprase is highly prized in its best colour—apple-green, but it can be olive green, pale green and whitish. Its density ranges from almost opaque to translucent;

Jasper — an exception in the Chalcedony group because it is opaque. Colour range is solid brownish-orange, yellow-beige, muted green and greyish;

Tiger Eye occurs in many shades and mixes of shades, but is best known as brown yellow, pink, and red with a silky lustre, seems to have received its name from its bands resembling the eye of a tiger. Blue and grey variety Tiger Eye is known as Hawke Eye, while green is called Wolf Eye. Other shades have numerous names including Tigerite.

PART FOUR

Healing Stones

This section deals with physical health, preparing your personal crystal and attuning the mind to it, procuring the energy of a gemstone you either can't afford or cannot obtain, self-healing, absent healing, healing through energy points (chakras) and the links between energy points, gland and organs, care and practical cleaning and a technique for meditation.

This is followed by a list of the most important healing stones, individually described, this time with reference to their holistic rather than their astrological properties. This chapter is followed by a glossary of ailments and their treatment in past ages and the present, in which many other stones are included. The reader may like to refer back and forth between this and the preceding, astrological section, thereby enhancing the benefits to be derived from both.

First, notes on how health and mental harmony is affected by stones and crystals.

O thorn in my heart,
Sister of hell;
Go back to the rose
And these messages tell;
Her love will not poison
For Emerald I wear;
I've a blue Topaz spoon
And a Sardonyx chair;
Go thou, go back now,
Hasten you home,
Sard against sorcery
Your catacomb.

Precious Health, Precious Stones

The root of all illness is poison through imbalance. Holistic treatment is based on the theory that disturbances of the parts disease the whole. So what is required, and what natural healing provides, is a treatment for the whole body or rather, for the whole person. It does not confine itself to patching up individual organs, as orthodox medicine is too often compelled to do. Of course the latter is frequently required — a broken bone cannot be repaired by rubbing it with a crystal. Ideally, orthodox and alternative medicine should be combined. The result would be a noticeable fall in the use of drugs and a faster recovery rate, with few or no side effects.

There is one more requirement, however self-help. "Physician, heal thyself" is a good maxim for all of us, and there are countless ways, well publicized nowadays, in which we can hope to ward off ill health and in the process achieve balance and happiness. We can heal your spirit, physical and honour by becoming a Vegan, take exercise, breathe and stand correctly, lay off tobacco and drink, even take barefoot walks along secluded sandy beaches letting the silicon work into our bodies from the undersides of our feet. Obviously, it is pointless to call in counsel from outside until we have determined to make the effort to help ourselves.

Unfortunately, few people seem to have grasped this basic fact. The average person turns to natural medicine only after all else has failed, and after years of punishing and ignorant abuse of his or her long suffering body. Thus the natural healing practitioner has to deal with destruction caused by drugs, the ravages of time and much else, as well as the ailment immediately apparent. Fortunately, holistic healers are seldom materialistic. They are ready to devote many hours to each client's welfare, unlike orthodox doctors who are forced by necessity to book in the sick at quarter hour (or shorter) intervals, hand them a prescription, or refer them to a specialist and send them on their way. Thus holistic methods can bring about healing at the deeper levels where the illness originated. Holistic medicine is not "band aid".

The previous section, on jewels of the zodiac, indicated the connections between particular stones and the astrological planets and signs, thus showing how we can improve our lives by living more closely in harmony with our immediate section of the universe. That in itself is a major contribution to health. This part of the book goes further. It describes the active, healing properties of stones, how we can use them to help ourselves and how healers can help us through them. How does this happen?

All healing is a transfer of energy from one source to another. A natural healer seems to transmit energy, in some mysterious way, from or through his or her own person to another human being. Sometimes the transfer is from plants to man or from man to plants. Often man benefits through the will of an animal. Pets, looking fondly at their masters or mistresses when they are ill, are wishing them well, and so healing them. Modern research bears this out. The work of the Crawford Centre in Melbourne, Australia, the findings of the Friedman Study, the results produced by such distinguished specialists as Roger Mugford, the British animal behavioural consultant, and Aaron Fletcher of the University of Pennsylvania all tend towards the same conclusion: that owners of pets live longer lives and suffer less from ill health than those who lack such companionship.

But this chapter concerns Earth's gems, which are matter in its purest form, and which heal by transmitting energies gathered from the rest of the universe to which they are linked by their elements and composition. When we are ill, unhappy, or in whatever way out of sorts, it means that we have allowed ourselves to get off-key with our surrounds and celestial bodies which influence us. By their power of transmitting the energies that are vital to us, minerals can greatly help to restore the balance.

So, as a first step in the process of elementary self-healing, make use of your birthstones, be aware of their powers, fondle them, wear them, place them near you and look at them. At night they can bring healing if placed on a bedside table slightly above the level of the owner's head under the bed or mattress is not as good unless specified in this book or by a natural therapist who knows their stuff.

Next study the descriptions of stones in the following pages which concentrate specifically on their healing properties, and then the list of ailments, both physical and spiritual, and of the stones that can help to remedy the problem. In the process of healing by stones, energy flows from the stone with unstoppable force. But first, it must be warmed to room temperature at least, and possibly rubbed, to activate its vibrations. It is these vibrations that act on the subject to correct his or her own rhythms. It is the stone, moreover, which is doing the work here, simply by virtue of proximity. The person has merely to let it act.

But beyond this process of simple self-help there is the ancient art of healing others, an art dismissed in the materialistic centuries but now returning borne along on a steady tide.

How can a person tell whether he or she possesses this power? It certainly owes nothing to academic attainment, sharp wits or "braininess". It is a matter, rather, of concentration and sensitivity. It is these qualities, and these alone, which will unlock a stone's essence, and whether or not one possesses them one must find out for oneself. One must simply remember that since healing by stones can open up the higher channels of the spirit or soul clogged and blocked by the excesses of rational thought, the healer's own mind must be cleared of debris before useful work can begin. Remember too that the lists just mentioned, which of course are intended as much for the use of the healer of others as of the individual applying a healing remedy to the self, are based on general findings only. The practitioner's skill and personal vibrations are also a factor and so the lists should be used as a springboard for free experiment.

It will be noted, too, that a few ancient and powdered recipes are listed. These are included for fun, and for the sake of curiosity, to illustrate some ancient ideas. They are definitely not advocated by this author. The virtue of gemstones lies in their tints, their reflectivity and their energies.

Attuning Your Mind to Crystal
But first, how does the would-be crystal healer start? How is the healing process performed?

The healing is conducted through the medium of a stone, rather in the manner of crystal gazing. For the novice, the best choice is a piece of Rock Crystal of the quartz variety, one and a half to two inches long, which should be cleansed before use in pure, cool water, preferably mineral water, and allowed to dry in the shade, not in the sun because minerals were born in the dark caverns of the earth. It should not be dried with a towel, as adhering fluff will collect negativity. Nor in the ocean water, it leaves an unwanted surface film containing other minerals, vegetable matter and remnants of sea animals contained in ocean, lake, river and other flow water. Likewise salt water will leave salt crystals.

To attune your mind to the mineral, play some soft, gentle music, or perhaps a recording of Whale song, Dolphins at play, rain, or a cat purring. Then place the crystal at eye level beside a lit candle and focus on the flame. This will have the effect of anaesthetizing the optic nerve, thus cutting out distractions, which is what happens in crystal gazing. With half-shut eyes watch the light expand and let the glow illuminate the far edges of the room. Inhale deeply; exhale slowly, deliberately breathing onto the crystal.

Now transmit yourself in imagination to some particularly well-loved setting and think of yourself lingering there. Almost at once, your own vibratory rate will begin to adjust itself to the crystal's and your higher channels will clear. Slowly rise and take your crystal to a peaceful, light place, indoors or outdoors, and, without the candle, concentrate on the stone until its body-light expands. Let its energy field fuzz the air around you while you breathe in the crystal's vibrations. Your own energy will blend with the crystal's as you breathe out. Your melody has been created.

Carry your crystal with you, constantly fondle it and, when you are alone, at any time of the day or night, imagine your body, your mind and the crystal in perfect harmony. After a bad experience or a disturbing day, clear your stone with mineral water and let it dry as already described. If need be, light the candle and start the process again from scratch.

People who are drawn to your energy, and remember that it will be amplified when you are carrying your crystal, will get excited and suddenly touch your crystal if you are wearing it or they may ask to touch your crystal. Don't panic because you can easily give it a quick clearing. Stay calm, smile and let them touch your crystal, they obviously need healing.

After the touch, smile straight at the person, blow on your crystal, rub it in both your hands, hold it for about a minute, then let it hang free if you are wearing it or put it back in its resting place. Continue with your conversation.

Your warming actions changed the rate of the crystal's vibrations at least twice which cleared it. Then you let it return to its natural pace in tune with you.

You will find your crystal will bring peace, acting on your mind like a memory chip in a computer.

From then on, for those who find themselves gifted with this faculty, the healing of others will be an easy step. Only remember that, although each variety of gemstone has its own individual vibrations, and thus its own potential for energy and power, it cannot transmit and amplify these forces until stimulated either through heat or manipulation and will sleep if placed under room temperature.

Absent Healing
Amplification of the crystal's energy is the key to healing through this medium, in which a mental image of the recipient is evoked, wrapped round with the crystal's light. More often than not, when this is done, the truly affected areas, which may be quite different from those in which the pain occurs, will reveal themselves in patches or bursts of

muddy or angry colours, marring the even light that constitutes what is known as the aura. The latter, a sort of rainbow of colours mainly around the head, may be a genuinely multi-coloured phenomenon but usually reveals itself by a predominance of two or three. Distinct, strong tints and clarity are all important in the healthy aura. If these colours are broken, muddy or faded, the practitioner mends them by feeding the energy of another gem with the mind's eye. Stones of the Zircon family, with their fine display of light and colour range, are generally the best for this purpose, but as Zircons may be expensive or hard to obtain, the solution may well be a visit to one's local museum.

There the tyro healer can study selected minerals not more than four or five at one sitting and having visualized them thoroughly, will return home, bring out his/her Rock Crystal and allow the image of the stone or stones studied in the museum to work through it to the recipient. If, however, the gem itself can be acquired, place the Zircon next to the Rock Crystal or in the palm of the hand and concentrate fully on the afflicted aura, to send it healing and strength. Hold the aura as steady as possible in the mind's eye for a few seconds and then bathe it mentally with the light from the Rock Crystal. Finally stabilize the aura in the same mental fashion with Labradorite.

All vegetable and animal matter constantly radiates trillions of fine, hair like, sky-blue arrows the physical manifestation and gauge of the life force which hug the body and flow freely at an even and constant strength when the subject is well, but when continuance of life is in question or the subject is notably weak, the arrows become erratic or sparse. Working with the same Rock Crystal, clear (white) Topaz or Aquamarine, the healer will attempt to coax the emanations back into their proper form. If the subject responds, gently nourish with Rhodonite or Rhodocrosite, in the manner described above. These stones carry the power of unconditional love. Use Rhodonite for the mature Individual, Rhodocrosite for the young. For plants and animals, follow the described procedure with a mental bath of Dioptase.

Though the techniques described above can be used with the client present, they are applicable most of all to the branch of the art known as absent healing, when the subject may be anywhere in another room, another country or another continent, and most probably will not know that healing is taking place. Because of the esoteric quality of such healing, this is in fact the best way. But whether the recipient is present or absent, his first need will be for peace. This means that the healer must himself be relaxed and tranquil, able to make full use of his gems with their properties and health giving powers.

Earlier in this chapter the vibrations of minerals were spoken of. Very few of us, left to ourselves, are sensitive enough to feel them, but here is a method of learning how to do so which requires no more than a little patience.

Begin with a nest of Amethyst crystals. First rub your palms together, place your outstretched hands just above the stones. Hold them there for a few seconds. If you don't feel a sensation of buoyant coolness try again, and you soon will. This exercise was demonstrated to many "doubting Thomases" in the rock department of Harrods store in Knightsbridge, London. Their changes of expression from disbelief to the wonder and joy of achievement were memorable to behold.

Gem Elixirs
Now here's a subject which, in this author's opinion, should not be entered lightly. The only gemstones and crystals which can be seeped in clean water to concoct health-safe gem elixirs are highly polished, non-porous varieties because a porous mineral such as sulphur could do damage to a person or animal who is allergic to sulphur. This may also apply to minerals containing copper, aluminium, zinc, lead, mercury, nickel arsenic and others. Beware. For this reason instructions on making Gem Elixirs are not included in this book – The Healing Power of Crystals.

Chakras, Energy Points and the Physical
The concept of Chakra originates in Hindu texts, the word deriving from the Sanskrit for "turning wheel" or just "wheel".

In Indian traditional medicine, and typically, Chakras are thought of and seen by some as round or flower-like vortexes of rotating energy on the surface of the subtle body of all living beings in the animal kingdom.

If we are well these force centres, which are focal points for both transmission and reception of giving and receiving energies, are believed to have an ever-increasing fan-like shape.

There are minor and major Chakras, the major situated in channels running either side of the spine and while Indian medicine tells us there are seven major Chakras it also indicates the importance of two minor Chakras which must be also be kept spinning and transmitting.

The first, known as "the wishing tree" is located just below the heart at the solar plexus. The wishing tree has the ability to absorb energy from the sun and to determine our destiny. The second is located at our belly button and it governs life-force and the will to live.

It is obvious there are energy points all over our bodies from the tip of our heads to the toes. Those trained in Chinese acupuncture treat these many energy points as does a well-schooled masseur.

In the west we have lost the way a little and treat seven Chakras only so we are obviously missing out. Chakras and Energy Centres are thought to be different, but as the line is subtle we know that treating one is as good as treating the other.

Energy through Colour

Finally, there are three other factors in healing by stones which deserve special consideration. The first is colour and its importance as a source of power. It is no doubt stating the obvious to say that colour is one of the great pleasures of life. It dazzles us in the paintings of a Gainsborough or a Van Gogh. We respond with emotion to the spectacle of a beautiful sunset. These things bring excitement to our senses and refreshment to our souls. Have we ever realized that they also restore our bodies? Imagine how much more power colour has if it exudes from a mineral.

The nine "Chakras" are closely associated with the principal energy centres in the body and they work through colour. Each responds to a particular set of colour vibrations which it transmits to the area of the body beneath its control, either directly or through other, minor energy points. In this way they perform their principal role which is to procure for each one of us physical, psychological and spiritual help.

Each energy point can operate more effectively if matched with an appropriate stone. It will also do best on the day of the week traditionally associated with its dominant colour, also authenticated by ancient esoteric lore which has been set through trial and error. The following charts show these correspondences at a glance. On the appropriate day in each week focus the mind on the appropriate colour and stone (where there is more than one stone, exercise your preference), concentrating your thought on the area of the body controlled by the energy point for approximately five minutes. If you feel your body particularly drained, this exercise can be conducted more often than once a week that is, on days not primarily linked with the energy point in question. Here, as in all other aspects of holistic practice, success will come through experience.

Chakras and Stones
Nine Major Energy Centres

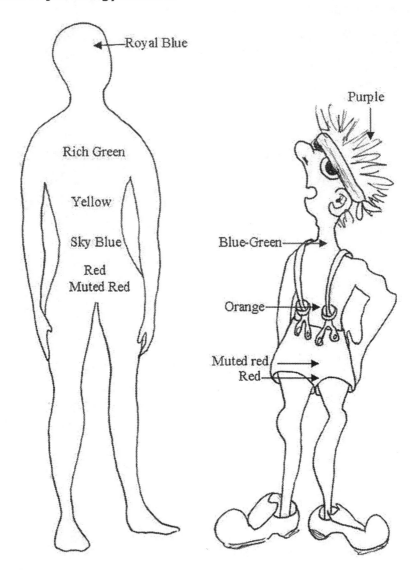

Royal Blue

Rich Green

Yellow

Sky Blue

Red
Muted Red

Purple

Blue-Green

Orange

Muted red
Red

Energy Centres are the same for men, women and our planetary creatures with the exception of the Creative Core which is positioned above the Base of Spine on the female and below the Base of Spine on the male.

Gemstones listed in the following table for chakra/day balance are relatively easy to obtain, particularly as one only needs a small specimen to energize the intended Chakra. Never use Moonstone on the spleen.

Energy Point	Day	Colour	Mineral
Heart, emotions affinity—air	Monday	rich green	Dioptase Malachite
Creative Core, art, creative development, affinity—water	Tuesday	red orange-red	Red Amber Red Spinel Red Zircon Red Diamond
Base of Spine, physical energy affinity—earth	Tuesday	muted red	Jasper Bloodstone Red Garnet
Crown, spirituality learning affinity—ether	Wednesday	purple pink-violet	Amethyst Charoite Stichtite Kunzite
Throat, speech communication affinity— ether & air	Thursday	blue-green	Chrysoprase Turquoise Chrysocolla Eilat
Solar Plexus, abdominal nervous system affinity— Air & fire	Friday	yellow	Citrine Heliodore
Brow, higher wisdom affinity—ether	Saturday	indigo royal- blue	Lapis, Azurite, Ceylonese Sapphire Tanzanite
Spleen, mirth, malice & melancholy affinity—fire	Sunday	orange	Fire Opal Orange Topaz Orange Citrine
Gut, deep physical power affinity— air, fire, earth and water	daily	white sky-blue electric-Blue	all clear gemstones Blue Topaz Aquamarine Blue Zircon Blue Spinel

Glands, Organs

Many believe there is a definite link between our Energy Points (Chakras) and the glands and organs of our body.

Put simply, to focus on chakra strengthening is to keep our glands and organs in good health.

Use the same minerals corresponding to colours as listed/suggested on the previous chart.

Correlation of Energy Points, Glands and Organs

Energy Points	Glands	Organs
Base of Spine muted red	adrenal	kidneys spinal column
Creative Core red	gonads	reproductive system
Solar Plexus yellow	pancreas	stomach gall bladder nervous system
Heart rich green	thymus	heart circulation vagus nerve
Throat blue-green	thyroid	lungs & bronchi vocal chords alimentary canal
Brow indigo & royal blue	pineal	lower brain nervous system ears & nose left eye
Crown purple	pituitary	upper brain right eye

Adrenal is located at the top of each kidney;

Alimentary Canal correlates to the system of nutrition, the passage through which food passes from mouth to anus;

Gonads...sexual gland related to the testacies or ovary;

Pancreas...gland near stomach discharging a digestive secretion;

Pineal...located at the base of the brain and attached to the mid-brain. It responds to light and is regarded by Biologists as an evolutionary relic of an eye which still exists in certain lizards at the top of the head. Its external projection is usually regarded as located in the middle of the forehead. Medically it is not connected to sight but depends on light to produce the hormone Melatonin which in the long run regulates sleeping patterns and is a regulator of thought. The Pineal is believed by many astute scholars as the point of contact between mind and matter and the pint of enlightened sight;

Pituitary...located at the base of the brain, above the roof of the mouth and behind the bridge of the nose. Medically it is the master gland of the body; esoterically it provides spiritual energy for the whole organism.

Thorax...cavity containing heart, lungs and bronchi;

Thymus...a gland-like structure in the upper thorax and neck, responsible for the formation of white blood cells which produce immune bodies to overcome and protect against infection;

Thyroid...situated in front of the trachea;

Vagus Nerve...the tenth cranial nerve which provides a secretion to involuntary muscles and the organs in the thorax and abdomen.

Polarity Therapy

Polarity Therapy believed to have been developed by Dr. Randolph Stone (1890-1981) is based on the balance of Yin/Yang and the flow of Chi through the body. You can administer yourself by understanding the connection between major energy points and the five ancient traditional elements.

Use suggested gemstones and colours suggested in the Energy Point Chart.

Polarity Chart

Energy Point	Seat	Correlation	Colour
Crown	spirituality	ether	purple
Brow	higher wisdom	ether	royal-blue
Throat	personality sound speech	ether air	blue-green
Heart	emotions	air	Rich-green
Solar Plexus	abdominal nervous system	air fire	yellow
Spleen	mirth melancholy malice	fire	orange
Gut	deep physical power & catalyst to all other energy points	earth fire air water	sky-blue electric-blue white
Creative Core	sexual energy artistic development creativity	earth water	red
Base of Spine	physical energy alignment	water	muted red

Ether is the prime element which promotes joy. Although Ether works with all other elements its strongest bond is with Air. Ether is essential to our connectedness to spirit, and general wellbeing. In the body, ether is balance and self-expression which if out of balance or weak, may be expressed in breathing difficulties and joint pain, grief and loneliness.

Air is movement, new beginnings and birth. Air's compass direction is east and its season is spring, Air imbalanced can result in nervous exhaustion, panic attacks, headaches, bronchitis, heart problems and neuralgia. Balanced air promotes unconditional love, devotion, and compassion.

Fire is transformative and is associated with willpower and creative force. Fire's compass direction is south and its season is summer. Too much fire results in a anger, bullying, resentment, stress and burn-out but when balanced, Fire encourages forgiveness and enthusiasm.

Water is the essence of malleability, metal health, the law of supply and personal communications. West is the compass direction of Water and its season is autumn. Imbalance of water shows in greed and over-indulgence, problems with bodily fluids and back pain, while balanced water encourages growth in business and emotional stability.

Earth is passive, stabilizing and nurturing. Earth is the great provider and is associated with material needs. The direction of Earth in space is north and her season is winter when many animals are in hibernation and new life is growing in the womb. When Earth is balanced we exude courage and contentment but when Earth is out of balance we suffer inflexibility in joints, the neck and develop weak bones. Earth is strongly associated with our intake of food meaning we cannot possibly consider ourselves in balance with Earth's nurturing qualities if we have anything to do with harming other living things.

Care and Cleaning

Like all other precious and beautiful objects not to mention people and our creatures, stones deserve to be treated with loving care. Recall first their origins in the dark bowels of the earth, and their subsequent sojourn, often lasting many centuries, nearer the surface but in regions often cold and damp. Therefore, handle them as this background suggests. Keep them in a dust proof case and, except for the rarest intervals, protected from all strong light. What are spoken of here particularly are minerals in their natural state. Gemstones which have been cut and polished are obviously toughened up for handling and display. They too are delicate, as will be shown in a moment. But uncut stones remain as vulnerable and sensitive as at the moment when they were retrieved from the earth. Treat them with no less gentleness and respect than you would a fine and aged sheet of rice paper!

Now to cleaning itself. If a stone is very dirty, with for instance mud or hard soil to be removed (a state an uncut stone may very well be in when you first acquire it), begin by soaking it in cold water to soften the dirt, which can then be removed with the aid of a "shaggy dog" tooth-brush. Be careful never to chip, scrape or pick at the stone, which could easily suffer damage. If, instead of dirt, there are foreign minerals adhering, take the stone to a museum, a lapidary club or lapidary shop and ask an expert to remove them. But think carefully about this step because the adhering material may be adding extra strength or mystery to the parent stone. The cleaning of stones is more complex than might be thought, and it is surprising that few books dealing with minerals bother to mention it. For instance, it is wrong to suppose, though very natural to do so, that all minerals and crystal nests can be washed under running water. On the contrary, this can cause some to disintegrate. Members of the gypsum family (for example, the Desert Rose) take particularly unkindly to water. This is hardly surprising since they are among the main constituents of plaster of Paris, fertilizers, and cement. The same applies to the calcite family, the basic compound of chalk and limestone.

Other minerals on the danger list include Apophyllite, Sulphur, Halite, Natrolite, Adamite and Auriochalcite, together with all powdery crystals such as often occur in Azurite, Chalcopyrite, Bornite and Citrine, the last mentioned being, almost invariably, Amethyst reheated by man. If these minerals are dusty, it is best to blow on them, stand them close to an electric fan, or place them in a safe spot which is also exposed to the wind. Alternatively, brush them with a small paintbrush of the finest quality or with a camera lens brush with a puffer bulb. Do not put them in the Sun.

The majority of large crystals such as Tourmaline, Aquamarine, Rock Crystal and other quartz varieties can be cleaned under cool, running water, rinsed by rainfall, or even washed in luke-warm water containing a drop of cloudy ammonia. Be sure to rinse afterwards as the film from the chemicals will not only detract from the lustre of the stone but also attract negativity or other energy. After bathing let the stone dry in a shady spot in the open air, or inside on a clean sheet of paper. A towel leaves unwanted fibre particles.

And with some stones and gemstones particularly Malachite, Azurite, Chrysocolla, Fluorite, Pearls, Amber and Jet avoid detergents and ammonia altogether.

Turning now to gems of the cut and ornamental variety, here is some guidance on the treatment of particular stones.

Solid Opal, when not in use, and particularly if stored in an air-conditioned room, a bank vault, or a velvet-lined box, should be placed in an unsealed plastic bag with a drop of water. A solid Opal should be immersed in cold water about once a month, and should never be worn while sun-bathing, swimming, washing up or cooking. If this has inadvertently happened, replenish its thirsty structure with an immediate drink. Opal doublets and triplets must be left severely alone, for if touched by even a drop of water, or accidentally exposed to heat, they may turn white, lift from their backing, or separate from their crystal or plastic dome.

Amber and Jet both take a high polish, are easily scratched, matt on contact with body acids and perfumes, and have low melting points. On account of their fragile characters both will disintegrate and eventually crack on exposure to air. To halt this process, even if they are not being worn, polish them regularly with a soft cloth and a whiff of beeswax or simply polish with a soft cloth. Do not let other jewellery touch them — their softness will cause them to rub. Store them in darkness and wrapped in a soft cloth. When fashioned as beads thread them on silk or cotton as metal will certainly damage them beyond repair.

Turquoise can be rubbed with a soft cloth but must be kept away from heat or it will fuse. Swift discolouration occurs through contact with body oil and cream. Body acids, body

Turquoise can be rubbed with a soft cloth but must be kept away from heat or it will fuse. Swift discolouration occurs through contact with body oil and cream. Body acids, body lotions, creams and perfumes cause discolouration too, so wear Turquoise on the outside of a garment whenever possible. If worn on the skin rinse in warm water with a couple of drops of Ammonia to remove body oils.

Tanzanite, Fluorite and Dioptase jewellery must be protected with high settings.

Hematite, sadly, will lose its sheen after about six months' solid wear; there is nothing to be done about this. Jade and Jadeite are tough, but can break if knocked.

Pearls are a difficult gemstone to advise on, as there are so many grades. Generally a light shampoo will not hurt them, but they should not be subjected to ready-made jewellery dips, lemon juice or any acid.

Mother of Pearl and Coral should be cleaned in the same way as pearls, shells, ivory, and all seed jewellery.

Diamonds can be soaked in jewellery dips and cleaned with a "shaggy dog" toothbrush and a little ammonia. Jewellers often clean Diamonds by ultrasonic water heating (that is, heating through the operation of high frequency sound waves). This is a dangerous practice, as the smallest flaw in a crystal can lead to a split stone. For the same reason Emeralds, which have natural striations of colour in the very best, and countless flaws and inclusions in most, can be destroyed by this method. Instead, clean Emeralds with luke warm water laced with a sniff of shampoo, and rinse afterwards.

Rubies, Sapphires, Topaz, Spinels and Zircons are other precious stones which should not be tortured by ultrasonic as they often lose colour. A good soak in shampoo and water softener is a much better idea.

That famous rock, Lapis Lazuli, seems to stay clean all by itself, but if thoughtlessly handled will need a professional polish every now and then.

The care and cleaning of minerals and crystals is an enormous subject, which a lifetime's study would hardly be sufficient to master, but the key to it all is tenderness and respect. No owner or wearer, even the veriest novice, who cultivates that spirit is likely to go far wrong.

Esoteric Cleansing

This can be considered as complementary to practical care, and many weird and wonderful rituals have become attached to it over the centuries. Here is one authentic method.

Sit cross legged with the back of the hands resting on the thighs in the pyramid position and your stone placed at forehead level. In imagination surround the stone with light and transport it to the edge of a sandy shore to be lapped by the incoming tide. This vision need only be held for a few minutes, as the ocean is a natural disinfectant, and powerfully remedial. Your stone is now regaining harmony from the silicon rich sand, silicon being the most prolific element on earth and the one all minerals and crystals are attuned to.

Still in imagination, take your stone to a mountain stream and dunk it. Finally, dry it by a fire spiced with frankincense an aromatic resin obtained from African and Asian trees.

After this imaginary, meditative operation, physically rinse your stone in mineral water the bottled kind will do — and let it dry naturally in a shady spot. Cleansed, as it should now be, both physically and spiritually, it is a perfect medium for the esoteric healing act.

Meditation

The wartime Resistance heroine Odette Hallowes, awarded the MBE in 1945, The George Cross in 1946, and the Legion d'Honneur in 1950, found relief from excruciating pain at the hands of her tormentors by means of a technique little considered today by the majority of people of a practical turn of mind: the technique of meditation. It is said her salvation was to concentrate on the ever changing coloured light thrown off by an opal ring which had by luck or perhaps by providence been left on her finger, thus utilizing a means of mental escape from unbearable physical suffering similar to that which other torture victims have been known to employ. Is it coincidental that the Opal in ancient times was reputed to be "The Stone of Justice" and "The Rainbow Bridge between Heaven and Earth"?

Meditation, that key to transcendence of worldly cares, can avail itself of many aids, including crystals and stones. Here is a lovely technique which a friend of mine learned from a female Shaman of a North American tribe.

To practice it you will need a blanket, a largish feather (my friend used a brightly coloured macaw feather), four incense sticks , a Rock Crystal measuring at least four inches in length, a smaller crystal or ornamental stone of whatever sort you care to choose, and a quiet, semi darkened space in which to work.

Always buy very good quality incense sticks or cones or if preferred use essential oil burners, again the quality of the oil is important. Beware of candle quality the best being those made of soy. Buddhist temples throughout the world favour Nag Champs which is a blend of natural ingredients, resin, herbs and masala; other choices are Sage, Lavender, Frankincense and Myrrh.

To begin, having decided on your meditational theme, lodge it firmly in your mind and write it on four separate pieces of paper. Place these individually with the four lit incense sticks or essential oil burners in north, south, east and west positions round you. Spread the blanket on the floor and briskly flick the feather around as a means of banishing any patches of negativity. If at this stage you find the scent of the incense or oil too heady, it may be extinguished. To cleanse crystal or any other ritual tools pass through the incense smoke or hold over oil burners several times.

Seated cross legged on the blanket, rest the backs of your hands on your legs, cradle the large crystal in your right palm and the smaller stone in your left. This attitude is known as the "power-house" position, and forms a triangle, echoing the shape of the pyramids. Now breathe regularly and deeply, completely exhaling your breath each time. Close or half close, your eyes, and imagine your body in its present pose surrounded by light. Coax the light until its fullness touches the paper placed near the incense. See the subject from all angles, let it fill your being, understand why it is there, what you must do about it, and who you should pass it onto if anyone. Sometimes, when subjected to this close and unblinking scrutiny, the subject is seen to lack merit. In that case, discard it.

Should placing the subject on paper, or fixing it in your mind, prove too difficult a task, try an alternative method. After you have positioned your body in the power house pose and surrounded yourself with light, imagine a wheel containing seven segments of colour. These are the colours of the rainbow red, orange, yellow, green, blue, indigo and violet. Whirl the wheel. When the motion stops, you will see your subject in one of the segments. Then, as in the first exercise, dwell upon it, observe it with great care, and, if appropriate, apply to it the powers of healing. And, as before, think of how to transfer it for the benefit of others.

When the time has arrived to conclude the meditation, never cut it off suddenly, for as the mind has been working the physical senses have been put to sleep. Wake them gently while still holding the power-house pose. Fade out the image until you see only colour or light. Once again breathe deeply and return the body to life by wriggling your toes, fingers, head, limbs and trunk. Ease yourself to your feet and sign off with a long, cool drink of water, preferably energized by the presence in the glass of Fluorite, a stone which brings oxygen to the bloodstream.

As a luxurious extra, and if you have the time and inclination, lie flat on the floor covered by your meditational blanket and allow yourself to fall asleep. On waking you will feel strong, relaxed and happy. Often you will find that problems you had not even meditated about will have been solved too!

Meditation can be practiced during the daytime or at night, each with a different purpose. Night meditation is generally practiced with the aim of opening the higher channels of the mind, whereas day meditation is for physical energy, nourishment of the body and spirit, and healing. The best of both worlds can be obtained, in a manner of speaking, by meditation at sunrise. No need to stay up alone to indulge in this. Better still is to do it with friends. Before you launch into this euphoric adventure, take a glass of water which has stood in the night air. If you fancy an elixir let freshly cleansed Aquamarine, the life force stone, be placed in the glass. Choose as your vantage-point a hill, a cliff, or some other spot with a view of the eastern horizon, and find a place where you will be comfortable. Bare your feet and your head and arrange your crystals beside you. Position your body in the pyramid shaped power house attitude and be absolutely sure that your palms are exposed to the first streamers of light which herald the Sun and illuminate the sky. You will benefit from the positive ions showered on Earth — magnesium, aluminium, iron and zinc, among others.

From here on all is easy as you are on automatic pilot. Go ahead and enjoy the atmospheric effects of sunrise. Meditate and know that this is an opportune moment for administering healing to others.

Twilight meditation can be equally therapeutic, especially after watching a sunset. The only preparation I personally make for this exercise is to wear a cotton headband containing a Rock Crystal and a sliver of Azurite or a small piece of Lapis. One could equally well wear a crystal pendant or necklace and carry the Azurite or Lapis. Together these minerals assemble suitable ions for this period between night and day when the Sun's centre is below the horizon and the passive side of nature prepares to dominate the active.

Before meditating, there are basic rules that should be followed. Because of negative vibrations picked up from oneself and others, it is wise to start with a bath or shower, and since during meditation body temperature sometimes drops a little, make sure to be warm and comfortable. Never attempt meditation on a full stomach or after consuming alcohol, and certainly not in a crowded room or within earshot of an argument or a party.

Beyond that, there are no rules. Meditation is always therapeutic, with or without stones. Moses used it on the mountain, before receiving the Ten Commandments, and the greatest sages have resorted to it. One thing is certain: the Crystal Healer or any other healer for that matter will do no good without a spirit of calmness and recollection, which is what meditation, when properly practiced, ensures.

Alphabetical list of Healing Stones

Alexandrite

Here is a stone of stunning optical properties. Always a colour-change gemstone at its best by day, its colour is an intense grass-green and by artificial light Alexandrite undergoes a transformation into a soft columbine-red or a gentle raspberry-pink. Since green is the colour of new growth and pink the shade of impartial love, the Russian name for Alexandrite, "Stone of Good Omen", could not be more apt.

The Alexandrite has a positive electrical charge which stays for hours after rubbing and an energy factor which changes with its colour. But potent though this stone looks, it radiates sensitivity. In physical healing it bypasses the actual ailment and goes straight to the root of the problem, acting on the head and spine areas, effectively rebalancing the dry, the moist, the hot and the cold in their correct proportions. Worn by day and night, its beneficial properties soon show. The head feels roomier, the memory improves, and eyesight is clearer and the neck muscles are relieved of tension.

The Alexandrite is expensive because it is rare. A variety of chrysoberyl, it was discovered as recently as 1831, so compared to most gems its history is short. Though tests to establish its efficacy in natural medicine will certainly continue, it has already proved its worth. It transmits inner peace by developing magnanimity of heart and should be valued and used extensively.

Amber

This time hardened resin is associated with healing powers galore and rightly so. Retsina, the pine cured, resinated Greek wine, soothes irritated throats as well as raising depressed spirits, while nature's way with wounded vegetation is to heal a plant's cuts with its own secretion of resin. Ancient ointments (not to be copied) consisting of powdered Amber mixed with various combinations of oil were similarly applied to human wounds, but this stone's real power lies in the curing of chest complaints such as asthma, bronchitis, coughs, raw throats, headaches caused through chest and throat inflammation, and toothache.

Certain modern healers are reverting to the old custom of mixing powdered Amber with honey as an internal medicament. Beware of this! It is no more than a money making racket and can be dangerous to those who take it. Certainly swallow no such mixture except on the advice of an orthodox medical practitioner. Amber heals perfectly well from the outside and this is how it should be used.

For healing purposes, wear it between the levels of chest and ears or, if you prefer to carry it that is, to use it as a touchstone place it in a top pocket or in a silk sack on a loose string round the neck. Do not cover the throat chakra with Amber as it has the wrong vibrations for this area. Similarly do not wear a large piece of Amber for too long a period. Amber is inclined to keep the wearer's energy circulating inwardly instead of allowing it to flow out, thus stunting its owner's physical strength.

Properly used, Amber brings benefits on every level. For meditational purposes it is best to use only the clear fluorescent type found in the Dominican Republic and Sicily. Most other Amber works on the physical level (only) although Opaque varieties are gentler in character and promote understanding towards others, probably because they contain trillions of sub microscopic air bubbles and possibly droplets of water and/or calcite. Many actors and actresses wear Amber and Amethyst in combination jewellery on stage. They are convinced these stones help their performances.

Pressed Amber, which is a mass of small pieces welded together under gentle heat, has almost the same essence as the natural form. The same is generally true of what are known as "inclusion" pieces that is, Amber inset with small insects, bird feathers, pine needles, flowers and anything else the once sticky substance embalmed. However, not long ago, a specimen entombing a large lizard was found. When tested for healing purposes it emitted a hefty, negative energy!

Amethyst
This stone, always esteemed, should be accounted especially precious in the hectic world of today, for it heals during cat-naps, induces meditation, and is thus invaluable for healing and comforting those suffering from stress or from psychosomatic illness. Even cancer, as many researchers now recognize, can be precipitated by mental strain, and the Amethyst, coloured red by irradiated iron, contains the very element with which orthodox practitioners fight the disease. Iron is one of the six active body minerals essential for life. It strengthens the muscles, enriches the blood and increases resistance to infection, so here too the Amethyst has an invaluable part to play.

It is anciently believed to be the stone of piety and keeps its wearers from falling into the sin of drunkenness. Bishops' rings are traditionally mounted with Amethyst and that holy monarch, Edward the Confessor, had an Amethyst ring stone. Still in the royal collection, it was once renowned as a charm against contagious diseases.

There was an ancient belief that the Amethyst changed colour when placed near poisoned food. This almost certainly stemmed from the fact that it shows colour variations in its single crystals. It is attuned to the higher sensitivity of the crown energy point which inspires second sight especially if coupled with lapis lazuli.

Used in combination with a Bloodstone, the Amethyst was once strapped over the area of a blood clot and after a fortnight or so the obstruction was often reported clear.

Sometimes the result is permanent; sometimes the subject will need to repeat the treatment periodically and an orthodox medic must be consulted.

Worn with Carnelian, Amethyst restrains the overactive and also the bossy at home, at work or in public life. Did we begin by saying that this was truly a stone for today!

Aquamarine
Every energy has its colour and the colour of our body's life force is sky-blue. This is the colour of the Earth as seen from space and the tint reflected in the blue of the Aquamarine.

When assessing a person's health many crystal practitioners work through an Aquamarine to gaze at the surrounding life force, which manifests itself to those sensitive enough to see them in trillions of fine, hair like blue arrows. If this radiating energy is steady and of constant strength throughout its flow (that is, not patchy), then all is well. If however it is seen to thin out here and there, the indications are that physical strength is on the wane. In this case healing should be applied to the inner centres through the throat chakra, using the Aquamarine as a stabilizer. When the blue arrows strengthen, the subject begins to recover. If the life force insists on leaving the body, which means that the person is dying, the Aquamarine can hold it for a little time until the departing person is prepared. But the healer must act with care. If the life force is held in for too long, the dying person will suffer.

Aquamarine once bore the title "All Life". The Romans valued its natural six sided form, so wore Aquamarine earrings, a favoured decoration, with their crystals uncut, not understanding that a stone can be cut or even powdered and still retain its original properties, the stone's internal "building blocks" of atoms and molecules being as much present then as before. Aquamarine is a gem that must be listened to, not "ordered about". Its powers will depend on its owner's receptiveness and it will work on the level that he or she is able to attain.

Apart from the virtues attributed to it in the past, modern practitioners find this blue wonder stone improves eyesight, calms eye itch, is an effective balm for swollen feet and a fine soother of jangled emotions and nerves. Its essence being liquid, it refines the faculties of the intuitive mind and removes discordant vibrations.

Aventurine
With its soft energy and slightly iridescent, metallic beauty, this stone was put to beautiful use by the Russian craftsman and designer Carl Fabergé (1846-1920) and also by the Chinese. Its less practical applications, like those of the Carnelian, have, however, lately been overlooked.

Aventurine can be brownish in colour, when it belongs with the feldspar family and is called the Sunstone; or yellow-brown or greenish-yellow, in which case it is known as Aventurine Quartz. Both varieties act as a general tonic on the physical level, with special application to the central nervous system.

On a higher level this is a stone for meditation, and for encouraging malleability of mind.

Azurite
Azurite can open the floodgates of cosmic truth and reveal to its wearers the essential purposes of their life. As such, it is a stone for highly evolved souls. People find it an aid to their psychic development but will also discover that its effects last a limited time because slowly but inexorably this royal to midnight blue stone changes into another mineral, the bright green Malachite.

During its working life as an Azurite, however, it frees channels along which its wearers might fear to tread. In particular it can complete the opening of the "third eye", the faculty which enables its owner to see and feel the approach of good and evil happenings. In the same way it can be used to transfer the energy of positive and negative vibrations from its manipulator to another person.

Little is known of the Azurite's powers on the level of physical healing, but its hallmark is harmony and encouragement of the qualities of sympathy and tenderness in all their forms. Thus it can assist when a person's ailment is caused through disappointment, aggression or hate.

Azurite operates almost entirely on the spiritual level alone.

Bloodstone

Holding mightier than Mars energy but still relating to that planet, the Bloodstone, with its traces of Plutonian influence, can weigh too heavily on the mind. For that reason, in healing it should always be used in combination with Rock Crystal and Rose Quartz, which will alleviate its oppressive effects.

Containing iron impurities, this stone works with the blood-stream against cramp and light headedness. Its corrective properties also enable it to break down deep-rooted diseases and counteract over-indulgence, aggression, obsession and violence.

More cheerfully, in its lighter aspects, the Bloodstone encourages a sunny disposition as it sweeps dross from the chakras.

Blue John

There is a strange belief, many centuries old, that the spirits of certain children unhappily aborted, often in the ordinary way of nature, roam about the world in desperation and confusion seeking an earth mother from whom they can take nourishment. The mother, when found, mysteriously loses strength and in recent years some astonishing esoteric cures have been accomplished through the medium of the banded fluorite known as Blue John with which crystal practitioners have treated the "mother's" blood before it reaches the spirit child. Once this is done the child is "born" and both woman and infant can be freed by an esoteric severing of the spiritual natal cord.

There is a scientific reason for the efficacy of the stone in that fluoride in the laboratory can be heated with acid to give off bubbles of acid gas. The stone can be similarly stimulated by the crystal practitioner. But while Blue John is doing its work, other stones will be needed as well: Aquamarine for life force; Magnetite for polarization (that is, for aligning the spine to the magnetic forces of Earth); and Dioptase to strengthen the heart. These are for the "mother". The child spirit, now released, must also be treated as the practitioner thinks fit. No other fluorite works with such success as Blue John in restoring women from the effects of mysterious weakness. Doubtless this is because of the Blue John's concentric purple-blue banding, which is now thought to be caused by radiation from uranium.

Blue John also brings relief to mediums and other sensitives who are overworked and giving too much of themselves. If you live in the country, or any unpolluted area, a chunk or small nodule of Blue John in a bowl of tap water can also be left outside the house, in the fresh, cleansing air, overnight. It provides an excellent pick-me-up in the morning or any time if kept in the fridge.

Bowenite

Often called "The Gentle New Jade" or "Korean Jade", this stone is an unusual, transparent to translucent, hard variety of serpentine. It is usually tinted pale sea-green touched with yellow, though the New Zealand variety is a magnificent deep greenish-blue. But whatever its colour this stone is invaluable because of its content of magnesium. It is established that the human body should contain twenty one grammes of this mineral. If its magnesium count falls below that figure, depression and insomnia set in and Bowenite helps to cure both. It also relieves indigestion and acts as a general antiseptic.

By itself an important throat chakra stone, when worn with Chrysoprase, Bowenite has the additional virtue of enhancing spiritual vision and sharpening the wearer's perceptions.

Carnelian

Once a stone in King Solomon's breastplate, this now unjustly overlooked gem clears the mind for deep concentration and, when coupled with Amethyst, purifies the consciousness, reverses negative attitudes and develops higher mental awareness. In meditation it induces a better understanding of the true meaning of life and thus offers a key to wisdom.

As both the Carnelian and the Amethyst have iron as a colouring agent, they can be used in combination to benefit the blood stream, combat depression and help their owners to shake off sluggishness and become vigorous and alert.

Chalcopyrite and Bornite

These stones go together like the proverbial horse and carriage. Chalcopyrite is linked with Jupiter, Bornite with Venus. Employed in combination they can help to terminate one of the most agonizing and frustrating states of mind, that of chronic indecisiveness. Beware, however, never to use them to tamper irresponsibly with other people's lives. Both Jupiter and Venus are justice loving planets, and fiery with it. Any spiteful hanky-panky could rebound on your own head!

Chalcopyrite and Bornite are used by mediums in contacting the deceased. But here they are effective on two conditions only. First the departed must be recently dead and have been personally close to the medium; secondly the deceased should have left unfinished some action of which the completion is truly urgent.

It is important to recall that Chalcopyrite and Bornite are major ores of copper, a mineral vital to our bodies as an activating element to enable the amino acid Tyrosine to work on the pigmentation of the hair and skin. Copper also helps to convert the body's iron into the oxygen carrying pigment contained in the red blood cells. As Chalcopyrite and Bornite are not only rich in copper but also comprise a fair amount of iron, sufferers from anaemia and edema, two diseases caused by copper and iron deficiency, obviously benefit from their actions.

It is a household truism that if food is cooked or heated in copper pans, Vitamin E, Folic Acid and Vitamin C are destroyed, so strong is the mineral's action. Copper also remains in the body of a dead person long after the other minerals have disappeared, as witness the hair still found to be in good condition when caskets containing the bodies of men and women from the Tudor period were opened recently.

Both Chalcopyrite and Bornite can act with great benefit on the general running of daily life. But so powerful are their energies that after a certain amount of use they will shatter into small pieces.

Chrysocolla, Eilat
Here are two minerals not often used in physical healing but shown by recent tests to be powerfully efficacious against weakness of the bones and lack of pigmentation in hair or skin. These minerals, both copper based, likewise help the absorption of Vitamin C into the body and assist iron assimilation.

On the spiritual plane, both Chrysocolla and the Eilat Stone can ward off attacks from lower entities such as poltergeists. They are efficient ESP (extrasensory perception) agents which work by opening the throat energy point.

Ideally, tradition holds, both these closely related stones should first come into one's possession as a gift.

Chrysoprase
Here is one of nature's most contradictory stones. The colouring of the Chrysoprase, which runs from translucent emerald through apple-green to yellow-green, is due to the presence of nickel, a metallic element which contributes to many allergies. Yet Chrysoprase purges its wearers both physically and spiritually, from the lowest plane upwards. It is a case of a little poison acting as a vaccine, as with the Diamond.

Both on account of its outgoing influence, which promotes inner clarity and discipline, and of its tint, this protective and strikingly beautiful mineral is often likened to the Jadeite of Upper Burma, though Chrysoprase is the more adept of the two in deflecting negative vibrations before they reach the higher senses. As jewellery or a touchstone, this mineral is believed to help correct nervous disorders, to steady the brain before bursts of activity, to calm sufferers from convulsions and hysteria and to help eliminate anxiety. Its "watchdog" personality is worn by some to protect from over violent reactions and to filter discordant facts until balance is obtained.

The nickel tinted variety of this gem, the most sought after, comes from Australia. But here, as always, personal choice is important, and some may prefer the paler types which occur in the USA, the Urals and Brazil. A chromium green chalcedony called Mtorodite, from Zimbabwe, is also on the market. In all respects except the colouring agent this stone resembles Chrysoprase, but unlike the latter it has yet to show holistic results.

One curious characteristic of the Chrysoprase is its fidelity to its owner. On changing hands, or when an owner has died, it may show no response at all in the possession of a stranger, which is doubtless why this most personal of gems was once buried with the deceased in Iron Age Japanese graves.

Citrine
Natural Citrine was originally an Amethyst transformed by being reheated and burnt in Earth's crust. Then man took a hand, learning to "cook" this stone artificially. But whether in its natural or man-made form, the energy of this rare and highly desirable gem is so similar as to make little or no difference.

Citrine is of various colours. The very orange shade helps the spleen; yellow Citrine acts on the solar plexus; the orange brown, "madeira" variety is used in Crystal healing, where it relieves the sufferings of introverted personalities by encouraging rational and positive thought. Combined with Amethyst, it purifies the blood and clears the mind. Often it is even more helpful than Amethyst as a means to meditation. This is understandable since the violet of Amethyst and the gold of Citrine are both head colours.

Coral
Filled with negative vibrations, a legacy of Coral hunters, this ocean gemstone nevertheless does its best, and its healing properties, mainly efficacious against calcified joints and skin eruptions, have been recognized since ancient times.

Coral's astrological correspondence is with our Moon, as befits its watery genesis, and in a chart with a positive placement can have a beneficial influence on anyone born under the same ruling mass. When negatively aspected, however, it can produce arguments and depression. It will often balance a chart with an abundance of fire.

Those who find Coral an attractive stone to wear should follow tradition and respect its natural form. This means wearing it as pieces of twig or cut stems, never fashioned into beads.

Agatized Coral is a strikingly different gem, in which the original calcite has been replaced by fine grained Quartz in

the course of geological changes, yet the essentially protective character of Coral remains. Agatized Coral has a reputation of calming the nerves, aiding the digestive system and creating physical harmony of a gentle but pervasive kind.

Diamond
The purest substance in nature and one of the hardest (ten out of ten on the Mohs Scale), the Diamond can be fashioned into the neatest and sharpest of cutting edges and as such has helped to bring into existence one of the marvels of modern medicine, the art of micro-surgery.

Using a Diamond blade instead of the old fashioned stainless steel is, for a surgeon, the equivalent of switching from manual to power assisted steering in a car. It requires virtually no pressure so there is minimal scar tissue after the wound is healed, while the blade's smooth cutting track minimizes bleeding. Bruising and after pains are alike greatly reduced. Blue and Yellow Diamonds of the highest quality are both used. Best of all, however, are the first grade, clear white stones. With the addition of a fibre optic light attached to the blade's feather weight titanium handle, the surgeon gets a clear view both of and through the blade which is invaluable in deep cavity operations.

Cost unfortunately prevents these miracle blades from being adopted for general use; and cost, too, disqualifies the Diamond as an instrument of holistic healing, since few can afford the two carat stone which is the smallest needed to produce any results. An uncut Diamond of clear quality could be used, but such stones are hard to obtain, and the quality of light refracted from industrial Diamonds, which are readily available and would be acceptable in terms of price, is so poor as to render them useless.

Tradition endowed the Diamond with a wonderful range of powers, from curing lunacy to driving away the Devil. It was believed to bolster up courage and, above all, to ensure longevity. Thanks to carbon, the single element in its composition, it was also esteemed as a vaccine a tradition scientifically based. It is unrivalled in its hard surface lustre and dispersion of light (fire). When rubbed, it produces a positive electrical charge.

Last but not least, the Diamond is the modern token of love brought about by heavy advertising from those who benefit financially. But its coveted reputation as a girl's best friend should not be allowed to rest, as it usually does, entirely on the Diamond's over bloated market value. Rather this magnificent gem, through its purity and durability, offers moving proof of total perfection expressed in a single element.

Dioptase
This stone rivals the Emerald (see next entry) in the beauty of its colouring and in its holistic powers. As its nickname indicates, its metallic element is copper, a substance used by nature, in combination with iron, to prevent fatigue and promote resistance to disease. (It also converts iron into the pigment needed by the red blood cells.)

For holistic purposes, Dioptase pendants should be worn mid chest. Alternatively, a clump of unset Dioptase crystals should be held in the left hand each day for about five minutes, for the third finger of this hand is believed by many to emotionally channel directly to the heart, seat of unconditional love and all the generous instincts and source, when healthy, of all physical and mental strength.

Nor does Dioptase confine its healing powers only to humans. Sick animals, birds, and plants have been restored to health by it. Two birds which the author looked after were flooded with Dioptase light, in accordance with the esoteric technique of healing already described, for two minutes a day, then small crystals were placed in the sick bay. Soon both creatures were on the mend. The plants were similarly bathed in the gemstone's rich, green fire, and then soaked in water esoterically infused with Dioptase. The sick animal was a cat, a frightened street dweller with an appalling abscess on its forehead. It would allow no one near, so was mentally surrounded with Dioptase by two devoted pet lovers at hourly intervals for three weeks. Once again, the treatment worked. Before long, the cat was spotted scampering about, exhibiting a bald patch of perfectly healed skin where an infected hole had once gaped.

Although the brittleness of this stone disqualifies it for cutting, many a magnificent rich green pendant has been fashioned round a nest of natural Dioptase crystals. Its colour is traditionally linked with nonphysical forces and Dioptase itself sharpens the ESP faculties and promotes guidance from higher planes.

Emerald

From the unfathomable depths of this much admired stone come healing vibrations for those afflicted with eye diseases. Testimony to this power has come down to us from ancient times, for in the effigies of gods and goddesses the eyes are often of solid Emerald. Today we can still benefit.

Here are a few hints on how to utilise this gemstone for healing purpose. When working on your own eyes, simply gaze at the Emerald. If treating those of another who is actually present with you, transfer the energy. Alternatively, take a tumbler full of water and soak an Emerald in it overnight. Soak cotton wool pads in the elixir, wring them partially dry and place them over the closed eyes for about ten minutes twice a day. This treatment is good not merely for diseased eyes. Bloodshot and tired eyes benefit also. If you are unable to get hold of an Emerald, a third method may be used. That is simply to think about an Emerald, transferring the energy to the eye area and the back of the head.

This third method also produces brilliantly beneficial results when applied to the problems of the heart and middle chest. The Emerald is effective too in soothing those with nervous tensions and high blood pressure. On the mental plane it brings tranquillity and balance, hence also learning and wisdom.

Healers may find that it takes some time before they feel thoroughly at ease with this stone, so they should start by working on such comparatively minor complaints as headaches, asthma, the common cold and scalding. Later they will find the Emerald can be used to ease pain through skin ulcers, food poisoning, and skin cancer and, many believe, certain other cancers as well.

Ancient crystal practitioners used the Emerald to help relieve the pain of women in childbirth, as an antidote to poison, and for strengthening the memory. Worn by married women, it was thought to guarantee their fidelity to their husbands. Snakes were supposed to be afraid of Emeralds and these gems were also highly regarded as a talisman against evil and the plague. Most important of all was the reputation of the emerald as a link with divine forces.

Fine quality Emeralds are expensive and hard, to come by but for healing purposes this does not matter because fortunately for both healers and their clients, a "mossy Emerald", that is, one which is not quite clear, serves just as well.

Garnet

Black, pink-red, yellow-brown, orange or green you can take your pick of all these colours when choosing a Garnet, which should properly be regarded less as a single stone than as a member of a vast gemstone family. All Garnets, however, have this in common: they hold a little of most metals but are basically composed of aluminium, silicon and oxygen, and though different stones will be found to suit different subjects and healers, holistically speaking all are viable and can be classed as one.

The Garnet's healing character is that of a knight in shining armour. It will send its vibrations straight to the battle front, where other stones have made no impression, and is powerfully effective in lifting depression and strengthening the recipient's will. It is good for treating arthritis and other ailments resulting from calcification. Recently, too, it has been used to help childless couples, aided in this by its high metallic composition and working on the would-be parents both physically and emotionally.

Used in meditation, it brings a sense of relief from material burdens, giving peace and calmness of mind, but working more obviously through the logical rather than the spiritual faculties. When carried in the pocket of an overactive or restless child, or worn as a string of beads, Garnet will have the effect of channeling the youngster's energy into fewer and less frenetic areas.

Two varieties of Garnet have uses of their own: the orange coloured stone assists in strengthening the base of the spine, and the green one invigorates the heart.

Heliodore

This lemon to rich-yellow transparent crystal is about to come into its own as an incorruptible medium of spiritual illumination.

Often showing radioactivity and generally thought to be coloured by iron, both of which are emitted by the Sun, the Heliodore indeed resembles a solid chunk of golden light, and in healing radiates corresponding warmth. It consoles, rejuvenates and achieves its particular power through its ability to reconcile the conscious and the unconscious mind.

Although the Heliodore works through the solar plexus, it actually relates to the circulatory system and heart, where it operates to energize the inner self and the intellect.

Hematite

There are a number of ailments in the cure of which iron is needed and in these cases the pretty, shiny, steel grey Hematite is the answer. Used in combination with Malachite, or Dioptase, Hematite is believed to relieve inflammation of the joints, increase resistance to disease and to prevent fatigue, particularly during pregnancy. The ancients described Hematite as one of the antidotes to melancholy.

Hematite is also and often coupled with clear quartz to amplify its stabilizing energy. Worn as a bracelet or carried as tumble stones in a lower garment pocket one will reap many benefits from this gentle ore of iron because it works with the base of the spine, helping to balance the body and therefore assist clear, logical thinking. Hematite has also been reported to relieve aching limbs, hips and headaches. Yet Hematite by itself should not be worn around the neck, throat or as earrings because it is not an enlightening gemstone and these areas deserve higher energy.

Jade, Jadeite

Jade and Jadeite are two entirely distinct minerals with different holistic values, but they are frequently confused and even thought of as one and the same. For that reason it seems sensible to list them together, the better to highlight both their differences and similarities.

Like most gemstones, Jade and Jadeite both contain silicon and oxygen. In addition, however, Jade's composition includes magnesium and calcium, while Jadeite holds sodium and aluminium.

Jade is composed of a mass of fibrous, hair-like crystals, while Jadeite crystals are granular.

Containing as it does three of the minerals most needed by the body, that is calcium, iron and magnesium, Jade is a natural medicament for those with high blood pressure, and also for diabetics, those suffering from heart and circulatory problems and people with kidney complaints. It should be worn by pregnant and lactating women, whose condition causes calcium, iron and magnesium to be drained from their bodies at this time.

Jadeite, which in its emerald green variety adds a touch of chromium to its other mineral constituents, is a muscle strengthener. It also helps correct perspiratory problems, to counteract the effects of sun stroke and, like Jade, is an excellent remedy for high blood pressure.

Both Jade and Jadeite bring peace through serenity and cleanse the energy centres. The green tints of both minerals strengthen the heart chakra while the pink-violet variety of Jadeite induces devotion and favours mystical temperaments.

Jade derives its name from the Spanish word for "colic", which the Conquistadors nicknamed "jada" after the Mexicans had taught them to cure their stomach complaints by touching the affected area with this stone. The geological term for Jade is Nephrite, from the Greek word "nephro" meaning kidney, hence the English "Nephritis" meaning inflammation of the kidneys.

Those acquainted with the legend of the Golden Fleece will remember the Jade axe mentioned in the story which cured kidney complaints.

Jadeite means "like Jade", but the differences should now be clear.

Jasper

This opaque variety of orangey quartz was famous among the ancients for extracting the poison from snake bites. In early times too it was revered as the supreme rain bringer and it was also believed that it would lower the blood pressure if engraved with the likeness of a lion.

Today it has largely lost favour as a healing stone. Nevertheless it can help those beset by emotional problems, whether these are caused by feelings of guilt, the loss of loved ones or fear of the future. Its power to strengthen and console such sufferers is well proven.

Jet

This intensely black stone began its existence about one hundred and eighty million years ago when branches and trunks of enormous monkey puzzle trees then flourishing on Earth broke and fell into pools of stagnant water. The waterlogged wood then sank to the waterbed where it was covered with mineral rich mud and decaying life, which both compressed the embryonic stone and induced chemical changes.

Jet comprises 12 per cent mineral oil. It also shows traces of sulphur, aluminium and silicon, which the skin absorbs when the stone is worn. If friction is applied to the Jet it develops static electricity and, since in reality it is a sort of brown coal, it proceeds to burn, emitting a pungent smell. Sufferers from sinus blockage, the common cold and breathing difficulties are sometimes encouraged to inhale burning essence of Jet. In ancient times the stone was used against toothache, headache, epilepsy, dropsy, loose teeth and swollen feet.

At one time Jet was also invoked as a test for virginity. The stone would be steeped for three days in water or alcohol, removed and given as an elixir to the lady whose virtue was questioned. If the effect was diarrhoea, as well it might have been one may well think, the test was negative. In Spain Jet is still used to ward off the Evil Eye. It is carried in the form of a carving known as a higa, which depicts a hand with the Sun pressed between two fingers. Nowadays neglected as a stone to bring good luck, throughout the Bronze Age it was considered one of the most propitious and magical of all amulets and talismans.

Labradorite
When in trouble wear Labradorite. Carry a slice or chunk of this stone in your pocket, place it above the car's dashboard, by the kitchen sink or behind your head whilst sleeping anywhere you choose, in fact. But be sure to let light catch its iridescent colours which rival a tropical butterfly's wings.

This beautiful extension of a common field rock has an internal structure of repeated layers of microscopically small crystals lying side by side and head to heel. The pale grey, translucent variety of this stone gives better results than the dark, opaque sort. In the former case the light plays more effectively on the stacked crystals which, on account of the optical interference they suffer, produce yellows, pinks, greens, blues and violet-blues, and violet in different shades.

The composition of Labradorite includes tiny plates of iron. These are helpful in straightening the spine and bringing the vertebrae in line with the magnetic north and south poles on our planet, an effect known as polarization. When the stone is used for healing purposes, salt should be taken with food. This gem is now just starting to be recognized. It is the stone of today and of the future.

Lapis Lazuli
This gem contains specks of brassy yellow or silver coloured iron, and occasionally of gold too. In fact it is a mixture of at least five separate minerals, which makes it technically a rock and a mineraloid not a stone or a mineral.

It has a corrective energy directed towards the self which shields the wearer during the process of spiritual development and it allows its wearer to draw wisdom from natural sources. As a result the recipient's emotions are not ignored but appreciated for what they are an invaluable means of restoring body and mind.

Lapis should be used on the centre forehead, which will also help the crown chakra, either held in position under a band or worn as earrings or a short necklace.

Lapis Lazuli should not be worn for long periods at a time, not even two consecutive days, because such is its strength that it can elevate the higher senses until a receptive wearer may want nothing else but its refining energy, leaving no thought for the body which houses the spirit.

Lapis can be a fine transmitter in the hands of a practitioner channelling health to a subject.

Most sensitives, however, should cleanse with Lapis rather than use it for the purpose of direct healing until the recipient's strength and self-assurance are perceived.

So many healing virtues are attached to this rock that it is difficult to specify the most important. The ailments against which it is particularly efficacious include disorders of the blood, epilepsy, severe stomach pains, vomiting, and diarrhoea, Rickets and brain disease. Lapis is the ultimate emotional sanctuary.

Magnetite

Also known as Lodestone and once called The Lovers' Charm, this mineral is renowned for its magnetic attraction to iron and also for pointing to the north and south poles when hung from a thread. Hence it was thought that it would reconcile quarrelling couples if the wife carried a lodestone and her husband iron shavings.

Today its magnetic energies are used for correcting spinal alignment and thus for relieving headaches caused through bad carriage and other discomforts associated with the lack of polarity.

In association with brown or smoky quartz, Magnetite is thought to be a suppressive agent for cancerous growths in their early stages.

In conjunction with Carnelian, it encourages concentration and promotes wisdom.

The ancients described Carnelian, Hematite, Magnetite and Malachite as antidotes to melancholy. On the basis of modern findings they would seem to have been correct

Malachite

Malachite is coupled in healing with iron stones because the body absorbs iron more often when copper is present and Malachite is a copper ore. By itself Malachite promotes physical harmony and has a long reputation for helping those with bone calcification, rheumatism, arthritis and relaxing a cramped limb. Malachite is often thought of as a gemstone to strengthen the heart muscle, and helps to ease menstrual disorders such as PMT, period pains and menopause. Anciently Malachite won accolades for strengthening hair and eyesight, calming an itch, and helping the bowel recover from bouts of diarrhoea.

Moonstone

A gemstone much used in the past as a cure for lunacy.

However its lustre, its most important healing quality, acts on its wearer's negative and positive emotions and is therefore a two edged weapon when dealing with conditions of the mind. Most modern practitioners restrict it to the physical side, where it is particularly helpful in cases of obesity, water retention and vomiting. Poor quality Moonstone, which looks almost opaque is of little help in healing, either to practitioner or owner, but the clearer, blueish variety curbs selfishness and vindictiveness.

Moonstone should not be used on the solar Plexis energy centre for the obvious reason the gemstone corresponds with the Moon and not with our Sun. That said if carried, worn by one with a predominant Moon in their chart it also has a generally uplifting effect.

In India the Moonstone is a sacred gem and thought to be lucky if given by a groom to his bride.

Obsidian

When a practitioner finds frustration blocking the healing process, he turns to Obsidian to counteract the offence. This is because Obsidian itself is said to hold negative energies. This of course is rot and an old lady's tale because no mineral holds negative energies; its perfect composition wouldn't allow it.

A mineral with dirt or dust on its outside may be in need of cleaning to rid it of adhering dirt or human body oils, as does jewellery that has been worn by another person or by one who has been ill.

In fact Obsidian is not a stone but a form of natural glass, which has no internal structure but starts in a liquid form. If, for instance, you look carefully at very old church windows, you will see the glass in them is thicker at the bottom than at the top and under magnification the flow lines are obvious.

The healer works on the liquid properties of this natural glass which we call Obsidian. First he transfers the subject's negative energy to the outside of the glass, then mentally heats the latter to an elevated temperature. Then comes the moment for a snap deep freeze which purges the surface of the Obsidian and the client's mind with it. To complete the treatment the client should be immediately bathed in a mental emulation of Rose Quartz, followed by Aquamarine.

Opal

Bringing miraculous order to a wealth of patterns and colours, this, the loveliest variety of our most abundant mineral, quartz, unites heaven and earth in a union of water and fire. It is the stone of hope and justice, the enemy of greed and corruption in all their forms, the support of the righteous but only the righteous in war and in the courtroom. Upstart and tyrannical monarchs, exploiting the miseries of their subjects, were once terrified of this gem. Alexander the Great proudly wore an Opal in his girdle but Queen Victoria was suddenly afraid to wear one, because, many believe, her grandson and heir apparent to the British throne Prince Albert Victor, her physician-in-ordinary Sir William Withey Gull and James Stephen, tutor to Prince Albert were personally associated with Jack the Ripper's frenzied murder spree in Whitechapel on November 1888. Yet that tough personage was a profuse collector who amassed more Opals than any other monarch, even giving one to each of her daughters on their wedding days.

For reasons only known to them, the last two Emperors of Russia and their families believed that Opal held the qualities of the "Evil Eye" and withdrew for the rest of the day after contact with even the smallest of these stones.

The pure tints of the Opal have been aptly likened to an innocent child's love. The Opal is considered capable of opening the "third eye" and above other minerals is used by mystics to lead them into supernatural realms.

It is a modern fallacy that Opal is too strong to wear near any part of the body except the extremities. This foolish misinterpretation of ancient and wise stone lore has been our loss, since Opal protects all the areas of the body that emit heat and all the energy points of attunement, that is, those that receive and dispatch power through colour. The predominant Opal tints to use on these zones are as follows:

> Crown: violet and pinkish
> Brow: deep blue with yellow, violet and paler blue
> Throat: soft greens and pale blue
> Heart: the brighter the green the better
> Solar Plexus: yellow
> Base of Spine: rich red
> Spleen: orange purple

In general one should hold the stone near the area concerned for about five minutes daily, depending on one's individual reactions and sensitivity. But provided a clear and strong image of the stone is evoked, healing can occur without the presence of the Opal, on the same principal as absent healing.

In the old days, as a rule, Opal was either burnt or powdered. Today we know that far more effective results are obtained by not tampering with the stone in this way but using its light, colours and dancing patterns in the gemstone's beautiful entirety to tap nature's vital forces for Opal is not efficacious only in the psychic realm.

It is of real aid in making good deficiencies on the physical level and, with zones and colours correctly matched as above, will work wonders in feeding the undernourished parts.

This becomes understandable once it is realized that the basic symptom of all disease is colour acting in the wrong places, vibrating out of tune, and thus causing disharmony.

Opal also acts as protective substance for certain tiny, oceanic growths known as Diatoms. Life on Earth could not go on without the Sun and water, fire and fluid, yet these pairs of opposites cannot meet without a mortal clash, so Diatoms have developed skeletal Opal structures which shield their softer parts from salt dehydration and the ocean's crushing pressure while allowing warmth and light to nourish them. When minuscule water bound entities die, their exquisite shells sink down, adding about three million tons of Opal Silica a year to the sedimentary rocks on which they come to rest. Modern industry uses this Silica in water repellent ointments and lubricants, so the Opal has this very practical use in addition to all its others.

It also teaches a lesson. Man cannot live without water and its life giving and purging powers. Indeed water covers roughly three quarters of the surface of planet Earth and man's own constitution is approximately three-quarters fluid.

Opal, in addition to silicon and oxygen, contains more water than any other mineral up to twenty two per cent. Thus it mirrors the Sun through water, the key of life, speaking to us in an alphabet of colours we understand.

Pearl
This ocean gem is beautiful as a jewel but of less consequence in healing. From antiquity onwards, Pearls were regarded as symbols of chastity and guardians of maidenhood, but their medical virtues were rated low.

A natural Pearl does not begin forming through a grain of sand as commonly believed. In its natural state a Pearl is conceived when the marine creature inside its shell is damaged or if foreign substance such as a parasite, burrows between the unfortunate creature's mantle and the shell, lodges itself in the mantle muscle and dies.

From then on a Pearl grows like a kind of cancer because the afflicted creature, in a gallant effort to ease its pain and protect itself, first forms a sac around the irritant and then coats the sac with a calcium and aragonite secretion called nacre.

But natural Pearls are rare and can be considered "no more" so enter the cultured Pearl.

Divers "capture" wild shell fish "slaves-to-be" and deliver them to a factory where they undergo the attentions of (mainly) female staff who open their shells, fasten their feet with clamps, then make up to ten incisions on the mantle of each victim, forcing lumps of another, dead clam into the cut, (sometimes accompanied by a small bead). This "Frankenstein" operation completed, the afflicted creatures live in plastic buckets three feet below water level for about three years. They are then brought to the surface where the Pearls are removed, the foreign substance having rotted in the intervening, formative period.

If all this sounds (and is) monstrous, it has to be said that the glorious, unique Pearl is not found fully formed on the sea shore, the river bank or ocean bed. Usually this soft marvel of luminosity is prised from a living, breathing child of Neptune which may go through its torture at least one more time before dying in an unsavoury, smelly mass of seething maggots and other sea creatures imprisoned in a pool or similar closed area.

Many healers past and present have considered Pearls to hold negative energies of a kind to foster human greed. In the light of the foregoing description this conclusion is hardly surprising. Yet maybe a flash from an X-ray camera could put paid to any harmful vibrations emanating from this beautiful jewel. Also to be considered are its constituents of calcium and lime. These could help encourage the human body to produce the 20 per cent bone replacement every adult needs each year and even help women with menstrual cramp problems and calcium deficiencies.

Peridot
Some say the inhabitants of legendary Atlantis gazed into the rich green velvety depths of the Peridot and chose it as their favourite gem. It was

prized by the Crusaders, who found in it the virtue of trust, while the Victorians believed it imparted gracious manners and serenity.

Comprising magnesium, iron and silicon, the Peridot fosters cardiovascular health, converts blood sugar to energy and promotes muscle functioning. It also counteracts some of the physical effects of alcohol. But crystal practitioners use it mainly in the settle ailments of the digestive system, stomach acidity and unwanted calcium deposits.

Its refined and delicate vibrations make it helpful to the timid, while its very gentleness, in notable contrast to the powerful physical force of many other minerals, relates it to the heart and balances the higher mind.

Rhodocrosite
Only discovered about fifty years ago, Rhodocrosite also called "Inca Rose", like its cousin Rhodonite, is new in holistic terms. It is found in two varieties: the sunset coloured stone of gem quality; and the white lined, rose or baby-pink semi-precious gemstone. Recent tests have shown that both have beneficial properties, emitting light vibrations which cheer the depressed, preserve youth, and retard the process of ageing, and helping to coax back the life force into young but sickly subjects as described at the start of this section.

Rhodonite
This gem, like its cousin Rhodocrosite, just described, is young and thus relatively untested in healing terms. But this gem quality crystal, the colour of crushed strawberries, and its opaque form are a mineral of the present and future.

Rhodonite carries a healing energy tuned to the thyroid gland where, thanks to its manganese content, produces the hormone thyroxin. It also has beneficial effects on the central nervous system, countering irritability, refreshing the bodies of the tired, weak and old (see, again, the start of this section), and aiding digestion and muscles.

The Rhodonite is best worn on the third finger of the left hand, from which position, attuning itself to the heart, it induces compassion, harmony and sensitivity to the higher values.

Rock Crystal
To the Greeks Rock Crystal, otherwise clear quartz was holy water frozen by the gods on Olympus. To the Japanese it was the solidified breath and saliva of their sacred dragons, traditionally depicted by artists as violet or white.

It has sparkled down the centuries from princely diadems and ecclesiastical crowns and glowed more somberly among the urns and tombs in impressive burial vaults.

Most cut quartz is hewed sphere shape, and these carefully fashioned "rounds" were once used to treat livestock, produce better harvests and call down rain or alternatively the warmth of the Sun.

It was, and still is, the stone most favoured for crystal gazing or scrying, for its lustre quickly freezes the optic nerve, with the result that outside impressions are suppressed and the eye is released to gaze at what is within. This and the energy inherent in quartz, accounts for its overall reputation and powers of healing. Its vibrations, which begin at about room temperature, resonate with the triple time; waltz like beat of life, giving this mineral a coordinating role in all holistic practice.

Whether held by a person, placed on an animal or positioned in close proximity to vegetation, Rock Crystal enlarges the aura of everything near it. It even increases the healing powers of other minerals.

Healers who operate by touch rather than by working through gems nonetheless often find that they obtain swifter results when the subject holds a clear piece of quartz. This is because the mineral steps up energy and clears chakra blockages.

Scrying with clear quartz also has a healing aspect, since the process of obliterating external distractions facilitates meditation and the development of the higher self, thus opening channels for the transference of energy from practitioner to recipient in the course of absent healing. In short this common and inexpensive stone holds a place of unique importance in the universe of gems.

Rose Quartz
Unobtrusive though it is, this stone should never be underrated. The minuscule crystals of which it is composed give it amazing durability, and the addition of a whiff of titanium — a metallic element of profound strength — not only accounts for its agreeable colouring but gives a tumbled piece the power to work on scar tissues, soothing and softening them and easing pain.

Coupled with Hematite, this pale pink gemstone works wonders on aching bones and bruised skin. Directing its energies mainly through the heart and eyes, it calms the spirit and banishes fear. Violent personalities cannot survive in its vicinity.

Ruby

In today's world perhaps the most important use in healing for Ruby is its ability to connect the person using it to their higher mind and to sharpen their ability to communicate on all levels, which includes receiving clarity of instruction from their guides.

Of the Ruby, eastern mythology says: "This gem is a drop of blood from Mother Earth's heart"; and certainly in terms of healing it is diseases of the blood which are the focus of its special powers. Some say Rasputin made use of a Ruby in treating the haemophiliac son of Tsar Nicholas II of Russia. There is also an ancient Burmese belief that a Ruby worn near or inserted into the flesh of a warrior would prevent him bleeding if wounded. Crystal practitioners use Rubies as treatment for anaemia, poor blood circulation heart disease, and for cleansing the blood. The liver also benefits from the Ruby's purifying action, as does the brain.

In times past the Ruby was considered efficacious against envy, nightmares, loss of or damage to property, and unfaithfulness in a spouse. It was thought to alleviate pain when worn and to pale or turn black if its owner's life came under threat. It will be found that it promotes disinterested love and acts on the level of extrasensory perception as a perfect channel of loving communication.

Like the Diamond, it also has a vital role in microsurgery. Though the Diamond is harder and almost unbluntable unless abused, the Ruby is possibly its superior as a cauterizing instrument.

All this, and beauty too!

Sapphire

Related to the Ruby (a fact few people are aware of), this remarkable stone comes in a whole range of colours, each with its healing virtues, associations and range of powers. Best known and best loved is the cornflower blue variety, the austere beauty of which is reflected in its effects. The least passionate of stones, dark blue Sapphires act directly on the intellect, and perhaps for that very reason is often the subconscious choice of those who wish to suppress their emotions and fall back instead on the reassurance of status and wealth. In healing terms it is excellent against fevers, and illness brought on by afflictions of the nerves.

By contrast, the cornflower Sapphire and other vibrant blues are reputed to lengthen life, keep their wearers looking young, fortify the heart, nourish the central nervous system and heal eye infections.

The almost opaque Star Sapphire has a generally calming effect, helpful in curing stomach ulcers and restraining the over practical.

The pink-violet Sapphire encourages selfless love. If worn with the traditional dark blue Sapphire it will help its owner to a more humane and sympathetic outlook on life, less narrowly legalistic and more open to the natural emotions.

Padparadjah (orange Sapphire) improves the character of the selfish, particularly those of an apparently extrovert nature who in reality seldom think about anybody except themselves. The energy of this Sapphire works effectively through the spleen, curbing the hastiness sparked off by irritability and encouraging its wearers to think before they act.

Sodalite

In appearance Sodalite is similar to Lapis Lazuli but its effects are different and confusion of the two is unfortunate. Sodalite's main holistic purpose is to impart youth and freshness to its wearer and to those who are treated by its vibrations.

Sodalite could be called "the stone of mental change or transformation", for it brings back joy and relieves the heavy heart. Placed just above the head during sleep, it can make a sad person wake up full of effervescence and bounce.

Sick animals and house plants will respond to a Sodalite used in combination with Dioptase and Rock Crystal. However, do not try to place a pendant on an animal, a procedure which could be dangerous and to which it would very properly take exception. Instead, amass a generous number of the stones and place them near the pet's favourite spot. In the case of house plants, soak the minerals in water for twenty four hours, then remove them and treat the plant with the elixir thus produced.

Spinel

Up to the end of the middle Ages, the Spinel was admired for the magnificent stone it truly is and was credited with the same healing powers as other valuable gems of like colourings. This was before the study of precious stones became a science. Sadly this beautiful crystal then lost its popularity because both in its appearance and in its elements as then known it too closely resembled the Ruby and Sapphire.

We now know that first grade Spinel is far rarer than most of the stones it could be mistaken for. Unfortunately, however, the trade still retains the outdated mentality of those early gemmologists, with the result that the public have not been given the chance to rediscover it for themselves. In fact it is similar in composition to many Garnets, though far lovelier in its sparkling clarity and wonderful range of hues.

It is a hardwearing stone more so indeed than the Garnet, Zircon, Emerald, Peridot or Jadeite and occurs in the same crystal systems as the Diamond.

Magnesium and aluminium make up the pure, clear white variety of this stone, other chemicals, most often iron and chromium, entering in as impurities to account for its coloured forms, with zinc producing the very scarce blue. These colour differences allow the Spinel to be used in holistic work in place of many Garnets, in particular to promote the functions of nerve and muscle, to diminish stress and to fight the effects of stomach acidity and depression.

The planets Venus and Uranus are co-rulers of this stone, with the result that the Spinel, on the spiritual plane, is effectively directed towards promoting general idealism through harmony, creativity and in particular the making of music.

Topaz
An excellent touchstone or pocket companion, white Topaz especially helps those who suffer from nerves or insomnia. Topaz of all colours is used to ease coughs and throat disorders, nerve ailments, catarrh, children's diseases such as measles, as well as scabby skin punctures and gout. In Roman times Topaz was used to ward off the effects of black magic and, if strapped over a woman's abdomen during her menstrual period, was reputed to alleviate her pain and discomfort.

As a talisman the most important, indeed unique, virtue of this stone was to protect its owner against sudden death. It is also, in common with certain other gems, said to be helpful in putting its owner in touch with life in other parts of the galaxy.

Tourmaline
Here we have a master physician of the mineral world, with remarkable properties and a harlequin personality. Its myriad tints are the result not of impurities, as is usually the case, but of the contributions made by each single original crystal in this lovely stone's composition.

In times past the Tourmaline was classed as a mineral magnet rather than as a gemstone. The reason for this was its unique electrical energies which cause it, when rubbed or heated, to produce in each of its crystals a positive charge at one end and a negative charge at the other.

In healing its principal function is to produce polarity, an invaluable virtue since a perfectly aligned spine with feet and senses equally firmly planted on the ground makes it possible to give and receive on all levels.

Each Tourmaline crystal contains aluminium, boron, iron, lithium, magnesium, potassium, silicon and sodium, with most gems showing trace elements of other much needed body chemicals.

Magnesium is associated with common and Epsom salts which cleanse the system; it is the curative essence of ocean water and is necessary for a good memory.

Boron has been used down the ages as a treatment for diseased vocal chords, sore throats and throat inflammations.

Potash is found in "miracle waters" and with Fluorine, another common mineral, is used in shrinking troublesome varicose veins and in preserving healthy teeth, bones, nails and hair.

Other uses to which Tourmaline can be put are as a cure for indigestion, lethargy, excessive weight gain and loss, gout and the intense pain of neuritis. The last mentioned ailment can be relieved by the action of Tourmaline in feeding the muscles and releasing trapped nerves when the cranium joints are reslotted into their correct position through the force of its magnetism.

Tourmaline acts well in combination with gold. Rather than encasing the gem in this metal, however, it is better to use an open claw setting which allows the electrical properties of this mineral magician to act without obstruction.

Although Tourmaline is principally effective in physical cures, it is also of assistance to the higher mind through its action in clearing the chakras and removing bodily pain. It is a lovely stone and those who possess one, and particularly those who have been given one, are exceptionally fortunate.

Turquoise
The fame of this stone dates back to the earliest times. It is associated with Hator, daughter and wife of the Egyptian Sun God Ra, who protected her father and husband from all who rebelled against him and was feared as "the eye of Ra". Later it was esteemed by the North American

Indians, who believed that it contained the essence of the harshness of winter and would thus ensure that its wearer would show severity towards his enemies. The Buddha used Turquoise to call up spiritual help when he wished to free himself from an unknown and particularly frightening entity. Stories about Turquoise can likewise be found in Persian, Bedouin, Chinese, Mexican, Tibetan and Turkish mythology. The stone has always been worn as a protection against dark forces. Above all it is the talisman most favoured by horse and rider and by lovers as a guarantee of mutual fidelity.

Aluminium, alongside copper and a small amount of iron are the elements composing this opaque but attractive mineral. In healing its principal action is on the throat chakra, though it need not be placed directly over that area since it transmits its energy to all the body zones, particularly the higher abdomen. It is used holistically to cure headaches, eye ailments, fevers, leg, foot and loin problems, and counteracts the negativity which, coming at us in heavy doses, can entangle our lives to the point of chaos and insanity.

It can be used effectively in conjunction with Lapis Lazuli to deflect lowering influences and to harmonize the higher self. It can be set with silver, which does not affect its vibrations, and American Indian craftsmen have often mounted it in this way. But it is even stronger when surrounded or engraved with gold and as such is a necessary filter for other influences and a powerful talisman.

Whatever its shade, this ancient jewel will be found effective as long as its owner feels at ease with the colour of his or her choice. Turquoise exercises a particularly definite influence for better or worse according to the circumstances. It is a stone in which one man's meat is another man's poison and all the more fascinating for that.

Zircon
This many-coloured, transparent gem should not be under estimated either as a jewel or as a means to holistic healing. Thought by the ancient Greeks to strengthen the mind and bring joy to the heart, the Zircon once took precedence over almost all gemstones on account of its lustre and its dazzling reflection of light, in this respect often rivalling the faceted Diamond. Containing the radioactive element of uranium, the rare metal thorium (used in electrical apparatus) and the precious metals zirconium and hafnium, both of which are employed in the nuclear industry, the Zircon holds within itself the essence of the Sun and Jupiter, which carry the energy of existence.

The overriding characteristic of this crystal is its vitality, which some believe acts with great effectiveness when a person is recovering from brain damage, venereal diseases and acute skin disorders. It also helps disperse fluid in the lungs and works to counteract inertia and ailments of the spleen. On the spiritual plane Zircon promotes self-development and the extension of the higher mind, an effect particularly noticeable when the heat treated sky-blue variety is used.

Although similar to the Diamond in its lustre and light, the Zircon is less authoritarian in character but still firm in its direct action on physical and psychological states of being.

Glossary of Healing Stones

This Glossary of Stones names many minerals which have been suggested in various healing lists throughout the world, throughout history and in the present.

Mankind has always turned to natural healing, more often after all else fails, and sometimes with an approach which has logic such as wearing Hematite (an iron ore) for strengthening the blood (we take oral iron supplements) alongside bazaar remedies such as ridding the body of chicken pox by wearing a Pearl or a Topaz. Though it is said the English Queen Elizabeth 1st tried to cure her pock-marked complexion with a poultice made of Pearls dissolved in vinegar mixed with cow dung!

This list of illnesses, symptoms, physical and spiritual conditions indicates the minerals once and sometimes still believed appropriate to the treatment and/or improvement of each ailment. Detailed descriptions of the principal stones are given in the preceding pages.

Symptom: State	Rocks and Stones
Abdominal Colic	White Coral
Accidents (prevention of)	Yellow Carnelian
Acidity	Green Jasper, Bismuth, Peridot, Dolomite
Ageing (to retard process)	Rhodocrosite, Sapphire, Diamond, Sodalite
Aggression (moderation of)	Bloodstone
Alcoholism	Amethyst
Allergies	Zircon
Anaemia	Metallic Sphalerite, Bloodstone, Citrine, Chalcopyrite, Ruby
Anger	Carnelian/Amethyst
Angina	Bornite, Emerald, Dioptase
Animals' Illnesses	Dioptase
Arthritis	Apatite, Malachite, Garnet, Azurite
Asthma	Amber, Lapis Lazuli, Rose Quartz
Aura (strengthening of)	Zircon
Aura (protection of)	Diamond
Aura (stabilization of)	Labradorite
Babies (physical development)	Rhodocrosite, Sodalite, Dioptase, Chrysocolla, Chalcopyrite
Backache	Sapphire, Magnetite, Hematite
Bad Temper	Heliotrope, Emerald
Belching	Beryls
Benevolence (promotion of)	Jade
Bile Ducts	Jasper, Emerald
Biliousness	Emerald
Bites (venomous)	Sulphur, Emerald, Sard
Bladder	Jasper, Jade, Tourmaline
Bleeding	Bloodstone, Ruby
Blood Circulation	Ruby, Bloodstone, Amethyst
Blood Cleanser	Tourmaline, Red Coral, Ruby, Amethyst

Symptom: State	Rocks and Stones
Blood Clots	Amethyst, Bloodstone, Hematite
Blood Pressure (high)	Jadeite, Jade, Chrysoprase Emerald
Blood Pressure (low)	Ruby, Tourmaline
Body Fluids (cleansing of)	Halite
Body Repair (promotion of)	Apatite, Tourmaline
Boils	Sapphire
Bones (aching)	Magnetite, Spinel, Rose Quartz
Bones (health of)	Angel Skin and White Coral Calcite
Bowel	Yellow Jasper
Brain	Pyrolusite, Pyrite, Ruby, Green Tourmaline
Brain Damage	Zircon
Brain Tonic	Coral, Lapis Lazuli
Breathlessness	Magnetite, Amber, Jet
Bronchitis	Amber, Jet
Brow Energy Point	Blue Play on Black Opal, Lapis Lazuli, Azurite, Iolite
Bruises	Rose Quartz
Burns	Chrysoprase, Jadeite
Calcification	Garnet, Calcite, Scapolite, Coral, Pearl
Cancer	Amethyst, Brown and Rose Quartz, Smoky Quartz, Magnetite, Obsidian
Cancerous outer skin growths	Amethyst, Emerald, Amethyst
Catarrh	Topaz
Cauterizing (for use in surgery)	Diamond, Ruby, Sapphire
Cell Rejuvenation	Rhodonite, Jasper
Cellular Structure	Indicolite
Central Nervous System	Aventurine
Chakra Blocking (removal of)	Azurite, Lapis Lazuli, Bloodstone

Symptom: State	Rocks and Stones
Change of Life	Lapis Lazuli, Garnet, Pearl Fluorite
Chastity (promotion of)	Sapphire (very dark blue)
Chest (relief of pains in)	Amber, Emerald, Dioptase
Chicken Pox	Pearl, Topaz
Childbirth (pain during)	Emerald
Childbirth (to encourage)	Verdite, Emerald
Cholera	Malachite
Circulation (improvement of)	Blue John, Ruby
Clarity of thought	Jade
Cold (common)	Emerald, Jet
Coldness	Topaz, Opal
Colic	Malachite, Jade
Colon	Yellow Jasper
Colour (skin tone)	Iron Stones
Concentration	Carnelian
Concern (alleviation of)	Sodalite
Constancy	Opal
Constipation	Ruby
Consumption	Pearl
Convulsions	Diamond, Blue Zircon
Corns	Rub with Apatite
Coughs	Amber, Topaz
Courage	Diamond and all orange stones
Cramp	Limestone, Bloodstone
Creativity (to encourage)	Spinel, Smoky Quartz
Crown Energy Point	Purple gemstones, Pink Sapphire, Siberite, Iolite
Deafness	Tourmaline
Delirium	Zircon
Delusions	Carnelian
Depression	Spinel, Dolomite, Rhodocrosite, Bowenite, Lapis Lazuli, Jade, Garnet, Selenite

Symptom: State	Rocks and Stones
Devotion (to increase)	Pink-Violet Jadeite
Diabetes	Diamond
Diarrhoea	Malachite
Digestion	Olivine (Peridot)
Dizziness	White Sapphire
Disease (contagious)	Dioptase
Disease (general)	Dioptase, Amethyst
Drunkenness	Amethyst
Dysentery	Emerald
Ear Trouble	Sapphire, Amber, Tourmaline
Eczema	Sapphire
Edema (swelling)	Chalcopyrite, Bornite Diamond, Moonstone, Jet
Endurance	Jade
Energy	Amber, Jasper, Peridot
Envy (to dispel)	Ruby
Epilepsy	Onyx, Jasper, Jet, Tourmaline, Lapis Lazuli
ESP (to develop)	Dioptase, Lapis Lazuli, Ruby
Evil Eye (protection from)	Jet, Turquoise
Eye Ailments (general)	Emerald, Dioptase, Turquoise
Eyes (bloodshot)	Emerald
Eye Itch	Aquamarine
Eyesight	Goshenite, Malachite, Rose Quartz, Aquamarine, Variscite, Emerald
Eyes (watery)	Aquamarine
Fainting	Lapis Lazuli
Faithfulness (to encourage)	Ruby
Fatigue	Metallic Sphalerite, Staurolite, Dioptase, Hematite
Fear (to dispel)	Rose Quartz, Emerald
Feet (health of)	Aquamarine, Jet
Fertility (to increase)	Verdite, Orange Sapphire

Symptom: State	Rocks and Stones
Fever	Chrysoprase, Sapphire, Peridot
Fidelity (promotion of)	Turquoise, Pink Diamond
Flatulence	Emerald, Green Garnet, Peridot
Fluid (excess)	Jade, Diamond, Heliodore
Fluid (lack of)	Moonstone, Scapolite
Food Poisoning (to regain strength after)	Emerald
Forgetfulness	Tourmaline, Emerald, Moss Agate
Fractures (to aid healing)	Magnetite, Calcite
Frights (recovery from)	Lapis Lazuli, Opal
Frustration (to dispel)	Obsidian
Gall	Hiddenite
Gallstones (to recover from)	Dolomite, Jasper, Coral
Gastric Fever	Jasper, Emerald
Gastric Ulcer	Emerald, Sapphire, Peridot
General Tonic	Tourmaline, Tiger Eye, Amber, Sard, Padparadjah, Aventurine, Blue John
Glands (swollen)	Topaz
Goitre	Amber
Good Wit (to sharpen)	Diamond, Operculum
Greed (moderation of)	Opal
Grief	Lapis Lazuli
Growth (promotion of)	Sphalerite, Galena
Gums (health of)	Pyrolusite
Gut (umbilical area)	White & blue Topaz, Aquamarine
Haemorrhages	Ruby
Hemorrhoids'	Pearl, Coral
Hay Fever	Jet, Zircon
Hair (health of)	Opal, Quartz, Tourmaline, Malachite, Chrysocolla, Smithsonite
Hands (swollen)	Aquamarine, Moonstone
Happiness (promotion of)	Sunstone

Symptom: State	Rocks and Stones
Harmony	Opal, Spinel, Rhodonite, Jade, Jadeite, Moonstone
Headache	Turquoise, White Tourmaline, Amber, Jet, Hematite, Emerald
Heart (strengthening of)	Green Garnet, Emerald, Dioptase, Opal, Turquoise
Heartache	Lepidolite, Blue Topaz
Heart attacks (prevention of)	Dolomite, Dioptase
Heartburn	Rock Crystal, Peridot, Dioptase, Emerald
Heart Disease	Ruby, Dioptase
Heart Energy Point	Dioptase, Emerald
Hepatitis	Calcite, Dolomite
Herpes	Dolomite, Jadeite, Lapis Lazuli
Hysteria	Lapis Lazuli, Turquoise
Idealism (promotion of)	Spinel
Idleness (to stop)	Emerald, Aquamarine, Morganite, Heliodore, Goshenite
Ignorance (to dispel)	Heliodore, Carnelian
Incest (against ill effects of)	Lapis Lazuli, Turquoise
Indigestion	Tourmaline, Jasper, Dolomite, Peridot, Bismuth
Indulgence (to prevent)	Amethyst, Bloodstone
Infections	Amethyst, Smoky Quartz Brown Quartz
Inflammations	Topaz, Spinel
Inner growth (to encourage)	Lapis Lazuli, Chrysoprase
Insanity	Rock Crystal, Citrine, Amethyst, Sard, Topaz
Insomnia	Jacinth, Bowenite, Topaz
Inertia	Zircon
Intellect	Heliodore, Sapphire
Intermittent Fevers	Chrysoprase, Tourmaline
Intestine (health of)	Yellow Jasper
Intuition (increase of)	Sapphire, Lapis Lazuli

Symptom: State	Rocks and Stones
Invisibility (to become)	Opal, Sardonyx
Iron Assimilation (into body)	Chrysocolla, Turquoise, Hematite
Irritability	Rhodonite, Carnelian, Rose Quartz, Lapis
Irritated Throat	Amber, Tourmaline
Irritated Spirit	Spinel
Itching	Malachite, Azurite, Dolomite
Jaundice	Coral, Jadeite
Jealousy	Apophylite, Obsidian
Joint Inflammation	Hematite, Dioptase, Amethyst
Justice (promotion of)	Opal
Kennel Cough (in dogs)	Amber, Jadeite, Hematite, Rock Crystal
Kidney (treatment of)	Nephrite Jade
Laryngitis	Tourmaline, Amber
Legs (to strengthen)	Aquamarine
Lethargy	Carnelian, Ruby, Tourmaline
Life-force (to increase)	Aquamarine, Blue Topaz, Blue Spinel, Blue Zircon
Lightning (to dispel fear of)	Spinel
Liver (treatment of)	Jasper, Jade, Labradorite, Hiddenite, Emerald, Ruby
Longevity (promotion of)	Diamond, Zircon
Love (caring, promotion of)	Pink Diamond, Ruby, Pink Sapphire, Rhodonite, Rhodocrosite
Lumbago	Sapphire, Magnetite
Lunacy	River Pebbles, Moonstone, Chalcedony, Rock Crystal, Amethyst, Citrine
Lungs (care of)	Amber
Lung Fluid (to dispel)	Zircon, Diamond, Heliodore, Yellow Sapphire, Amber
Malaria	Turquoise
Malleability of Mind	Aventurine

Symptom: State	Rocks and Stones
Malignancy	Alexandrite, Malachite, Azurite, Amethyst, Magnetite, Carnelian, Garnet
Mania	Pearl, Coral, Scapolite
Measles	Pearl, Topaz
Melancholy	Tourmaline, Lapis Lazuli, Sardonyx
Memory	Moss Agate, Emerald, Tourmaline, Pyrolusite
Menopause	Diamond, Ruby
Menstrual Disorders	Topaz, Staurolite, Jet, Rose Quartz, Pink Quartz, Tourmaline
Mental Burdens	Amethyst
Metabolism (stimulation of)	Sodalite
Migraine	Jet, Hematite, Magnetite
Mind Strengthener	Zircon
Morality (promotion of)	Jade, Jadeite
Mouth Ailments	Heliodore, Yellow Sapphire
Mumps	Topaz
Multiple Sclerosis	Tourmaline, Blue John, Rose Quartz, Lapis Lazuli, Jadeite All with Gold
Muscles (toning up)	Dolomite, Fluorite, Tourmaline, Spinel, Peridot, Jadeite
Nails (to strengthen)	Pearl, Opal, Calcite, Rhodocrosite
Neck Tension	Alexandrite, Hematite, Magnetite
Negative Energies (to dispel)	Turquoise, Lapis Lazuli
Negative Energies (to avoid)	Pearl, Azurite, Obsidian
Negativity (to counteract)	Lapis Lazuli
Nephritis	Nephrite Jade
Nerve Cells (healthy activity of)	Chrysoprase
Nerves (to steady, to strengthen)	Dolomite, Jade
Nervousness	Lapis Lazuli, Sapphire, Jadeite
Neuritis	Tourmaline

Symptom: State	Rocks and Stones
Nightmares	Jet, Turquoise, Padparadjah, Bowenite, Hematite, Ruby
Nobility (reinforcement of)	Opal, Alexandrite, Diamond
Nose Bleeds	Sapphire, Ruby
Nostrils (blocked)	Amber, Jet
Obesity	Tourmaline, Heliodore, Diamond, Zircon
Oral Contraceptive Balancer	Dolomite
Pain (general)	Lapis Lazuli, Ruby, Tourmaline
Pancreas	Jasper, Bloodstone
Passion (to arouse)	Orange Sapphire, Verdite
Passion (to cool)	Emerald, Blue Sapphire, Amethyst
Perception (to sharpen)	Bowenite, Carnelian
Perspiratory Problems	Jadeite
Physical Harmony	Agatized Coral, Blue John
Pigmentation (improvement of)	Chrysocolla
Plague	Ruby, Pearl
Poison (antidote)	Emerald, Unicorn Horn, Zircon
Popularity (to increase)	Turquoise, Citrine
Pregnancy (for strength during)	Chrysolite, Jasper
Protection	Diamond, Zircon
Purity (to encourage)	Diamond, Jade
Quarrelling (between couples)	Magnetite
Quinsy	Topaz, Amber, Jet
Red Blood cells	Bornite, Chalcopyrite
Rejuvenator	Irish Fairy Stone
Renal Disease	Jade
Refining Energy (promotion of)	Lapis Lazuli
Rheumatism	Malachite, Azurite, Chrysocolla, Turquoise

Symptom: State	Rocks and Stones
Rickets	Calcite, Coral, Pearl
Righteousness	Jade, Jadeite
Ringworm	Diamond, Calcite, Zircon
Sacral Energy Point	Fire Opal, Red Spinel
Sadness	Ruby, Orange Sapphire
Saliva (excess of)	Diamond, Zircon
Scalding	Emerald
Scar Tissue	Rose Quartz
Sciatica	Sapphire, Tourmaline
Self-Expansion	Opal, Zircon, Diamond
Serenity	Jade, Jadeite
Sexual appetite (to arouse and increase)	Red Spinel, Red Amber
Sexual Higher Guidance	Orange Sapphire
Sexual Impotency and Infertility	Verdite, Orange Sapphire
Shingles	Jadeite, Lapis, Lazulite, Chrysoprase
Sighing	Aquamarine, Emerald, Morganite Goshenite, Heliodore
Sinus	Jet
Skin Colour (to improve)	Hematite
Skin Problems	Sulphur, Topaz, Carbuncle, Pearl, Zircon
Sleeping sickness	Amethyst
Sluggishness	Carnelian, Amethyst
Smell (loss of)	Tourmaline
Snakebite	Emerald, Jasper
Sneezing	Zircon
Solar Plexus Energy Point	Citrine, Heliodore
Spasms	Carnelian, Dolomite
Spine (general health of)	Jasper, Labradorite, Magnetite
Spine (alignment of,)	Hiddenite, Magnetite, Labradorite

Symptom: State	Rocks and Stones
Spleen Energy Point	Orange Zircon, Hessonite,
Stabilizer (in mental health)	Onyx, Lapis Lazuli, Azurite
Stomach Pains	Lapis Lazuli, Peridot
Stomach Upsets	Bloodstone, Aquamarine, Emerald, Heliodore, Morganite Peridot
Stomach Strengthener	Jasper
Stomach (swollen)	Pearl, Emerald
Strength (to increase)	Magnetite, Ruby
Stress	Dolomite, Lapis, Spinel
Sunstroke	Chrysoprase, Jadeite
Sweats	Green Sapphire
Taste (improvement of)	Topaz, Tourmaline
Teeth (loose)	Jet
Teeth (strengthening)	Angel Skin, Calcite
Telepathy (to induce)	Dioptase, Garnet, Ruby
Tempest (charm against)	Emerald
Tenderness (to promote)	Rhodonite, Pink Sapphire, Alexandrite, Rose Quartz, Ruby, Kunzite
Third Eye (to open)	Opal, Azurite, Lapis Lazuli, Iolite
Throat (to cure ills in)	Tourmaline, Turquoise, Hematite, Amber
Throat Energy Point	Chrysoprase, Turquoise, Ruby
Thyroid (regulation of)	Lapis Lazuli, Rhodonite
Tiredness	Pyrite, Amber
Tonsillitis	Tourmaline, Amber
Toothache	Jet, Amber
Tranquillity (to promote)	Emerald, Jade, Jadeite
Tumours	Jet, Amethyst, Sapphire
Ulcers (eyes)	Sapphire
Ulcers (general)	Tourmaline
Ulcers (skin)	Emerald
Ulcers (stomach)	Sapphire, Peridot

Symptom: State	Rocks and Stones
Unity (promotion of)	Opal
Urinary Ailments	Amber, Jade
Varicose Veins	Aquamarine, Amber, Opal
Venereal Disease	Zircon
Vertigo	Sapphire
Violence	Bloodstone, Rose Quartz
Virtue (to increase)	Jade, Sapphire, Pearl
Vocal Cords (protection of)	Amber, Jet, Tourmaline
Vomiting	Emerald, Lapis Lazuli
Warts	Emerald, or rub with Appatite
Wasting Disease	Magnetite, Jasper
Weak Muscles	Tourmaline, Moonstone
Weakness (general)	Hematite
Whooping Cough	Amber, Topaz, Coral
Wickedness (to dispel)	Sapphire, Ruby, Opal, Diamond
Wild Beasts (taming of)	Diamond
Will Power (to strengthen)	Ruby, Red Coral, Garnet
Wisdom (promotion of)	Carnelian, Amethyst
Worms	Casiterite, Ruby
Wounds	Garnet, Ruby

PART FIVE

Angel Stones

Angelic Hierarchy According to Medieval Studies

The word "angel" comes from the Greek word "angelos" meaning messenger.

In the 4th or 5th Century A.D., a Middle Eastern scholar named Dionysius the Areopagite — a Christian theologian and philosopher — studied references to angels in biblical scriptures and other popular non-biblical sources. He concluded that there are nine orders, also called choirs, of heavenly hierarchy split into three triads;

1. comprises angels closest to god which are Seraphim, Cherubim and Thrones;
2. is formed of Powers, Virtues and Dominions;
3. is composed of those closest to mankind — Angels, Archangels and Principals.

Angels, also called Guardian Angels, number many and rank lowest in the heavenly choir.

Angels, whose duties relate to delivering god's messages to mankind, deal directly with people.

Angels are easily recognised because they wear plain white robes, have two medium-sized, feathered wings and wear sandals embellished with gems belonging to the Quartz family — Rose Quartz, Pink Quartz, Star Rose Quartz, Amethyst, Rock Crystal, plus Amber (fossil resin).

Archangels are the seven ambassadors of god who mediate between him and Angels. Their duties are concerned with politics, military matters, commerce and trade. Each Archangel holds a separate position of command in the other, higher seven orders.

Archangel Michael has been placed as prince of the Seraphim. Archangels Gabriel and Michael are mentioned by name in the New Testament while Raphael and Lucifer appear in the Old Testament.

Contrary to popular belief Lucifer and Satan have never been referred to as the same beings. Lucifer was a beautiful Archangel cast from heaven to live on Earth after leading and losing a war against Michael the Archangel.

Archangels more usually appear in the form of fair-headed men with two large, feathered wings and leg-bands embellished with garnets of all colours, Kunzite and Aquamarine.

Principalities protect leaders of people and religion. Their numbers are infinite because each nation, country, town and community has its own Principality. Their duties are to inspire the arts and science and to promote protection of animals by man from the cruelty of man.

Principalities have the power to interfere in human affairs to invoke god's will and they have the ability to aid individuals in battle.

Principalities more usually have two large golden wings, carry a sceptre; and wear a crown embellished with jewels of Pink Onyx, Rhodonite, Rhodocrosite and Turquoise.

Powers are warrior Angels who fight the devil's army and all other evil spirits who attempt to wreak chaos through human beings. They are the bearers of conscience and the keepers of history.

Powers wear golden war regalia embellished with clear and colourless gemstones which emit strong light to defy the dark. Anciently believed to be the Zircon and Spinel but recently the Diamond has been added.

Virtues are angels of grace who carry god's miracles to earth and promote courage and valour when needed. Their major duty is to ensure the cosmos remains in order. Virtues govern all nature and control the behaviour of our planet's seasons, our moon, the stars, and even the sun. There are many different descriptions of Virtues but they are believed to be very large and surrounded by glaring light which explains their other name "the brilliant ones". Virtues favour cornflower-blue Sapphires, Ceylonese Sapphires, Lapis Lazuli, Azurite and Labradorite.

Dominions manifest the glory of god through their divine beauty of appearance. Their duty is to regulate the assignments of all lower angels. Dominions are considered the royal family of the angelic host so they accordingly wear courtly regalia. Their illuminated swords are decorated with Peridot, Emerald, Dioptase, Diopside, and multi-coloured Tourmaline.

Thrones are god's vehicle for divine justice, so their duty it is to carry out his decisions precisely and without mercy. Their bodies appear as fiery, multi-coloured Tourmaline wheels, the rims decorated with hundreds of gleaming eyes hovering on six wings covered with eyes. Hence their nick-name "the many eyed ones".

The lower choir of Angels, Seraphim and Cherubs need Thrones to access god.

Thrones favour green Jasper, Opal, Chrysoprase, Jade, Jadeite and Tourmaline.

Cherubim also known as Cherubs are keepers of the book of knowledge, charioteers and guardians of holy places including the gates to the Garden of Eden. Their appearance has changed over time. Originally Cherubs were terrifying, powerful critters with four wings and four heads each – the head of a man, an ox, a lion and an eagle but in this instance angel evolution has set in.

Cherubs are now easily recognisable as chocolate-box pretty, well-rounded babes with blonde, curly hair and two tiny wings. Cherubim favour yellow stones, particularly Topaz and Citrine.

Seraphim are in attendance upon god and constantly sing his praise. And are often referred to as "the burning ones" because the light they radiate is so pure no mere mortal can look upon them. Their duty is to regulate the heavens.

They number four, have four wings each and wear red stones—Spinel, Tourmaline, Zircon, Diamond, Ruby, Agate, Fire Opal and black Opal with red flashes.

Today few people care which rank an angel holds because an angel is an angel and may appear to anyone, regardless of religious or non-religious backgrounds or beliefs.

It is an interesting fact that the angels in all three major religions — Christian, Jewish and Muslim — share an almost common mythology of these heavenly beings, based on divine revelation and canonical writings.

According to the bible, angels have some form of spiritual body but have the power to change and appear in other forms. The bible assigns male gender to angels yet Matthew 22:30 seems to indicate angels are sexless.

Islam is clear about angels. Evidently Allah created them from light to be messengers of his god and they are neither male nor female.

Then in later Jewish tradition Michael is the angel of mercy; Gabriel the angel of justice; Raphael the angel of healing; and Uriel the angel of illumination.

North American Indians believe in holy spirits or angels, Hinduism has myriad spiritual beings called the "Shining Ones" who inhabit a higher plane and act in the capacity of angels, while those who follow a Buddhist way of life refer to angels as Devas or Celestial Beings. Celtic mythology has its angels called Faeries and Norse mythology has its Valkyries.

Angels have been around forever and are given credence in modern history by great, respectable leaders and by certified sane scientists.

In 1778 George Washington credited his success at Valley Forge to "an inspiring visit from a heavenly being."

In 1985 a Russian space scientist defected and then told the world that six cosmonauts working on routine medical

experiments aboard the Soyuz Seven space station, were bombarded by a brilliant orange cloud from outside the orbiting laboratory.

When their eyesight adjusted they saw a band of glowing angels, seven giant figures with wings and mist-like halos. They appeared to be hundreds of feet tall with a wingspan as great as a jetliner. This information was officially reported by three cosmonauts — Leonid Kizim, Vladimir Solevev and Oleg Artkov. Twelve days later another two men and one woman cosmonaut joined the team who also witnessed the seven angels.

Then let's not forget angels called "Elementals" who bless us with nature's therapeutic effect. Their domain is the outdoors where they are constantly showing themselves to believers and doubters alike, their minerals are Fossilised Wood, Fossils, Opal, Dioptase and Flint.

It is recorded that Abraham Lincoln referred to angels at the end of his first Inaugural Address in Washington D.C. on March 4th 1861 with the words "The mystic chords of memory, stretching from every battlefield, and patriot grave, to every living heart and hearth-stone, all over this broad land, will yet swell the chorus of the union, when again touched, as surely they will be, by the better angels of our nature."

Anniversaries

Anniversaries are important — ask any husband who has forgotten his wife's birthday — and nations as well as individuals celebrate them. So it is not surprising that over the centuries traditions have accumulated linking them with the planets and with particular precious stones.

Here then is another way of associating our lives with the rhythms of the whole universe. Earlier sections of this book have described the stones we should each possess or wear according to our birth signs, as well as those that can help us in sickness and in health because they too harness the planetary powers of which we stand most in need. Owning or carrying the right jewel on the occasion, let us say, of our tenth wedding anniversary or our twenty-fifth or fifty-fifth birthday is no more than an additional way of reinforcing such beneficent influences. It can be fun, too, throwing a party where such stones are worn or displayed. They have the good effect of reminding us of the powers that influence us from outside this Earth, however light-hearted the occasion of that reminder.

The chart printed here shows these connections at a glance anniversary number, ruling planet, and matching stone. But how are they arrived at? If we want to discover this we should look back first of all to the "Note on Numerology" printed on pages 8 and 9. This states in simple form the law of numerology, according to which all numbers are reduced to single digits, and lists the number traditionally allocated to each planet in our Solar System by astrological lore. (The Sun, 1; Mercury, 5; and so on.) Once grasped, these two pieces of information make it easy to calculate which planet and which anniversary correspond. For example, a twenty fifth wedding anniversary will be under the sign of Neptune, because the number astrologically associated with Neptune is 7, and the number of the anniversary, 25, breaks down numerologically in the following way: 2 + 5 = 7. Now, look back to see what birth sign is ruled by Neptune.

Answer: Pisces. So the stone attributed to the anniversary in question should logically feature among those worn by Pisceans. And so it proves.

Not that everything is completely cut and dried. Why, for instance, Stichtite is designated for an eighth anniversary, corresponding to Saturn's number, and Amethyst for a seventeenth, which is equally Saturn-linked, and not the other way round, is indeed a matter of traditional gemmological wisdom rather than cold logic. But the main principle holds.

Dwarf Planet Pluto is not added to the numbered Anniversary list as a ruling body mainly because Astrologers don't always agree on Pluto's number.

One interloper into the column of planets or satellites is Sirius, the Dog-Star, well known to the sages of Sumeria and Ur of the Chaldees, and to certain primitive African tribes, as already explained. Here it is designated for a fiftieth or hundredth anniversary. For the former, it is fittingly matched with Dioptase, the "Congo Emerald", both on account of its colour (reflecting those flashes of green emanating from Sirius)

and also because the first fine quality crystals of this stone are thought to have been formed at about the time that Sirius was moving closer to Earth. For the latter, it is matched with a red or white Diamond, appropriate to Sirius's colour change, already described, and with a brightness reflecting the Sun (100= 1, the Sun's astrological number). It should also be noted that Lapis Lazuli, a second stone for a centenary, was worn by the priest-seers of Ur and ancient Egypt for the purpose of making contact with Sirius.

For any anniversary over a hundred, tradition dictates a "Jew's Eye", which, being interpreted, means simply "any worthy stone". Well what was good enough for Methuselah...These additions apart, the chart is self-explanatory, except for the last column which presents a sea of muddles. For the "Traditional Emblems" for different anniversaries which have reached down the ages are both illogical and incomplete. Why is there an emblem for a twenty third anniversary and not for a twenty fourth? More importantly, what sense are we to make of the value of some of the "gifts"? Why is china earmarked for a twentieth anniversary when Zircon, Garnet, Amethyst, Topaz, Crystal, Moonstone and even Agate, all more valuable except in rare cases, are specified for the preceding years? What lies behind the choice of modestly priced Coral to mark a thirty fifth anniversary when a precious Sapphire is to be given for a twenty third?

These lists have evidently become confused with time, or at least the reasons underlying their arrangement now elude us. And to make confusion worse confounded, several writers on the subject seem to have invented lists of their own. But what matter? Let us practice on the level of national festivities and see how the sums work out.

Are you a patriotic Frenchman of strong republican principles wishing to celebrate the storming of the Bastille on 14th July, 1789 the famous Quatorze Juillet? If you were throwing your party in the year of grace 1988,* you were separated from that historic event by 199 years. So: 1+9+9=19, and 1+9=10. You thus knew your planet, which is the Sun (astrological number 1); and because the number of intervening years had run right off the chart, you reverted to the figure 1 for your anniversary year too. Conclusion: your friends should have brought you Sulphur, preferably paper wrapped.

Perhaps you are English, keen to celebrate the exploits of the only man who went into Parliament with the right idea Guy Fawkes and are reading this book in the year 2000. The Gunpowder Plot was discovered on 5th November 1605. Thus the time-lag here will be 395 years and the sum will go as follows: 3+9+5=17; then 1+7=8. Conclusion: the ruling planet is Saturn (astrological number 8); and your guests must arrive bearing Stichtite or Bronzite.

Whether you are an American and it is George Washington's Birthday, a Swiss whose National Day commemorates the famous occasion on which William Tell shot the apple from his son's head, or an Australian opening a can of Foster's lager to toast the raising by Captain Cook of the English flag on the shores of Botany Bay, the procedure is the same: follow the rules of numerological calculation, and the chart will do the rest.

One final point. All anniversaries have their significance of course, but the most important day in any of our lives has got to be the one on which we were born. So, while each year may bring its appropriate gift, make sure every baby you know starts off with a present of his or her precious crystal, talisman, and bedside rock.

* Denotes a mineral or gemstone match for the traditional emblem.
INT Internationally recognised

Anniversary Stones			
Anniversary Planet/Satellite		Minerals/Gemstones	Traditional Emblem
1	Sun	Sulphur (*wrapped in paper)	Paper (UK, AU; US)
2	Moon	Desert Rose	Cotton INT[1]
3	Jupiter	Chalcopyrite/Bornite	Leather INT
4	Uranus	Wulfenite, *Fossil Plant	Fruit or Flower (US)
5	Mercury	Staurolite, *Fossil Wood	Wood (UK and US)
6	Venus	Irish Fairy Stone, *Candy Cavern Quartz	Candy (US) Iron (UK)
7	Neptune	Apophylite, *Native Copper	Copper (US) Wool (AU)
8	Saturn	Stichtite, *Bronzite	Bronze, Pottery INT

9	Mars	Jasper, Youngite, *Opalised Wood	Willow, Wood INT
10	Sun	Vanadinite *Casiterite	Tin (UK, AU.)
11	Moon	Calcite, *Pyrite	Steel (USA, AU)
12	Jupiter	Aurichalcite, *Agate	Agate (UK, AU) Silk, Linen (INT)
13	Uranus	Charoite * Moonstone	Moonstone (UK, AU, USA), Lace (INT)
14	Mercury	Vesuvian Lava, *Moss Agate	Agate (INT)
15	Venus	Marcasite, *Rock Crystal	Crystal (UK, AU, USA)
16	Neptune	Fluorite, *Topaz	Topaz (INT)
17	Saturn	Venus' Hair, *Amethyst	Amethyst (UK, AU, USA)
18	Mars	Bloodstone * Garnet	Garnet (UK, AU, USA)
19	Sun	Zircon	Zircon (UK, AU, USA)
20	Moon	Aragonite, *Chinastone	China (UK, AU)
21	Jupiter	Amber	
22	Uranus/Pluto	Blue John	
23	Mercury	Tektite, Verdite, * white Sapphire	Sapphire (UK, AU, USA)
24	Venus	Malachite	
25	Neptune	Satin Spa, Native *Silver	Silver (UK, AU, USA) (Diamond Jubilee)
26	Saturn	Jet	
27	Mars	Ruby Zoisite, *Bronzite	Bronze (UK, AU, USA)
28	Sun	Phenacite	
29	Moon	Coral	
30	Jupiter	Chrysocolla, *Pearl	Pearl (INT)
31	Uranus	Onyx	

32	Mercury	Tiger Eye	
33	Venus	Dioptase	
34	Neptune	Opal Fossil	
35	Saturn	Chonderite, *Coral	Coral (UK, AU, USA)
36	Mars	Bowenite	
37	Sun	yellow Zircon	
38	Moon	Pearl	
39	Jupiter	Eilat Stone, Hauyne	
40	Uranus	B.C. Jade, *Ruby	Ruby (UK, AU, USA)
41	Mercury	Uvarovite	
42	Venus	Azurite & Malachite	
43	Neptune	Chrysoprase	
44	Saturn	Benitoite	
45	Mars	Sunstone, *pink Sapphire	Sapphire (UK, USA, AU)
46	Sun	white Zircon	
47	Moon	Water Nodule, Selenite	
48	Jupiter	Turquoise	
49	Uranus	gem quality Casiterite, Peridot	
50	Mercury Sirius	Lapis Lazuli, Dioptase, *Native Gold/Nugget	Gold (UK, AU), Also known as "Silver Jubilee"
51	Venus	Andalusite	
52	Neptune	gem quality Euclase	
53	Saturn	yellow Topaz	
54	Mars	Morganite	
55	Sun	Heliodor, *Emerald	Emerald (INT)
56	Moon	Pearl	
57	Jupiter	Phosphophylite	
58	Uranus	Violane	
59	Mercury	Topazolite	

60	Venus	Star Sapphire *Diamond	Diamond (UK, AU, USA)
61	Neptune	Hiddenite	
62	Saturn	Lazulite	
63	Mars	Chrysoberyl	
64	Sun	Tsavorite	
65	Moon	Star Rose Quartz	
66	Jupiter	Gem Rhodocrosite	
67	Uranus	Gem Tugtupite pink Tourmaline	
68	Mercury	Gem Iolite Labradorite	
69	Venus	Imperial Green lavender Jadeite	
70	Neptune	blue Diamond	
71	Saturn	Lapis lazuli	
72	Mars	Gem Rhodonite	
73	Sun	red Zircon	
74	Moon	Gem Scapolite	
75	Jupiter	white Tourmaline *yellow Diamond	Diamond (UK, AU)
76	Uranus	Brazillianite	
77	Mercury	orange Sapphire	
78	Venus	Spinel	
79	Neptune	Kunzite	
80	Saturn	Tanzanite	
81	Mars	pink Diamond	
82	Sun	Gem Sphene	
83	Moon	Adularia Moonstone	
84	Jupiter	bi-colour Tourmaline	
85	Uranus	Diopside	
86	Mercury	Cat's Eye Chrysoberyl Tiger Eye	
87	Venus	Kashmir/Ceylonese Sapphire	

88	Neptune	Pigeon's Blood Ruby	
89	Saturn	Opal Pineapple	
90	Mars	pink Sapphire	
91	Sun	pale blue Zircon	
92	Moon	Water Opal	
93	Jupiter	Melonstone Tourmaline	
94	Uranus	Peridot	
95	Mercury	Black Opal, Pietersite	
96	Venus	Emerald	
97	Neptune	Aquamarine	
98	Saturn	pink Topaz	
99	Mars	Alexandrite	
100	Sun/Sirius	red or white Diamond Lapis Lazuli	

Envoi

This following vision, now known as Tantanka-Ohitika's "Dream of the Sacred Stone", is the note on which the author of this book wishes to take leave of her readers. Stones and gems are one of Nature's precious gifts. They bring healing and harmony, wisdom and courage, cheerfulness, generosity and joy, and their beauty enrich the world. They are given for our pleasure. Let us use and understand them to the full.

Tantanka-Ohitika's Dream

Around the early years of this century there flourished among the Sioux Indians a famous Medicine Man called Tantanka-Ohitika. In his youth he had received a vision which he loved to describe and which he recorded like this.

"At the age of ten I looked at the land and rivers, the animals and the sky above, and could not fail to realize that some great power had made them. I was so anxious to understand this power that I questioned the trees, the bushes and the flowers. Studying the mossy stones I saw that some seemed to have human features. Afterwards I dreamt that one of these stones appeared and said that by my quest to know the Creator, I had shown myself worthy of supernatural help. When in future, said the stone, I was curing the sick I had only to call upon its assistance and it would command all the forces of nature to aid me".

Acknowledgements

My forever thanks to Rivers Scott my editor and mentor, who unravelled my melee of tangled sentences and skillfully wove them into an understandable whole. His ingenuity is only overshadowed by his Etonian charm and my debt;

Special acknowledgement to Gary Lundquist for helping me with my calculations on the constituent elements of planets, and for his comprehensive range of knowledge. Few scientists would have bothered as he did with the layman's point of view;

I deeply appreciate the help given by Roger Harding, Curator of Gems at the British Museum, who nurtured my interest in the myriad, exquisite crystals not usually brought to public attention. His careful explanations and patience never flagged;

My appreciation and admiration to Elizabeth Gage – jewellery designer and goldsmith whose exquisite designs have taught me that jewels, gold and enamel can be used as an artist uses a pallet and that each individual piece is, in itself, a powerful healing tool;

Geologists Lin and Martin Searle dug deep for the infinitesimal detail I often required. Their long discussions went beyond the call of friendship;

I am grateful for the information supplied by Fred Birnie on his speciality of Jade and Jadeite;

Thanks to Helen Fraquer for sharing her extraordinary knowledge on amber and other minerals;

I am indebted to Denis Inkersole as my tutor at the City of London Polytechnic for his expertise and patience in Gemmology classes;

My gratitude to the "King of Opals" Rex Dallimore for his attention to detail in all sections referring to Opal;

Helen Muller who gave me the benefit of their knowledge regarding Jet;

Pamela Towlson generously extended her hospitality at the Royal Astronomical Society, allowing me to spend many hours sifting through records, books and photographs and letting me pick her brains. I thank her for remembering my cause and keeping me posted with snippets of interest;

I received much helpful advice on the western school of astrology from Betina Lee and Jeff Meddle — attached to the London Astrological Lodge;

Heartfelt gratitude to Manika Gosh who tutored and advised on the Indian school of astrology;

Thanks to John Clarke of the Sydney Astrological Centre for his time and caring attitude;

John Pyeman opened the floodgates of knowledge about the science of self-discipline and offered me valuable facts on mythology, numerology and other key matters;

Lessons with Master I. Ching tutor John Bineham advanced my Tao to a higher level where I was able to connect with higher knowledge. I thank you John.

Georgia Pitsillides contributed information on soluble minerals, vitamins and amino acids which helped me enormously in the section on healing;

My grateful acknowledgements also go to the many clients and healers I consulted, particularly Vera Van Der Sleesen and Elizabeth Draper;

Gordon Prangley and Dunstan Harrison from Bath/England who selflessly give their life to healing using their remarkable invention the gem lamp. I benefited physically from a treatment and was then honoured to observe the treatment of individuals, including an active little boy once condemned by orthodox medics to a short, confined lifestyle he had long outlived.

For encouragement to continue the mammoth task of studying while researching and writing this manuscript I thank Diana Altman, Sylvia Compton Miller, Marie Laure Lawson, Margaret Breton, Pauline Baker, Patrick Crosbie, Michael Sinel;

Christine Motley is remembered for her valiant typing;

Gabriela Ebert for her general knowledge on gemstones,

Sheila McErlane, and Barbara Sarik for personal reasons;

Gratitude to Oliver Caldecott, who believed in the value of the subject and put it to print;

There's a permanent place in my heart for Gloria Ferris who made light of dark days and through truth, gentle probing and an occasional crack of the whip brought my brain into focus.

Finally to Veronica Dickinson who without her enthusiastic support, advice and loving care this book – The Healing Power of Crystals" would never have grown beyond its embryo stage.

Bibliography for Sources of Reference.

Atkinson, Richard and Frances, *The Observer's Book of Rocks and Minerals* (William Clowes & Sons Ltd, Beccles & London).

Bariand, Paul (texts) and Bariand, Nelly (photographs) *The Wonderful World of Precious Stones in Their Natural State* (Abbey Library, London).

Bible, Old and New Testaments, Standard and Revised edns. Browning, Robert, *The Byzantine Empire* (Weidenfeld & Nicolson, London).

Bruton, Eric, *Diamonds* (2nd edn. NAD Press Ltd, London). Burland, C. A. *Peoples of the Sun* (Weidenfeld & Nicolson, London).

Child, John, *Australian Rocks and Minerals* (Periwinkle Press, 1963; rev. and enlarged edn, Landsdowne Press, Melbourne, 1969).

Crow, W. B. *Precious Stones* (Aquarian Press).

David, Dr Rosalie (ed.), *Mysteries of the Mummies* (The story of the Manchester University investigation) (Book Club Associates).

Dixon, Don, *Universe* (Houghton Mifflin, Boston).

Gubelin, Eduard, *Precious Stones* (3rd edn, Hallwag, Berne, 1973).

Kirkaldy, J. F. *Minerals and Rocks* (Blandford Press, London).

Leland, Charles Godfrey, *Gypsy Sorcery and Fortune Telling* (Dover Publications, New York).

Lons, Veronica, *The World's Mythology in Colour* (Hamlyn, London).

McLintock, W. F. P., *Gemstones in the Geological Museum,* 4th edn rev. Patricia M. Statham, based on 3rd edn, rev. P. A. Sabine (1951, 4th 1983).

Mailard, Robert (ed.), *Diamonds, Myth, Magic and Reality* (Crown Publishers, New York).

Malin, David and Murdin, Paul, *Colours of the Stars* (Cambridge University Press, Cambridge).

Mineralogical Record, *The, Tourmaline* — 1 (Mineralogical Record Inc.).

Murray, Margaret A., *The Splendour that was Egypt* (Sidgwick & Jackson, London). NASA, http://www.nasa.gov

Mineralogical Record, *The, Tourmaline* — 1 (Mineralogical Record Inc.).

Murray, Margaret A., *The Splendour that was Egypt* (Sidgwick & Jackson, London).

NASA, http://www.nasa.gov

Ollerenshaw, Arthur E., *Blue John Cavern and Blue John Mine* (no further details available).

Ollerenshaw, Arthur E., *The History of Blue John Stone* (no further details available).

Poynder, Michael, *The Price Guide to Jewellery 3000 BC-1950 AD* (Antique Collector's Club Ltd, Suffolk).

Read, H. H., *Rutley's Elements of Mineralogy* (Thomas Murby, London).

Royal Astronomical Society, numerous reference books.

Sauer, Jules Roger, *Brazil: Paradise of Gemstones* (Jules Roger Sauer, 1982).

Silverman, David P., *The Masterpieces of Tutankhamen*, Introduction and commentaries (Abbeville Press, New York).

ABS Science *"StarStuff"* with Stuart Gary, http://www.abc.net.au/science/starstuff

Temple, Robert K. G., *The Sirius Mystery* (Billing & Sons, Guildford and London).

Wikipedia the free encyclopaedia, http://en.wikipedia.org/wiki

Woolley, Dr Alan (ed), *Mineral Kingdom* (Hamlyn, London).

Wright, Esmond (ed.), *The Ancient World* (Hamlyn, London, 1969, rev. and updated 1979; Chartwell Book Sales Inc. New Jersey).

Index

256

Finis